# PREFACE

In *Introduction to Literature: Short Fiction*, we have retained from the third edition of *Introduction to Literature* works that consistently interest and stimulate class discussion and have discarded those that, for various reasons, no longer prove as engaging as they did. We remain committed to Canadian literatures and the larger historical and cultural contexts within which they operate. Over the last few decades, literature has helped change as it has been changed by an increasingly inclusive society that respects the rights and responsibilities of people of different genders, classes, cultures, and ethnic and religious backgrounds. We have preserved the compact size of the anthology while reflecting diverse audiences and authors and an ever-expanding canon of literature in English.

We have retained chronological order according to authors' dates of birth, have added dates of publication of all works (printed on the right at the end of each selection), and have revised the introduction to represent something of the history of short fiction. We feel that the benefits of historical order outweigh those of structural alternatives that highlight formal features or follow alphabetical order of authors' names or thematic arrangement. An emphasis on the historical conditions of production and reproduction of the genre helps students understand the writer not so much as mysterious genius but as social actor in specific historical and cultural contexts.

We have resisted thematic ordering to encourage a broad range of approaches and readings of the work. We do, however, offer a few suggestions toward a thematic approach in the introduction and indicate some connections between certain works in the brief author profiles and footnotes.

Selections have been considerably revised and enlarged to reflect changing needs, to provide updated material, and to represent a wider range of women's and postcolonial writing in English. This anthology includes new material, in both traditional and experimental forms, extending thematic, technical, and cultural range, while amplifying the history of the form and elaborating its powers and utility within and beyond the literary domain.

Footnotes, though kept to a minimum, are included for quick reference and to aid ready understanding without resources and reference books. Notes are provided for dialect or foreign phrases, some place names, mythological allusions, and folkloric references, for example. We have tried to resist the temptation to steer the reader toward particular interpretations by means of footnote material. Basic vocabulary found in most desk dictionaries is not included in footnotes, with the exception of a few words that we have found may give some difficulty or are being used in a non-standard sense. Like the glossary entries, the brief biographical profiles that precede each author's work are intended to be suggestive rather than comprehensive.

## ACKNOWLEDGEMENTS

If all writing is collaborative, it is especially so in the case of revising an anthology. This new edition builds on the success of previous editions and the impressive work of the editorial team of Wendy R. Katz, Kenneth A. MacKinnon, Richard J.H. Perkyns, and Gillian Thomas. I am grateful for their generous support of and contributions to the current edition. In addition, I thank those instructors who provided valuable suggestions for this edition: Nancy Batty, Red Deer College; J. Baxter, Dalhousie University; Joan Crate, Red Deer College; Robert Fleming, Kwantlen College; Jean Guthrie, Memorial University of Newfoundland; John Morgenstern, Mount St. Vincent University; Irene Ogrizek, Vanier College; Chris Petty, Red River Community College; Roger Ploude, University of New Brunswick; Birk Sproxton, Red Deer College; Dorothy Wells, St. Mary's University.

This edition is also the richer for the thoughtful feedback and suggestions of students and colleagues at the University of Saskatchewan, and, in particular, Ron Cooley, Len Findlay, John Lavery, David Parkinson, Doug Thorpe, and Lisa Vargo. I would also like to thank my editors at Harcourt Canada — Heather McWhinney, Martina van de Velde, Megan Mueller, Joanna Cotton, Stephanie Fysh, Emily Ferguson, and Anne Williams — and copy editor Faith Gildenhuys for their encouragement and valuable advice.

*Isobel M. Findlay*

# A NOTE FROM THE PUBLISHER

Thank you for selecting *Introduction to Literature: Short Fiction*, by Isobel M. Findlay, Wendy R. Katz, Kenneth A. MacKinnon, Richard J.H. Perkyns, and Gillian Thomas. The authors and publisher have devoted considerable time to the careful development of this book. We appreciate your recognition of this effort and accomplishment.

    We want to hear what you think about *Introduction to Literature: Short Fiction*. Please take a few minutes to fill in the stamped reader reply card at the back of the book. Your comments and suggestions will be valuable to us as we prepare new editions and other books.

# CONTENTS

| | |
|---|---|
| INTRODUCTION | 3 |
| Aesop (Sixth century B.C.) | 11 |
|    *The Dog in the Manger* | |
|    *The Fox and the Grapes* | |
|    *The Shepherd's Boy* | |
| James Thurber (1894–1961) | 13 |
|    *The Bear Who Let It Alone* | |
|    *The Little Girl and the Wolf* | |
| Anonymous (Collected by Joseph Jacobs, 1854–1916) | 16 |
|    *Cap o' Rushes* | |
| Nathaniel Hawthorne (1804–1864) | 20 |
|    *The Birthmark* | |
| Edgar Allan Poe (1809–1849) | 34 |
|    *The Tell-Tale Heart* | |
| Sarah Orne Jewett (1849–1909) | 39 |
|    *A White Heron* | |
| Charlotte Perkins Gilman (1860–1935) | 48 |
|    *The Yellow Wallpaper* | |
| James Joyce (1882–1941) | 61 |
|    *The Boarding House* | |
| D.H. Lawrence (1885–1930) | 67 |
|    *You Touched Me* | |
| Katherine Mansfield (1888–1923) | 81 |
|    *The Fly* | |
| Ethel Wilson (1888–1980) | 86 |
|    *We Have to Sit Opposite* | |
| William Faulkner (1897–1962) | 94 |
|    *A Rose for Emily* | |
| Ernest Hemingway (1899–1961) | 102 |
|    *In Another Country* | |

Langston Hughes (1902–1967) 107
*On the Road*
Tillie Olsen (b. 1913) 111
*I Stand Here Ironing*
Nadine Gordimer (b. 1923) 118
*Town and Country Lovers*
Margaret Laurence (1926–1987) 127
*The Loons*
Timothy Findley (b. 1930) 136
*Dreams*
Alice Munro (b. 1931) 153
*Boys and Girls*
Alistair MacLeod (b. 1936) 165
*The Boat*
Margaret Atwood (b. 1939) 180
*Happy Endings*
Toni Cade Bambara (b. 1939) 183
*The Lesson*
Thomas King (b. 1943) 190
*The One About Coyote Going West*
Donna E. Smyth (b. 1943) 199
*Red Hot*
Alice Walker (b. 1944) 204
*Nineteen Fifty-Five*
Lee Maracle (b. 1950) 216
*Yin Chin*
Guy Vanderhaeghe (b. 1951) 222
*Drummer*
Rohinton Mistry (b. 1952) 236
*Swimming Lessons*
Lynda Barry (b. 1956) 254
*Automatic Timer*

GLOSSARY 257

CREDITS 273

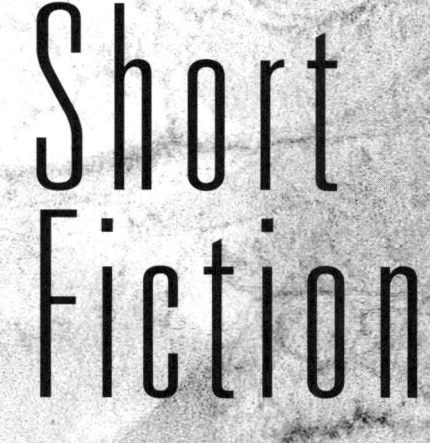

# Short Fiction

# INTRODUCTION

The short story, in the broad sense of a relatively brief fictional narrative in prose, is a very old literary form. In Western literary tradition, it derives from ancient Egyptian story-telling, Old Testament stories and Christ's parables, fables, folk tales, myths, legends, ballads, tales, sketches, and anecdotes. The telling of stories is a basic human activity in all cultures that persists even in the many stories that circulate and help fashion our sense of the global village or our journey on the Information Highway. Short fiction (from the Latin *fictio* — shaping or feigning), story, or narrative, once broadly defined in opposition to history or truth-telling and associated with "primitive" and oral cultures, is now widely understood to be a priceless repository and living repertoire of cultural, historical, and other knowledge that extends narrative's power and value far beyond the literary domain. In the interests of a more humane, just, and equitable society, writers and researchers create new narratives as well as counter-narratives that challenge dominant views not only in literary studies but also in history, law, philosophy, psychology, anthropology, and sociology, for example. All of us, and not only the investigative reporters, "have the story."

As a quite distinctive literary genre, however, the short story dates only from the nineteenth century with practitioners such as Edgar Allan Poe, Nathaniel Hawthorne, Guy de Maupassant, Anton Chekhov, and E.T.W. Hoffmann. The short story, in this more defined sense, is associated with changes in society and print culture in the early decades of the century and, in the American context, with a culture trying to define itself by difference from the old world of European and specifically British models and practices. The legitimation of the novel as a literary form in early nineteenth-century Britain is closely related to the bulk of the three-decker (or three-volume) novel, which aspired to educate and entertain with its sweeping panoramas of historical and social change and detailed compendia of bourgeois manners. Since British novels had no copyright protection in America, they were widely pirated and dominated the market. Such considerations played no small part in Poe's efforts to promote the short story as a literary form designed for the growing magazine and annual market in the interests of cultural nationalism — and an audience concerned to make the most of its leisure time. The spread of literacy and an increasingly urban society created a wide and eager audience for weekly and monthly periodical literature, for which short fiction was ideally suited.

Poe's 1842 review of Hawthorne, by some accounts, marked the canonization of the American short story as a unified design with a single effect. Often focussed on one character and/or episode, it typically deals with a single moment of crisis or conflict that reveals depths of character or makes a profound statement about life. The writing is characteristically intense and concentrated so that all aspects of the story — theme, character, setting, plot, point of view, tone, mood, and style — benefit from careful crafting. Poe's own "The Tell-Tale Heart" is an effectively claustrophobic version of this aesthetic, in its intense focus on physical and mental interiors, on the mythology of the evil eye converging with a new culture of surveillance, out of which come the first examples of detective fiction.

In Britain the short story gained prestige only gradually over the course of a nineteenth century concerned with the place and value of fiction more generally in debates on "the fiction question," "the art of fiction," and "candour in fiction." Given the dominance of the novel, the short story, "one of the blunders of the age," according to novelist Charles Reade, struggled in Britain to overcome its reputation as little more than a rest cure from the real labour of novel writing. With expanded audiences and developments in print technology as well as new magazines and the decline of the three-decker and the circulating library's control of household reading, the 1890s, however, proved a fertile period, when, as H.G. Wells put it, "short stories broke out everywhere." Because of the very different conditions of production, the British short story does not typically follow Poe's model of brevity or Henry James's valuing of proportion. In the case of Thomas Hardy, for example, as with many women writers, the short story is valued for "disproportioning" or "throwing out of proportion" and observing that which is typically overlooked or neglected.

It is an error, then, albeit a common one, to approach the short story as if it were a novel, or, still worse, the novel's poor relation. The short story, the product of a particular convergence of social, literary, economic, and other forces in the nineteenth century, has endured as a powerful and popular form of expression. Frank O'Connor is one writer who has found the short story remarkably receptive to the "romantic, individualistic, and intransigent," and undoubtedly it has proven a potent means for marginalized groups and individuals to speak the hitherto unspeakable and to challenge prevailing orthodoxies about, for example, human sexuality, racial difference, the decorum of public/private lives, and issues of human justice. Charlotte Perkins Gilman's "The Yellow Wallpaper" and Alice

Walker's "Nineteen Fifty-Five" are examples of women's stories as a form of resistance to a culture's grand narratives and habitual practices. The short story has proven a particularly valued form in Canada and postcolonial contexts more generally. Alice Munro and Margaret Atwood, for example, figure largely in most collections of short stories. Reading D.H. Lawrence, Katherine Mansfield, and others taught Nadine Gordimer how she might represent the realities of a divided South Africa. They and other short-story writers represented here are among the finest in the language, and it is our hope that their work will demonstrate the considerable richness, breadth, and potency of this literary form.

We have included in this section some examples of the more ancient forms of prose narrative. Before the age of mass literacy, it was common for the story to be used as a vehicle for teaching or preaching a specific moral. Fables, in general, narrate a simple story that exaggerates character and motive through the use of animal protagonists. They point to a highly specific moral that can usually be codified in a single sentence. The most widely known fables are traditionally ascribed to Aesop, a sixth-century B.C. Phrygian slave. However, surviving Egyptian papyri indicate that many of these fables were actually written nearly a thousand years earlier. They were retold many times by various writers, some of whom added their own original fables to the collection. A modern humorist, James Thurber, produced two volumes of fables that set out to parody the fable form while providing some sharp satiric comment. Ethel Wilson's "We Have to Sit Opposite" is a modern political fable of the struggles between civilization and barbarism and the implication of everybody in the "fear and folly" synonymous with Munich in the years leading to and during World War II.

The parable, like the fable, is a simple narrative that points the reader toward a specific interpretation of the story. Although its significance cannot always be codified in a single sentence, the parable nonetheless exists primarily as a "closed text" rather than one inviting a wide variety of readings. Similarly, the folk tale "Cap o' Rushes" employs a predictable narrative structure to lead to an ending meant to elicit only one response. Early pre-literary story forms such as the parable, fable, and folk tale continue to surface in twentieth-century literary stories. For example, Langston Hughes's "On the Road" owes something of its structure to the biblical parable. James Thurber's "The Little Girl and the Wolf" presents a modern parody of the folk tale best known as "Little Red Riding Hood." Readers of "Cap o' Rushes" will recognize not only one of the scores of variants of the Cinderella story but also the theme of the rejected loving daughter that Shakespeare used in *King Lear*.

While the modern short story owes some of its origins to such early forms as the fable, the parable, and the folk tale, it could not have come into being without the rise of the popular literary magazine in the nineteenth century. Thus began an association between the short story and periodical publication that continues to the present day. The majority of short stories are still published first in journals. Although it is usually much longer than either a fable or a parable, the nineteenth-century short story bears a closer resemblance to such forms than do its modern successors. For instance, Hawthorne's "The Birthmark," Poe's "The Tell-Tale Heart," and Sarah Orne Jewett's "A White Heron" appear to point the reader toward rather clearer moral conclusions than do any of the more recent stories reprinted here. Also popular with the nineteenth-century short-story reader and writer was a significant authorial presence in the narrative voice. The narrator of "The Birthmark" comments on the action, philosophizes, and moralizes in a manner that has now been all but abandoned. Still, it is a mistake to attempt to reduce even those stories to a singular or unproblematic message since they probe without resolving cultural contradictions exposed in times of crisis and conflict. Hawthorne's story is as much about gender politics and domestic abuse as it is about science's presumption to master the environment and human reproduction.

In addition to such narrative control, the nineteenth-century short-story reader and writer liked a story that had a sharp twist of plot or sudden reversal at its conclusion. In this respect, many writers were influenced by the tales of de Maupassant and Poe — works that often concluded with a bitter or ironic twist. Gilman's "The Yellow Wallpaper" exploits the horror story to tell a woman's story of confinement in marriage, creativity, professional competence, and mental illness. Twentieth-century writers, such as Timothy Findley in his macabre story "Dreams" or William Faulkner in "A Rose for Emily," continue to be fascinated by the style of Gothic horror and the supernatural so favoured by Poe.

The unexpected ending, the pronounced authorial presence, and the story with a clear-cut moral have not remained very popular with more recent short-story writers. One source of this change was the psychoanalytic theories of Sigmund Freud and others. The "stream-of-consciousness" technique, developed by such writers as James Joyce (in his later works) and Virginia Woolf, depicts the subjective, often irrational, working of a character's mind, rather than the character's actions or motivations presented more or less objectively. Although Poe and Gilman already focus attention on the inner life, many twentieth-century writers divert interest from the external events to the inner life of thoughts, feelings, dreams, and fantasies — or elaborate connections between external circumstances and inner realities. James Joyce, D.H. Lawrence, Katherine Mansfield, Tillie Olsen, Nadine Gordimer, and Margaret Laurence, for example, explore class, race, gender, religion, war, industrialization, and the contradictions of family as determinants of human emotion and behaviour.

The great complexity of the modern short story derives largely from the writer's handling of point of view, or the view from which the writer presents the action of the story. Examination of narrative technique often leads to fuller understanding. Of the stories included here, several ("The Tell-Tale Heart," "The Yellow Wallpaper," "A Rose for Emily," "In Another Country," "I Stand Here Ironing," "The Loons," "Boys and Girls," "The Boat," "The Lesson," "The One About Coyote Going West," "Nineteen Fifty-Five," "Drummer," "Yin Chin," "Swimming Lessons," and "Automatic Timer") use first-person narration. In each of these, the writer has invented a literary personage (or, as in Faulkner's case, a representative voice of the community) who speaks in character. These narrators have a limited point of view: they can tell readers only what they themselves know or what others tell them. The more mature narrator of "Boys and Girls," for example, reflects on her childhood view of her family while disclosing the gendering of identity, whereas in "I Stand Here Ironing" it is the mother's viewpoint that directs the narrative and supplements official and professional explanations of her daughter's actions. When the narrator of "Automatic Timer" tosses off a casual remark about Mexican whores, it is not the author who might be considered racist but a character in the story.

One way to probe characters' sense of reality is to provide the reader with a basis for suspicion or an ironic perspective. Generally, the authors of the first-person narrations included here develop some means whereby the narrator reveals himself or herself in ways that are not intended. Little inconsistencies, disparities between past and present, excessive self-justification, repetition, even trivial allusions to revealing details — all make one aware that what one is told is a compound of reliable and unreliable reportage. Such a method certainly presents interesting challenges to the reader's powers of interpretation. More than that, it reinforces, in a moving way, our sense of the relativity and frailty of the human perception of ourselves and others and of powerful differences of gender, of race and ethnicity, of age, and place.

An omniscient narrator is one who tells the story with a seemingly unlimited point of view or fund of knowledge about characters and their actions. Narrators are not necessarily omniscient, and even omniscience has its limits in "The Birthmark." Some writers prefer to limit the information they provide to the range of knowledge exhibited by the characters. While this kind of narrator does not take part in the action, objects and events are described from the perspective of someone inside the fictional world of the story. "A White Heron," for instance, illustrates this technique, and "The Boarding House" registers in turn the very different judgements of Mrs. Mooney, Mr. Doran, and Polly. Critics sometimes speak of such stories as having a central consciousness. In an increasing number of modern short stories, we are allowed only the characters' perspectives on the action. "On the Road" is told in the third person, but the reader understands the story from the viewpoint of its protagonist, Sargeant.

Our selection offers a wide variety of story lengths, which in their turn require a range of narrative techniques. On the one hand, there is the tale that the writer develops at a leisurely pace, which often allows for the filling in of minute details. "You Touched Me" and "The Boat," for example, are developed at some length, with many detailed images. Other stories are very short. Hemingway wastes no words in his portrayal of a bleak wartime Milan. Writers like Hemingway often rely on and focus attention on the stated and unstated, what is revealed and what concealed. Joyce does not reveal to his reader what passes between Mrs. Mooney and Mr. Doran at their climactic interview, leaving the outcome to the judgement and imagination of readers. Some authors focus vividly on a very few minutes in the lives of their characters: Sunday morning in Dublin in "The Boarding House" or the rail journey in "We Have to Sit Opposite." Brevity is the essence of "Automatic Timer."

Despite such variations, short-story writers must in general make the most of details of setting, character, plot, tone, mood, and diction. Stories such as Donna E. Smyth's "Red Hot" go further than those of Joyce and others in exploring the nature of evidence, considering the legal ramifications of gendered perception. In any case, writers must be able to shape an incident or set of incidents into a memorable scene immediately, without the luxury of lengthy development, drawing on such poetic devices as figurative and rhythmical language. Learning to swim is both a literal and a figurative concern for Rohinton Mistry. Like the essayists and poets, the short story writers explore and exploit language's role in shaping identity and community. In stories like "The Lesson," "Drummer," "The One About Coyote Going West," "Nineteen Fifty-Five," "Swimming Lessons," or "Yin Chin," the distinct idioms of narrators and characters, the mix of oral and written, speak to the conundra of cultural exchange, the linking of past and present, and the complex construction of national and other identities.

Crucial in all stories, both for dramatic impact and for psychological insight, are sharply observed details. Sometimes they are inserted unexpectedly, like the cigarette butts in Alistair MacLeod's story. Characters can be sketched in a sentence with the right details. In "The Boarding House," Polly "had a habit of glancing upwards when she spoke with anyone, which made her look like a little perverse madonna." Carefully observed settings, such as the industrialized landscape of Lawrence's World War I England, often have a symbolic meaning. A symbolic significance may also be conveyed by the title of a story, as, for example, "The Birthmark," "The Boarding House," "The Fly," "The Boat," or "The Lesson." Is there a connection between the "touch" in the title of Lawrence's story and Matilda's sudden change of heart, or between the walls enclosing the Pottery House and the boundaries of class, gender, and family? Such symbols provide controlling images that help to establish a sense of order (and meaning) in the story.

The following selection of stories illustrates not only a diversity of techniques but also a wide variety of themes. Like essayists and poets, writers of fiction will often seek inspiration from personal or closely observed experiences. Mistry explores immigrant accommodations, while Olsen and Maracle probe prejudice and uncover human dignity and capacity to survive. "The Fly" and "In Another Country" focus on problems of adjustment following war. Ideas about race, class, and culture emerge not only in a North American context, as in "On the Road," "The Lesson," "The Loons," "The One About Coyote Going West," and "Nineteen Fifty-Five," but in the South African background of apartheid in Gordimer's "Town and Country Lovers." While most of the stories are serious, they are not without humour. Writers such as Bambara, Wilson, and King explore themes that allow them to adopt a wryly humorous tone.

Given the variety of its historical origins and the diversity of literary modes and techniques that can be employed in the short story, it is best to approach the genre without fixed preconceptions or expectations. Indeed, many stories resist easy formulations, the clichéd and stereotyped, while others explore the realities of fiction and the fictions of reality. Margaret Atwood's "Happy Endings," for example, like King's "The One About Coyote Going West," focusses on the shaping power of stories; these stories do not allow the reader to forget that the writer is constantly involved in the technique of storytelling. The method is comparable to that of John Fowles, who constructs his novel *The French Lieutenant's Woman* in such a way that the action can move in a variety of different directions, or, in another medium, to the theatre of Bertolt Brecht, an influential playwright who insisted that viewers remain constantly aware that they are watching a play. Such playwrights as Luigi Pirandello and Thornton Wilder likewise experiment with the relationship between reality and illusion, when actors step out of the characters they are playing to discuss their roles; Woody Allen uses a comparable technique in his film *The Purple Rose of Cairo*. A story like "Red Hot" may upset preconceived notions about such a basic thing as plot: it partially concerns real people, uses quotations from actual newspaper reports, is divided into very short sections, and is narrated through a series of violently flashing images. This may suggest to the reader television channel surfing or the technique of the film docudrama, in which a fictitious story may be spliced with live footage to aid its authenticity. When such methods are employed, the reader never loses sight of the technique — or what it reveals about the connections between media representations and people's private behaviours. Similarly, stories as different from one another as "The Fly," "You Touched Me," "In Another Country," and "Dreams" may deliberately provoke a framework of reader expectations only to demand a radical change in perception by the end of the story.

Experimentation with technique is only one of many aspects of short fiction by which an author may stimulate a reader's responses.

Writers use multiple methods of amusing, exciting, or moving their readers by introducing them to the imagined worlds they create in their fiction. The selection that follows offers readers a wealth of styles and experiences; however much stories may have changed over the centuries, sharing stories remains at the heart of individual and collective life.

# Aesop *(Sixth century B.C.)*

No historical information exists about the legendary Aesop credited with the famous Greek fables. If such a person existed, he may have been a Greek slave in the mid–sixth century B.C. The fables were the work of several hands.

## The Dog in the Manger

A dog looking out for its afternoon nap jumped into the manger of an ox and lay there cosily upon the straw. But soon the ox, returning from its afternoon work, came up to the manger and wanted to eat some of the straw. The dog in a rage, being awakened from its slumber, stood up and barked at the ox, and whenever it came near attempted to bite it. At last the ox had to give up the hope of getting the straw, and went away muttering:

"Ah, people often grudge others what they cannot enjoy themselves."

## The Fox and the Grapes

One hot summer's day a fox was strolling through an orchard till he came to a bunch of grapes just ripening on a vine which had been trained over a lofty branch. "Just the thing to quench my thirst," quoth he. Drawing back a few paces, he took a run and a jump, and just missed the bunch. Turning round again with a one, two, three, he jumped up, but with no greater success. Again and again he tried after the tempting morsel, but at last had to give it up, and walked away with his nose in the air, saying: "I am sure they are sour."

"It is easy to despise what you cannot get."

## The Shepherd's Boy

There was once a young shepherd who tended his sheep at the foot of a mountain near a dark forest. It was rather lonely for him all day, so he thought upon a plan by which he could get a little company and some excitement. He rushed down towards the village calling out "Wolf, wolf," and the villagers came out to meet him, and some of them stopped with him for a considerable time. This pleased the boy so much that a few days afterwards he tried the same trick, and again the villagers came to his help. But shortly after this a wolf actually did come out from the forest, and began to worry the sheep, and the boy of course cried out, "Wolf, wolf," still louder than before. But this time the villagers, who had been fooled twice before, thought the boy was again deceiving them, and nobody stirred to come out to his help. So the wolf made a good meal off the boy's flock, and when the boy complained, the wise man of the village said:

"*A liar will not be believed, even when he speaks the truth.*"

# James Thurber (1894–1961)

Thurber was an American essayist and humorist whose work appeared in The New Yorker, *a magazine well known for its urbanity and wit.*

## The Bear Who Let It Alone

1 In the woods of the far west there once lived a brown bear who could take it or let it alone. He would go into a bar where they sold mead, a fermented drink made of honey, and he would have just two drinks. Then he would put some money on the bar and say, "see what the bears in the back room will have," and he would go home. But finally he took to drinking by himself most of the day. He would reel home at night, kick over the umbrella stand, knock down the bridge lamps, and ram his elbows through the windows. Then he would collapse on

the floor and lie there until he went to sleep. His wife was greatly distressed and his children were frightened.

2   At length the bear saw the error of his ways and began to reform. In the end he became a famous teetotaller and a persistent temperance lecturer. He would tell everybody that came to his house about the awful effects of drink, and he would boast about how strong and well he had become since he gave up touching the stuff. To demonstrate this, he would stand on his head and on his hands and he would turn cartwheels in the house, kicking over the umbrella stand, knocking down the bridge lamps, and ramming his elbows through the windows. Then he would lie down on the floor, tired by his healthful exercise, and go to sleep. His wife was greatly distressed and his children were very frightened.

3   *Moral: You might as well fall flat on your face as lean over too far backward.*

(1940)

## The Little Girl and the Wolf

1   One afternoon a big wolf waited in a dark forest for a little girl to come along carrying a basket of food to her grandmother. Finally a little girl

did come along and she was carrying a basket of food. "Are you carrying that basket to your grandmother?" asked the wolf. The little girl said yes, she was. So the wolf asked her where her grandmother lived and the little girl told him and he disappeared into the wood.

2   When the little girl opened the door of her grandmother's house she saw that there was somebody in bed with a nightcap and nightgown on. She had approached no nearer than twenty-five feet from the bed when she saw that it was not her grandmother but the wolf, for even in a nightcap a wolf does not look any more like your grandmother than the Metro-Goldwyn lion looks like Calvin Coolidge. So the little girl took an automatic out of her basket and shot the wolf dead.

3   *Moral: It is not so easy to fool little girls nowadays as it used to be.*

(1940)

# Anonymous *(Collected by Joseph Jacobs, 1854–1916)*

*Born in Australia, Jacobs was a folklorist and editor of the British journal* Folk-Lore. *Also a Jewish historian, he became revising editor of the* Jewish Encyclopedia. *"Cap o' Rushes" was included in his 1890 collection of stories,* English Fairy Tales. More English Fairy Tales *was issued in 1894.*

## Cap o' Rushes

1. Well, there was once a very rich gentleman, and he had three daughters, and he thought he'd see how fond they were of him. So he says to the first, "How much do you love me, my dear?"
2. "Why," says she, "as I love my life."
3. "That's good," says he.
4. So he says to the second, "How much do *you* love me, my dear?"
5. "Why," says she, "better nor[1] all the world."
6. "That's good," says he.
7. So he says to the third, "How much do *you* love me, my dear?"
8. "Why, I love you as fresh meat loves salt," says she.
9. Well, but he was angry. "You don't love me at all," says he, "and in my house you stay no more." So he drove her out there and then, and shut the door in her face.
10. Well, she went away on and on till she came to a fen, and there she gathered a lot of rushes and made them into a kind of a sort of a cloak with a hood, to cover her from head to foot, and to hide her fine clothes. And then she went on and on till she came to a great house.
11. "Do you want a maid?" says she.
12. "No, we don't," said they.
13. "I haven't nowhere to go," says she; "and I ask no wages, and do any sort of work," says she.
14. "Well," said they, "if you like to wash the pots and scrape the saucepans you may stay," said they.
15. So she stayed there and washed the pots and scraped the saucepans and did all the dirty work. And because she gave no name they called her "Cap o' Rushes."

---

1. Than.

16   Well, one day there was to be a great dance a little way off, and the servants were allowed to go and look on at the grand people. Cap o' Rushes said she was too tired to go, so she stayed at home.

17   But when they were gone, she offed with her cap o' rushes, and cleaned herself, and went to the dance. And no one there was so finely dressed as she.

18   Well, who should be there but her master's son, and what should he do but fall in love with her the minute he set eyes on her. He wouldn't dance with anyone else.

19   But before the dance was done, Cap o' Rushes slipt off, and away she went home. And when the other maids came back, she was pretending to be asleep with her cap o' rushes on.

20   Well, next morning they said to her, "You did miss a sight, Cap o' Rushes!"

21   "What was that?" says she.

22   "Why, the beautifullest lady you ever see, dressed right gay and ga'.[2] The young master, he never took his eyes off her."

23   "Well, I should have liked to have seen her," says Cap o' Rushes.

24   "Well, there's to be another dance this evening, and perhaps she'll be there."

25   But, come the evening, Cap o' Rushes said she was too tired to go with them. Howsoever, when they were gone, she offed with her cap o' rushes and cleaned herself, and away she went to the dance.

26   The master's son had been reckoning on seeing her, and he danced with no one else, and never took eyes off her. But, before the dance was over, she slipt off, and home she went, and when the maids came back she pretended to be asleep with her cap o' rushes on.

27   Next day they said to her again, "Well, Cap o' Rushes, you should ha' been there to see the lady. There she was again, gay and ga', and the young master he never took his eyes off her."

28   "Well, there," says she, "I should ha' liked to ha' seen her."

29   "Well," says they, "there's a dance again this evening, and you must go with us, for she's sure to be there."

30   Well, come this evening, Cap o' Rushes said she was too tired to go, and do what they would she stayed at home. But when they were gone, she offed her cap o' rushes and cleaned herself, and away she went to the dance.

31   The master's son was rarely glad when he saw her. He danced with none but her and never took his eyes off her. When she wouldn't tell him her name, nor where she came from, he gave her a ring and told her if he didn't see her again he should die.

32   Well, before the dance was over, off she slipt, and home she went, and when the maids came home she was pretending to be asleep with her cap o' rushes on.

---

2. Scots dialect for "gallant"; here, meaning "stylish."

33    Well, next day they says to her, "There, Cap o' Rushes, you didn't come last night, and now you won't see the lady, for there's no more dances."
34    "Well, I should have rarely liked to have seen her," says she.
35    The master's son tried every way to find out where the lady was gone, but go where he might, and ask whom he might he never heard anything about her. And he got worse and worse for the love of her till he had to keep his bed.
36    "Make some gruel for the young master," they said to the cook. "He's dying for the love of the lady." The cook set about making it when Cap o' Rushes came in.
37    "What are you a-doing of?" says she.
38    "I'm going to make some gruel for the young master," says the cook, "for he's dying for the love of the lady."
39    "Let me make it," says Cap o' Rushes.
40    Well, the cook wouldn't at first, but at last she said yes, and Cap o' Rushes made the gruel. And when she had made it, she slipped the ring into it on the sly before the cook took it upstairs.
41    The young man he drank it and then he saw the ring on the bottom.
42    "Send for the cook," says he.
43    So up she comes.
44    "Who made this gruel here?" says he.
45    "I did," says the cook, for she was frightened.
46    And he looked at her.
47    "No, you didn't," says he. "Say who did, and you shan't be harmed."
48    "Well, then, 'twas Cap o' Rushes," says she.
49    "Send Cap o' Rushes here," says he.
50    So Cap o' Rushes came.
51    "Did you make my gruel?" says he.
52    "Yes, I did," says she.
53    "Where did you get this ring?" says he.
54    "From him that gave it me," says she.
55    "Who are you, then?" says the young man.
56    "I'll show you," says she. And she offed with her cap o' rushes, and there she was in her beautiful clothes.
57    Well, the master's son he got well very soon, and they were to be married in a little time. It was to be a very grand wedding, and everyone was asked far and near. And Cap o' Rushes's father was asked. But she never told anybody who she was.
58    But before the wedding, she went to the cook, and says she:
59    "I want you to dress every dish without a mite o' salt."
60    "That'll be rare nasty," says the cook.
61    "That doesn't signify," says she.
62    "Very well," says the cook.
63    Well, the wedding day came, and they were married. And after they were married, all the company sat down to the dinner. When they

began to eat the meat, it was so tasteless they couldn't eat it. But Cap o' Rushes's father tried first one dish and then another, and then he burst out crying.

64 "What is the matter?" said the master's son to him.

65 "Oh!" says he, "I had a daughter. And I asked her how much she loved me. And she said 'As much as fresh meat loves salt.' And I turned her from my door, for I thought she didn't love me. And now I see she loved me best of all. And she may be dead for aught I know."

66 "No, father, here she is!" said Cap o' Rushes. And she goes up to him and puts her arms round him.

67 And so they were all happy ever after.

(1890)

# Nathaniel Hawthorne (1804–1864)

Massachusetts-born novelist and short-story writer, Hawthorne is best known for his examination of New England morality and consciousness. His penchant for allegory is apparent in "The Birthmark" (1843), in which science opposes nature.

## The Birthmark

1  In the latter part of the last century there lived a man of science, an eminent proficient in every branch of natural philosophy, who not long before our story opens had made experience of a spiritual affinity more attractive than any chemical one. He had left his laboratory to the care of an assistant, cleared his fine countenance from the furnace smoke, washed the stain of acids from his fingers, and persuaded a beautiful young woman to become his wife. In those days, when the comparatively recent discovery of electricity and other kindred mysteries of Nature seemed to open paths into the region of miracle, it was not unusual for the love of science to rival the love of woman in its depth and absorbing energy. The higher intellect, the imagination, the spirit, and even the heart might all find their congenial aliment in pursuits which, as some of their ardent votaries believed, would ascend from one step of powerful intelligence to another, until the philosopher should lay his hand on the secret of creative force and perhaps make new worlds for himself. We know not whether Aylmer possessed this degree of faith in man's ultimate control over Nature. He had devoted himself, however, too unreservedly to scientific studies ever to be weaned from them by any second passion. His love for his young wife might prove the stronger of the two; but it could only be by intertwining itself with his love of science and uniting the strength of the latter to his own.

2  Such a union accordingly took place, and attended with truly remarkable consequences and a deeply impressive moral. One day, very soon after their marriage, Aylmer sat gazing at his wife with a trouble in his countenance that grew stronger until he spoke.

3  "Georgiana," said he, "has it never occurred to you that the mark upon your cheek might be removed?"

4  "No, indeed," said she, smiling; but, perceiving the seriousness of his manner, she blushed deeply. "To tell you the truth, it has been so

often called a charm that I was simple enough to imagine it might be so."

5   "Ah, upon another face perhaps it might," replied her husband; "but never on yours. No, dearest Georgiana, you came so nearly perfect from the hand of Nature that this slightest possible defect, which we hesitate whether to term a defect or a beauty, shocks me, as being the visible mark of earthly imperfection."

6   "Shocks you, my husband!" cried Georgiana, deeply hurt; at first reddening with momentary anger, but then bursting into tears. "Then why did you take me from my mother's side? You cannot love what shocks you!"

7   To explain this conversation it must be mentioned that in the centre of Georgiana's left cheek there was a singular mark, deeply interwoven, as it were, with the texture and substance of her face. In the usual state of her complexion — a healthy though delicate bloom — the mark wore a tint of deeper crimson, which imperfectly defined its shape amid the surrounding rosiness. When she blushed it gradually became more indistinct, and finally vanished amid the triumphant rush of blood that bathed the whole cheek with its brilliant glow. But if any shifting motion caused her to turn pale there was the mark again, a crimson stain upon the snow, in what Aylmer sometimes deemed an almost fearful distinctness. Its shape bore not a little similarity to the human hand, though of the smallest pygmy size. Georgiana's lovers were wont to say that some fairy at birth hour had laid her tiny hand upon the infant's cheek, and left this impress there in token of the magic endowments that were to give her such sway over all hearts. Many a desperate swain would have risked his life for the privilege of pressing his lips to the mysterious hand. It must not be concealed, however, that the impression wrought by this fairy sign manual varied exceedingly, according to the difference of temperament in the beholders. Some fastidious persons — but they were exclusively of her own sex — affirmed that the bloody hand, as they chose to call it, quite destroyed the effect of Georgiana's beauty, and rendered her countenance even hideous. But it would be as reasonable to say that one of those small blue stains which sometimes occur in the purest statuary marble would convert the Eve of Powers[1] to a monster. Masculine observers, if the birthmark did not heighten their admiration, contented themselves with wishing it away, that the world might possess one living specimen of ideal loveliness without the semblance of a flaw. After his marriage — for he thought little or nothing of the matter before, — Aylmer discovered that this was the case with himself.

8   Had she been less beautiful, — if Envy's self could have found aught else to sneer at, — he might have felt his affection heightened by the prettiness of this mimic hand, now vaguely portrayed, now lost,

---

1. Hiram Powers (1805–1873), American sculptor. "Eve" refers to one of his statues.

now stealing forth again and glimmering to and fro with every pulse of emotion that throbbed within her heart; but seeing her otherwise so perfect, he found this one defect grow more and more intolerable with every moment of their united lives. It was the fatal flaw of humanity which Nature, in one shape or another, stamps ineffaceably on all her productions, either to imply that they are temporary and finite, or that their perfection must be wrought by toil and pain. The crimson hand expressed the ineludible gripe in which mortality clutches the highest and purest of earthly mould, degrading them into kindred with the lowest, and even with the very brutes, like whom their visible frames return to dust. In this manner, selecting it as the symbol of his wife's liability to sin, sorrow, decay, and death, Aylmer's sombre imagination was not long in rendering the birthmark a frightful object, causing him more trouble and horror than ever Georgiana's beauty, whether of soul or sense, had given him delight.

9  At all the seasons which should have been their happiest he invariably, and without intending it, nay, in spite of a purpose to the contrary, reverted to this one disastrous topic. Trifling as it at first appeared, it so connected itself with innumerable trains of thought and modes of feeling that it became the central point of all. With the morning twilight Aylmer opened his eyes upon his wife's face and recognized the symbol of imperfection; and when they sat together at the evening hearth his eyes wandered stealthily to her cheek, and beheld, flickering with the blaze of the wood fire, the spectral hand that wrote mortality where he would fain have worshipped. Georgiana soon learned to shudder at his gaze. It needed but a glance with the peculiar expression that his face often wore to change the roses of her cheek into a deathlike paleness, amid which the crimson hand was brought strongly out, like a bas-relief of ruby on the whitest marble.

10  Late one night, when the lights were growing dim so as hardly to betray the stain on the poor wife's cheek, she herself, for the first time, voluntarily took up the subject.

11  "Do you remember, my dear Aylmer," said she, with a feeble attempt at a smile, "have you any recollection, of a dream last night about this odious hand?"

12  "None! none whatever!" replied Aylmer, starting; but then he added, in a dry, cold tone, affected for the sake of concealing the real depth of his emotion, "I might well dream of it; for, before I fell asleep, it had taken a pretty firm hold of my fancy."

13  "And you did dream of it?" continued Georgiana, hastily; for she dreaded lest a gush of tears should interrupt what she had to say. "A terrible dream! I wonder that you can forget it. Is it possible to forget this one expression? — 'It is in her heart now; we must have it out!' Reflect, my husband; for by all means I would have you recall that dream."

14  The mind is in a sad state when Sleep, the all-involving, cannot confine her spectres within the dim region of her sway, but suffers

them to break forth, affrighting this actual life with secrets that perchance belong to a deeper one. Aylmer now remembered his dream. He had fancied himself with his servant Aminadab, attempting an operation for the removal of the birthmark; but the deeper went the knife, the deeper sank the hand, until at length its tiny grasp appeared to have caught hold of Georgiana's heart; whence, however, her husband was inexorably resolved to cut or wrench it away.

15   When the dream had shaped itself perfectly in his memory, Aylmer sat in his wife's presence with a guilty feeling. Truth often finds its way to the mind close muffled in robes of sleep, and then speaks with uncompromising directness, of matters in regard to which we practise an unconscious self-deception during our waking moments. Until now he had not been aware of the tyrannizing influence acquired by one idea over his mind, and of the lengths which he might find in his heart to go for the sake of giving himself peace.

16   "Aylmer," resumed Georgiana, solemnly, "I know not what may be the cost to both of us to rid me of this fatal birthmark. Perhaps its removal may cause cureless deformity; or it may be the stain goes as deep as life itself. Again: do we know that there is a possibility, on any terms, of unclasping the firm gripe of this little hand which was laid upon me before I came into the world?"

17   "Dearest Georgiana, I have spent much thought upon the subject," hastily interrupted Aylmer. "I am convinced of the perfect practicability of its removal."

18   "If there be the remotest possibility of it," continued Georgiana, "let the attempt be made at whatever risk. Danger is nothing to me; for life, while the hateful mark makes me the object of your horror and disgust, — life is a burden which I would fling down with joy. Either remove this dreadful hand, or take my wretched life! You have deep science. All the world bears witness of it. You have achieved great wonders. Cannot you remove this little, little mark, which I cover with the tips of two small fingers? Is this beyond your power, for the sake of your own peace, and to save your poor wife from madness?"

19   "Noblest, dearest, tenderest wife," cried Aylmer, rapturously, "doubt not my power. I have already given this matter the deepest thought — thought which might almost have enlightened me to create a being less perfect than yourself. Georgiana, you have led me deeper than ever into the heart of science. I feel myself fully competent to render this dear cheek as faultless as its fellow; and then, most beloved, what will be my triumph when I shall have corrected what Nature left imperfect in her fairest work! Even Pygmalion,[2] when his

---

2. Sculptor and king of Cyprus in Greek legend who hated women but fell in love with his own ivory statue of a woman. The goddess Aphrodite answered his prayers and turned his statue into a live woman, Galatea, whom Pygmalion married.

sculptured woman assumed life, felt not greater ecstasy than mine will be."

20   "It is resolved, then," said Georgiana, faintly smiling. "And, Aylmer, spare me not, though you should find the birthmark take refuge in my heart at last."

21   Her husband tenderly kissed her cheek — her right cheek — not that which bore the impress of the crimson hand.

22   The next day Aylmer apprised his wife of a plan that he had formed whereby he might have opportunity for the intense thought and constant watchfulness which the proposed operation might require; while Georgiana, likewise, would enjoy the perfect repose essential to its success. They were to seclude themselves in the extensive apartments occupied by Aylmer as a laboratory, and where, during his toilsome youth, he had made discoveries in the elemental powers of Nature that had roused the admiration of all the learned societies in Europe. Seated calmly in this laboratory, the pale philosopher had investigated the secrets of the highest cloud region and of the profoundest mines; he had satisfied himself of the causes that kindled and kept alive the fires of the volcano; and had explained the mystery of fountains, and how it is that they gush forth, some so bright and pure, and others with such rich medicinal virtues, from the dark bosom of the earth. Here, too, at an earlier period, he had studied the wonders of the human frame, and attempted to fathom the very process by which Nature assimilates all her precious influences from earth and air, and from the spiritual world, to create and foster man, her masterpiece. The latter pursuit, however, Aylmer had long laid aside in unwilling recognition of the truth — against which all seekers sooner or later stumble — that our great creative Mother, while she amuses us with apparently working in the broadest sunshine, is yet severely careful to keep her own secrets, and, in spite of her pretended openness, shows us nothing but results. She permits us, indeed, to mar, but seldom to mend, and, like a jealous patentee, on no account to make. Now, however, Aylmer resumed these half-forgotten investigations; not, of course, with such hopes or wishes as first suggested them; but because they involved much physiological truth and lay in the path of his proposed scheme for the treatment of Georgiana.

23   As he led her over the threshold of the laboratory, Georgiana was cold and tremulous. Aylmer looked cheerfully into her face, with intent to reassure her, but was so startled with the intense glow of the birthmark upon the whiteness of her cheek that he could not restrain a strong convulsive shudder. His wife fainted.

24   "Aminadab! Aminadab!" shouted Aylmer, stamping violently on the floor.

25   Forthwith there issued from an inner apartment a man of low stature, but bulky frame, with shaggy hair hanging about his visage, which was grimed with the vapors of the furnace. This personage had been Aylmer's underworker during his whole scientific career, and was

admirably fitted for that office by his great mechanical readiness, and the skill with which, while incapable of comprehending a single principle, he executed all the details of his master's experiments. With his vast strength, his shaggy hair, his smoky aspect, and the indescribable earthiness that incrusted him, he seemed to represent man's physical nature; while Aylmer's slender figure, and pale, intellectual face, were no less apt a type of the spiritual element.

26 "Throw open the door of the boudoir, Aminadab," said Aylmer, "and burn a pastil."

27 "Yes, master," answered Aminadab, looking intently at the lifeless form of Georgiana; and then he muttered to himself, "If she were my wife, I'd never part with that birthmark."

28 When Georgiana recovered consciousness she found herself breathing an atmosphere of penetrating fragrance, the gentle potency of which had recalled her from her deathlike faintness. The scene around her looked like enchantment. Aylmer had converted those smoky, dingy, sombre rooms, where he had spent his brightest years in recondite pursuits, into a series of beautiful apartments not unfit to be the secluded abode of a lovely woman. The walls were hung with gorgeous curtains, which imparted the combination of grandeur and grace that no other species of adornment can achieve; and as they fell from the ceiling to the floor, their rich and ponderous folds, concealing all angles and straight lines, appeared to shut in the scene from infinite space. For aught Georgiana knew, it might be a pavilion among the clouds. And Aylmer, excluding the sunshine, which would have interfered with his chemical processes, had supplied its place with perfumed lamps, emitting flames of various hue, but all uniting in a soft, impurpled radiance. He now knelt by his wife's side, watching her earnestly, but without alarm; for he was confident in his science, and felt that he could draw a magic circle round her within which no evil might intrude.

29 "Where am I? Ah, I remember," said Georgiana, faintly; and she placed her hand over her cheek to hide the terrible mark from her husband's eyes.

30 "Fear not, dearest!" exclaimed he. "Do not shrink from me! Believe me, Georgiana, I even rejoice in this imperfection, since it will be such a rapture to remove it."

31 "Oh, spare me!" sadly replied his wife. "Pray do not look at it again. I can never forget that convulsive shudder."

32 In order to soothe Georgiana, and, as it were, to release her mind from the burden of actual things, Aylmer now put in practice some of the light and playful secrets which science had taught him among its profounder lore. Airy figures, absolutely bodiless ideas, and forms of unsubstantial beauty came and danced before her, imprinting their momentary footsteps on beams of light. Though she had some indistinct idea of the method of these optical phenomena, still the illusion was almost perfect enough to warrant the belief that her husband

possessed sway over the spiritual world. Then again, when she felt a wish to look forth from her seclusion, immediately, as if her thoughts were answered, the procession of external existence flitted across a screen. The scenery and the figures of actual life were perfectly represented, but with that bewitching yet indescribable difference which always makes a picture, an image, or a shadow so much more attractive than the original. When wearied of this, Aylmer bade her cast her eyes upon a vessel containing a quantity of earth. She did so, with little interest at first; but was soon startled to perceive the germ of a plant shooting upward from the soil. Then came the slender stalk; the leaves gradually unfolded themselves; and amid them was a perfect and lovely flower.

33   "It is magical!" cried Georgiana. "I dare not touch it."

34   "Nay, pluck it," answered Aylmer, — "pluck it, and inhale its brief perfume while you may. The flower will wither in a few moments and leave nothing save its brown seed vessels; but thence may be perpetuated with a race as ephemeral as itself."

35   But Georgiana had no sooner touched the flower than the whole plant suffered a blight, its leaves turning coal-black as if by the agency of fire.

36   "There was too powerful a stimulus," said Aylmer, thoughtfully.

37   To make up for this abortive experiment, he proposed to take her portrait by a scientific process of his own invention. It was to be effected by rays of light striking a polished plate of metal. Georgiana assented; but, on looking at the result, was affrighted to find the features of the portrait blurred and indefinable; while the minute figure of a hand appeared where the cheek should have been. Aylmer snatched the metallic plate and threw it into a jar of corrosive acid.

38   Soon, however, he forgot these mortifying failures. In the intervals of study and chemical experiment he came to her flushed and exhausted, but seemed invigorated by her presence, and spoke in glowing language of the resources of his art. He gave a history of the long dynasty of the alchemists, who spent so many ages in quest of the universal solvent by which the golden principle might be elicited from all things vile and base. Aylmer appeared to believe that, by the plainest scientific logic, it was altogether within the limits of possibility to discover this long-sought medium; "but," he added, "a philosopher who should go deep enough to acquire the power would attain too lofty a wisdom to stoop to the exercise of it." Not less singular were his opinions in regard to the elixir vitae. He more than intimated that it was at his option to concoct a liquid that should prolong life for years, perhaps interminably; but that it would produce a discord in Nature which all the world, and chiefly the quaffer of the immortal nostrum, would find cause to curse.

39   "Aylmer, are you in earnest?" asked Georgiana, looking at him with amazement and fear. "It is terrible to possess such power, or even to dream of possessing it."

40   "O, do not tremble, my love," said her husband. "I would not wrong either you or myself by working such inharmonious effects upon our lives; but I would have you consider how trifling, in comparison, is the skill requisite to remove this little hand."

41   At the mention of the birthmark, Georgiana, as usual, shrank as if a red-hot iron had touched her cheek.

42   Again Aylmer applied himself to his labors. She could hear his voice in the distant furnace room giving directions to Aminadab, whose harsh, uncouth, misshapen tones were audible in response, more like the grunt or growl of a brute than human speech. After hours of absence, Aylmer reappeared and proposed that she should now examine his cabinet of chemical products and natural treasures of the earth. Among the former he showed her a small vial, in which, he remarked, was contained the gentle yet most powerful fragrance, capable of impregnating all the breezes that blow across a kingdom. They were of inestimable value, the contents of that little vial; and, as he said so, he threw some of the perfume into the air and filled the room with piercing and invigorating delight.

43   "And what is this?" asked Georgiana, pointing to a small crystal globe containing a gold-colored liquid. "It is so beautiful to the eye that I could imagine it the elixir of life."

44   "In one sense it is," replied Aylmer, "or rather, the elixir of immortality. It is the most precious poison that ever was concocted in this world. By its aid I could apportion the lifetime of any mortal at whom you might point your finger. The strength of the dose would determine whether he were to linger out years, or drop dead in the midst of a breath. No king on his guarded throne could keep his life if I, in my private station, should deem the welfare of millions justified me in depriving him of it."

45   "Why do you keep such a terrific drug?" inquired Georgiana in horror.

46   "Do not mistrust me, dearest," said her husband, smiling; "its virtuous potency is yet greater than its harmful one. But see! here is a powerful cosmetic. With a few drops of this in a vase of water, freckles may be washed away as easily as the hands are cleansed. A stronger infusion would take the blood out of the cheek, and leave the rosiest beauty a pale ghost."

47   "Is it with this lotion that you intend to bathe my cheek?" asked Georgiana, anxiously.

48   "Oh, no," hastily replied her husband; "this is merely superficial. Your case demands a remedy that shall go deeper."

49   In his interviews with Georgiana, Aylmer generally made minute inquiries as to her sensations, and whether the confinement of the rooms and the temperature of the atmosphere agreed with her. These questions had such a particular drift that Georgiana began to conjecture that she was already subjected to certain physical influences, either breathed in with the fragrant air or taken with her food. She

fancied likewise, but it might be altogether fancy, that there was a stirring up of her system — a strange, indefinite sensation creeping through her veins, and tingling, half painfully, half pleasurably, at her heart. Still, whenever she dared to look into the mirror, there she beheld herself pale as a white rose and with the crimson birthmark stamped upon her cheek. Not even Aylmer now hated it so much as she.

50   To dispel the tedium of the hours which her husband found it necessary to devote to the process of combination and analysis, Georgiana turned over the volumes of his scientific library. In many dark old tomes she met with chapters full of romance and poetry. They were the works of the philosophers of the middle ages, such as Albertus Magnus, Cornelius Agrippa, Paracelsus, and the famous friar who created the prophetic Brazen Head.[3] All these antique naturalists stood in advance of their centuries, yet were imbued with some of their credulity, and therefore were believed, and perhaps imagined themselves to have acquired from the investigation of Nature a power above Nature, and from physics a sway over the spiritual world. Hardly less curious and imaginative were the early volumes of the Transactions of the Royal Society,[4] in which the members, knowing little of the limits of natural possibility, were continually recording wonders or proposing methods whereby wonders might be wrought.

51   But to Georgiana, the most engrossing volume was a large folio from her husband's own hand, in which he had recorded every experiment of his scientific career, its original aim, the methods adopted for its development, and its final success or failure, with the circumstances to which either event was attributable. The book, in truth, was both the history and emblem of his ardent, ambitious, imaginative, yet practical and laborious life. He handled physical details as if there were nothing beyond them; yet spiritualized them all and redeemed himself from materialism by his strong and eager aspiration towards the infinite. In his grasp the veriest clod of earth assumed a soul. Georgiana, as she read, reverenced Aylmer and loved him more profoundly than ever, but with a less entire dependence on his judgment than heretofore. Much as he had accomplished, she could not but observe that his splendid successes were almost invariably failures, if

---

3. Albertus Magnus (1206–1280), German scholastic philosopher whose name was often associated with a book of alchemical "secrets." Heinrich Cornelius Agrippa von Nettesheim (1486–1535), German writer and physician who was reputed to be a magician. He was charged with heresy and his writings were suppressed by the Inquisition. Paracelsus (c. 1490–1541), German physician who devised a highly unconventional pharmaceutical system. The Brazen Head, a head of brass which knew all things and could speak, was supposed to have been created by Roger Bacon (c. 1214–1294?), the "famous friar," an English scholastic philosopher and scientist.

4. The Royal Society, founded in 1660, is the oldest scientific organization in Great Britain and one of the oldest in Europe. Its activities include the publication of its *Proceedings* and of *The Philosophical Transactions*.

compared with the ideal at which he aimed. His brightest diamonds were the merest pebbles, and felt to be so by himself, in comparison with the inestimable gems which lay hidden beyond his reach. The volume, rich with achievements that had won renown for its author, was yet as melancholy a record as ever mortal hand had penned. It was the sad confession and continual exemplification of the shortcomings of the composite man, the spirit burdened with clay and working in matter, and of the despair that assails the higher nature at finding itself so miserably thwarted by the earthly part. Perhaps every man of genius, in whatever sphere, might recognize the image of his own experience in Aylmer's journal.

52 So deeply did these reflections affect Georgiana that she laid her face upon the open volume and burst into tears. In this situation she was found by her husband.

53 "It is dangerous to read in a sorcerer's books," said he with a smile, though his countenance was uneasy and displeased. "Georgiana, there are pages in that volume which I can scarcely glance over and keep my senses. Take heed lest it prove detrimental to you."

54 "It has made me worship you more than ever," said she.

55 "Ah, wait for this one success," rejoined he, "then worship me if you will. I shall deem myself hardly unworthy of it. But come, I have sought you for the luxury of your voice. Sing to me, dearest."

56 So she poured out the liquid music of her voice to quench the thirst of his spirit. He then took his leave with a boyish exuberance of gayety, assuring her that her seclusion would endure but a little longer, and that the result was already certain. Scarcely had he departed when Georgiana felt irresistibly impelled to follow him. She had forgotten to inform Aylmer of a symptom which for two or three hours past had begun to excite her attention. It was a sensation in the fatal birthmark, not painful, but which induced restlessness throughout her system. Hastening after her husband, she intruded for the first time into the laboratory.

57 The first thing that struck her eye was the furnace, that hot and feverish worker, with the intense glow of its fire, which by the quantities of soot clustered above it seemed to have been burning for ages. There was a distilling apparatus in full operation. Around the room were retorts, tubes, cylinders, crucibles, and other apparatus of chemical research. An electrical machine stood ready for immediate use. The atmosphere felt oppressively close, and was tainted with gaseous odors which had been tormented forth by the processes of science. The severe and homely simplicity of the apartment, with its naked walls and brick pavement, looked strange, accustomed as Georgiana had become to the fantastic elegance of her boudoir. But what chiefly, indeed almost solely, drew her attention, was the aspect of Aylmer himself.

58 He was pale as death, anxious and absorbed, and hung over the furnace as if it depended upon his utmost watchfulness whether the

liquid which it was distilling should be the draught of immortal happiness or misery. How different from the sanguine and joyous mien that he had assumed for Georgiana's encouragement!

59 "Carefully now, Aminadab; carefully, thou human machine, carefully, thou man of clay," muttered Aylmer, more to himself than his assistant. "Now, if there be a thought too much or too little, it is all over!"

60 "Ho! ho!" mumbled Aminadab. "Look, master! look!"

61 Aylmer raised his eyes hastily, and at first reddened, then grew paler than ever, on beholding Georgiana. He rushed towards her and seized her arm with a gripe that left the print of his fingers upon it.

62 "Why do you come hither? Have you no trust in your husband?" cried he, impetuously. "Would you throw the blight of that fatal birthmark over my labors? It is not well done. Go, prying woman! go!"

63 "Nay, Aylmer," said Georgiana with the firmness of which she possessed no stinted endowment, "it is not you that have a right to complain. You mistrust your wife; you have concealed the anxiety with which you watch the development of this experiment. Think not so unworthily of me, my husband. Tell me all the risk we run, and fear not that I shall shrink; for my share in it is far less than your own."

64 "No, no, Georgiana!" said Aylmer, impatiently; "it must not be."

65 "I submit," replied she, calmly. "And, Aylmer, I shall quaff whatever draught you bring me; but it will be on the same principle that would induce me to take a dose of poison if offered by your hand."

66 "My noble wife," said Aylmer, deeply moved, "I knew not the height and depth of your nature until now. Nothing shall be concealed. Know, then, that this crimson hand, superficial as it seems, has clutched its grasp into your being with a strength of which I had no previous conception. I have already administered agents powerful enough to do aught except to change your entire physical system. Only one thing remains to be tried. If that fail us we are ruined."

67 "Why did you hesitate to tell me this?" asked she.

68 "Because, Georgiana," said Aylmer, in a low voice, "there is danger."

69 "Danger? There is but one danger — that this horrible stigma shall be left upon my cheek!" cried Georgiana. "Remove it, remove it, whatever be the cost, or we shall both go mad!"

70 "Heaven knows your words are too true," said Aylmer, sadly. "And now, dearest, return to your boudoir. In a little while all will be tested."

71 He conducted her back and took leave of her with a solemn tenderness which spoke far more than his words how much was now at stake. After his departure Georgiana became rapt in musings. She considered the character of Aylmer and did it completer justice than at any previous moment. Her heart exulted, while it trembled, at his honorable love — so pure and lofty that it would accept nothing less than perfection nor miserably make itself contented with an earthlier

nature than he had dreamed of. She felt how much more precious was such a sentiment than that meaner kind which would have borne with the imperfection for her sake, and have been guilty of treason to holy love by degrading its perfect idea to the level of the actual; and with her whole spirit she prayed that, for a single moment, she might satisfy his highest and deepest conception. Longer than one moment she well knew it could not be; for his spirit was ever on the march, ever ascending, and each instant required something that was beyond the scope of the instant before.

72  The sound of her husband's footsteps aroused her. He bore a crystal goblet containing a liquor colorless as water, but bright enough to be the draught of immortality. Aylmer was pale; but it seemed rather the consequence of a highly-wrought state of mind and tension of spirit than of fear or doubt.

73  "The concoction of the draught has been perfect," said he, in answer to Georgiana's look. "Unless all my science have deceived me, it cannot fail."

74  "Save on your account, my dearest Aylmer," observed his wife, "I might wish to put off this birthmark of mortality by relinquishing mortality itself in preference to any other mode. Life is but a sad possession to those who have attained precisely the degree of moral advancement at which I stand. Were I weaker and blinder, it might become happiness. Were I stronger, it might be endured hopefully. But, being what I find myself, methinks I am of all mortals the most fit to die."

75  "You are fit for heaven without tasting death!" replied her husband. "But why do we speak of dying? The draught cannot fail. Behold its effect upon this plant."

76  On the window seat there stood a geranium diseased with yellow blotches which had overspread all its leaves. Aylmer poured a small quantity of the liquid upon the soil in which it grew. In a little time, when the roots of the plant had taken up the moisture, the unsightly blotches began to be extinguished in a living verdure.

77  "There needed no proof," said Georgiana, quietly. "Give me the goblet. I joyfully stake all upon your word."

78  "Drink, then, thou lofty creature!" exclaimed Aylmer, with fervid admiration. "There is no taint of imperfection on thy spirit. Thy sensible frame, too, shall soon be all perfect."

79  She quaffed the liquid and returned the goblet to his hand.

80  "It is grateful," said she, with a placid smile. "Methinks it is like water from a heavenly fountain; for it contains I know not what of unobtrusive fragrance and deliciousness. It allays a feverish thirst that had parched me for many days. Now, dearest, let me sleep. My earthly senses are closing over my spirit like the leaves around the heart of a rose at sunset."

81  She spoke the last words with a gentle reluctance, as if it required almost more energy than she could command to pronounce the faint

and lingering syllables. Scarcely had they loitered through her lips ere she was lost in slumber. Aylmer sat by her side, watching her aspect with the emotions proper to a man the whole value of whose existence was involved in the process now to be tested. Mingled with this mood, however, was the philosophic investigation characteristic of the man of science. Not the minutest symptom escaped him. A heightened flush of the cheek, a slight irregularity of breath, a quiver of the eyelid, a hardly perceptible tremor through the frame, — such were the details which, as the moments passed, he wrote down in his folio volume. Intense thought had set its stamp upon every previous page of that volume; but the thoughts of years were all concentrated upon the last.

82  While thus employed, he failed not to gaze often at the fatal hand, and not without a shudder. Yet once, by a strange and unaccountable impulse, he pressed it with his lips. His spirit recoiled, however, in the very act; and Georgiana, out of the midst of her deep sleep, moved uneasily and murmured as if in remonstrance. Again Aylmer resumed his watch. Nor was it without avail. The crimson hand, which at first had been strongly visible upon the marble paleness of Georgiana's cheek, now grew more faintly outlined. She remained not less pale than ever; but the birthmark, with every breath that came and went lost somewhat of its former distinctness. Its presence had been awful; its departure was more awful still. Watch the stain of the rainbow fading out of the sky, and you will know how that mysterious symbol passed away.

83  "By Heaven! it is well nigh gone!" said Aylmer to himself, in almost irrepressible ecstasy. "I can scarcely trace it now. Success! success! And now it is like the faintest rose color. The lightest flush of blood across her cheek would overcome it. But she is so pale!"

84  He drew aside the window curtain and suffered the light of natural day to fall into the room and rest upon her cheek. At the same time he heard a gross, hoarse chuckle, which he had long known as his servant Aminadab's expression of delight.

85  "Ah, clod! ah, earthly mass!" cried Aylmer, laughing in a sort of frenzy, "you have served me well!" Matter and spirit — earth and heaven — have both done their part in this! Laugh, thing of the senses! You have earned the right to laugh."

86  These exclamations broke Georgiana's sleep. She slowly unclosed her eyes and gazed into the mirror which her husband had arranged for that purpose. A faint smile flitted over her lips when she recognized how barely perceptible was now that crimson hand which had once blazed forth with such disastrous brilliancy as to scare away all their happiness. But then her eyes sought Aylmer's face with a trouble and anxiety that he could by no means account for.

87  "My poor Aylmer!" murmured she.

88  "Poor? Nay, richest, happiest, most favored!" exclaimed he. "My peerless bride, it is successful! You are perfect!"

89 "My poor Aylmer," she repeated, with a more than human tenderness, "you have aimed loftily; you have done nobly. Do not repent that, with so high and pure a feeling, you have rejected the best the earth could offer. Aylmer, dearest Aylmer, I am dying!"

90 Alas! it was too true! The fatal hand had grappled with the mystery of life, and was the bond by which an angelic spirit kept itself in union with a mortal frame. As the last crimson tint of the birthmark — that sole token of human imperfection — faded from her cheek, the parting breath of the now perfect woman passed into the atmosphere, and her soul, lingering a moment near her husband, took its heavenward flight. Then a hoarse, chuckling laugh was heard again! Thus ever does the gross fatality of earth exult in its invariable triumph over the immortal essence which, in this dim sphere of half development, demands the completeness of a higher state. Yet, had Aylmer reached a profounder wisdom, he need not thus have flung away the happiness which would have woven his mortal life of the selfsame textures with the celestial. The momentary circumstance was too strong for him; he failed to look beyond the shadowy scope of time, and, living once for all in eternity, to find the perfect future in the present.

*(1843)*

# Edgar Allan Poe (1809–1849)

*Short-story writer, poet, critic, and essayist, this American author was a leading architect of the short fiction form. Poe's best-known tales are appreciated for their psychological intensity, an effect often created by a finely tuned first-person narrator. Poe valued the aesthetic over the didactic properties of literature.*

## The Tell-Tale Heart

1   True! — nervous — very, very dreadfully nervous I had been and am; but why *will* you say that I am mad? The disease had sharpened my senses — not destroyed — not dulled them. Above all was the sense of hearing acute. I heard all things in the heaven and in the earth. I heard many things in hell. How, then, am I mad? Hearken! and observe how healthily — how calmly I can tell you the whole story.

2   It is impossible to say how first the idea entered my brain; but once conceived, it haunted me day and night. Object there was none. Passion there was none. I loved the old man. He had never wronged me. He had never given me insult. For his gold I had no desire. I think it was his eye! yes, it was this! He had the eye of a vulture — a pale blue eye, with a film over it. Whenever it fell upon me, my blood ran cold; and so by degrees — very gradually — I made up my mind to take the life of the old man, and thus rid myself of the eye forever.

3   Now this is the point. You fancy me mad. Madmen know nothing. But you should have seen *me*. You should have seen how wisely I proceeded — with what caution — with what foresight — with what dissimulation I went to work! I was never kinder to the old man than during the whole week before I killed him. And every night, about midnight, I turned the latch of his door and opened it — oh so gently! And then, when I had made an opening sufficient for my head, I put in a dark lantern, all closed, closed, so that no light shone out, and then I thrust in my head. Oh, you would have laughed to see how cunningly I thrust it in! I moved it slowly — very, very slowly, so that I might not disturb the old man's sleep. It took me an hour to place my whole head within the opening so far that I could see him as he lay upon his bed. Ha! — would a madman have been so wise as this? And then, when my head was well

in the room, I undid the lantern cautiously — oh, so cautiously — cautiously (for the hinges creaked) — I undid it just so much that a single thin ray fell upon the vulture eye. And this I did for seven long nights — every night just at midnight — but I found the eye always closed; and so it was impossible to do the work; for it was not the old man who vexed me, but his Evil Eye. And every morning, when the day broke, I went boldly into the chamber, and spoke courageously to him, calling him by name in a hearty tone, and inquiring how he had passed the night. So you see he would have been a very profound old man, indeed, to suspect that every night, just at twelve, I looked in upon him while he slept.

4   Upon the eighth night I was more than usually cautious in opening the door. A watch's minute hand moves more quickly than did mine. Never before that night, had I *felt* the extent of my own powers — of my sagacity. I could scarcely contain my feelings of triumph. To think that there I was, opening the door, little by little, and he not even to dream of my secret deeds or thoughts. I fairly chuckled at the idea; and perhaps he heard me; for he moved on the bed suddenly, as if startled. Now you may think that I drew back — but no. His room was as black as pitch with the thick darkness, (for the shutters were close fastened, through fear of robbers,) and so I knew that he could not see the opening of the door, and I kept pushing it on steadily, steadily.

5   I had my head in, and was about to open the lantern, when my thumb slipped upon the tin fastening, and the old man sprang up in bed, crying out — "Who's there?"

6   I kept quite still and said nothing. For a whole hour I did not move a muscle, and in the meantime I did not hear him lie down. He was still sitting up in the bed listening; — just as I have done, night after night, hearkening to the death watches in the wall.

7   Presently I heard a slight groan, and I knew it was the groan of mortal terror. It was not a groan of pain or of grief — oh, no! — it was the low stifled sound that arises from the bottom of the soul when overcharged with awe. I knew the sound well. Many a night, just at midnight, when all the world slept, it has welled up from my own bosom, deepening, with its dreadful echo, the terrors that distracted me. I say I knew it well. I knew what the old man felt, and pitied him, although I chuckled at heart. I knew that he had been lying awake ever since the first slight noise, when he had turned in the bed. His fears had been ever since growing upon him. He had been trying to fancy them causeless, but could not. He had been saying to himself — "It is nothing but the wind in the chimney — it is only a mouse crossing the floor," or "it is merely a cricket which has made a single chirp." Yes, he had been trying to comfort himself with these suppositions: but he had found all in vain. *All in vain*; because Death, in approaching him had stalked with his black shadow before him, and enveloped the victim. And it was the mournful influence

of the unperceived shadow that caused him to feel — although he neither saw nor heard — to *feel* the presence of my head within the room.

8   When I had waited a long time, very patiently, without hearing him lie down, I resolved to open a little — a very, very little crevice in the lantern. So I opened it — you cannot imagine how stealthily, stealthily — until, at length a simple dim ray, like the thread of the spider, shot from out the crevice and fell full upon the vulture eye.

9   It was open — wide, wide open — and I grew furious as I gazed upon it. I saw it with perfect distinctness — all a dull blue, with a hideous veil over it that chilled the very marrow in my bones; but I could see nothing else of the old man's face or person: for I had directed the ray as if by instinct, precisely upon the damned spot.

10   And have I not told you that what you mistake for madness is but over acuteness of the senses? — now, I say, there came to my ears a low, dull, quick sound, such as a watch makes when enveloped in cotton. I knew *that* sound well, too. It was the beating of the old man's heart. It increased my fury, as the beating of a drum stimulates the soldier into courage.

11   But even yet I refrained and kept still. I scarcely breathed. I held the lantern motionless. I tried how steadily I could maintain the ray upon the eye. Meantime the hellish tattoo of the heart increased. It grew quicker and quicker, and louder and louder every instant. The old man's terror *must* have been extreme! It grew louder, I say, louder every moment! — do you mark me well? I have told you that I am nervous: so I am. And now at the dead hour of the night, amid the dreadful silence of that old house, so strange a noise as this excited me to uncontrollable terror. Yet, for some minutes longer I refrained and stood still. But the beating grew louder, louder! I thought the heart must burst. And now a new anxiety seized me — the sound would be heard by a neighbour! The old man's hour had come! With a loud yell, I thew open the lantern and leaped into the room. He shrieked once — once only. In an instant I dragged him to the floor, and pulled the heavy bed over him. I then smiled gaily, to find the deed so far done. But, for many minutes, the heart beat on with a muffled sound. This, however, did not vex me; it would not be heard through the wall. At length it ceased. The old man was dead. I removed the bed and examined the corpse. Yes, he was stone, stone dead. I placed my hand upon the heart and held it there many minutes. There was no pulsation. He was stone dead. His eye would trouble me no more.

12   If still you think me mad, you will think so no longer when I describe the wise precautions I took for the concealment of the body. The night waned, and I worked hastily, but in silence. First of all I dismembered the corpse. I cut off the head and the arms and the legs.

13   I then took up three planks from the flooring of the chamber, and deposited all between the scantlings. I then replaced the boards so

cleverly, so cunningly, that no human eye — not even *his* — could have detected any thing wrong. There was nothing to wash out — no stain of any kind — no blood-spot whatever. I had been too wary for that. A tub had caught all — ha! ha!

14   When I had made an end of these labors, it was four o'clock — still dark as midnight. As the bell sounded the hour, there came a knocking at the street door. I went down to open it with a light heart, — for what had I *now* to fear? There entered three men, who introduced themselves, with perfect suavity, as officers of the police. A shriek had been heard by a neighbor during the night; suspicion of foul play had been aroused; information had been lodged at the police office, and they (the officers) had been deputed to search the premises.

15   I smiled, — for *what* had I to fear? I bade the gentlemen welcome. The shriek, I said, was my own in a dream. The old man, I mentioned, was absent in the country. I took my visitors all over the house. I bade them search — search *well*. I led them, at length, to *his* chamber. I showed them his treasures, secure, undisturbed. In the enthusiasm of my confidence, I brought chairs into the room, and desired them *here* to rest from their fatigues, while I myself, in the wild audacity of my perfect triumph, placed my own seat upon the very spot beneath which reposed the corpse of the victim.

16   The officers were satisfied. My *manner* had convinced them. I was singularly at ease. They sat, and while I answered cheerily, they chatted of familiar things. But, ere long, I felt myself getting pale and wished them gone. My head ached, and I fancied a ringing in my ears: but still they sat and still chatted. The ringing became more distinct: — it continued and became more distinct: I talked more freely to get rid of the feeling: but it continued and gained definiteness — until, at length, I found that the noise was *not* within my ears.

17   No doubt I now grew very pale; — but I talked more fluently, and with a heightened voice. Yet the sound increased — and what could I do? It was *a low, dull, quick sound — much such a sound as a watch makes when enveloped in cotton*. I gasped for breath — and yet the officers heard it not. I talked more quickly — more vehemently; but the noise steadily increased. I arose and argued about trifles, in a high key and with violent gesticulations; but the noise steadily increased. Why *would* they not be gone? I paced the floor to and fro with heavy strides, as if excited to fury by the observations of the men — but the noise steadily increased. Oh God! what *could* I do? I foamed — I raved — I swore! I swung the chair upon which I had been sitting, and grated it upon the boards, but the noise arose over all and continually increased. It grew louder — louder — *louder*! And still the men chatted pleasantly, and smiled. Was it possible they heard not? Almighty God! — no, no! They heard! — they suspected! — they *knew*! — they were making a mockery of my horror! — this I thought, and this I think. But anything was better than this agony! Anything was more tolerable than this derision! I could bear those hypocritical smiles no

longer! I felt that I must scream or die! and now — again! — hark! louder! louder! louder! *louder!*

18 "Villains," I shrieked, "dissemble no more! I admit the deed! — tear up the planks! here, here! — it is the beating of his hideous heart!"

*(1843)*

# Sarah Orne Jewett (1849–1909)

Born in Maine, Sarah Orne Jewett responded to the rural landscape and ordinary people around her with what critics have called a "lyrical" fiction. She presents a meditation on experience rather than an incident-filled plot.

## A White Heron

### 1

1 The woods were already filled with shadows one June evening, just before eight o'clock, though a bright sunset still glimmered faintly among the trunks of the trees. A little girl was driving home her cow, a plodding, dilatory, provoking creature in her behavior, but a valued companion for all that. They were going away from the western light, and striking deep into the dark woods, but their feet were familiar with the path, and it was no matter whether their eyes could see it or not.

2 There was hardly a night the summer through when the old cow could be found waiting at the pasture bars; on the contrary, it was her greatest pleasure to hide herself away among the high huckleberry bushes, and though she wore a loud bell she had made the discovery that if one stood perfectly still it would not ring. So Sylvia had to hunt for her until she found her, and call Co'! Co'! with never an answering Moo, until her childish patience was quite spent. If the creature had not given good milk and plenty of it, the case would have seemed very different to her owners. Besides, Sylvia had all the time there was, and very little use to make of it. Sometimes in pleasant weather it was a consolation to look upon the cow's pranks as an intelligent attempt to play hide and seek, and as the child had no playmates she lent herself to this amusement with a good deal of zest. Though this chase had been so long that the wary animal herself had given an unusual signal of her whereabouts, Sylvia had only laughed when she came upon Mistress Moolly at the swamp-side, and urged her affectionately homeward with a twig of birch leaves. The old cow was not inclined to wander farther, she even turned in the right direction for once as they left the pasture, and stepped along the road at a good pace. She

was quite ready to be milked now, and seldom stopped to browse. Sylvia wondered what her grandmother would say because they were so late. It was a great while since she had left home at half past five o'clock, but everybody knew the difficulty of making this errand a short one. Mrs. Tilley had chased the horned torment too many summer evenings herself to blame any one else for lingering, and was only thankful as she waited that she had Sylvia, nowadays, to give such valuable assistance. The good woman suspected that Sylvia loitered occasionally on her own account; there never was such a child for straying about out-of-doors since the world was made! Everybody said that it was a good change for a little maid who had tried to grow for eight years in a crowded manufacturing town, but, as for Sylvia herself, it seemed as if she never had been alive at all before she came to live at the farm. She thought often with wistful compassion of a wretched dry geranium that belonged to a town neighbor.

3   "'Afraid of folks,'" old Mrs. Tilley said to herself, with a smile, after she had made the unlikely choice of Sylvia from her daughter's houseful of children, and was returning to the farm. "'Afraid of folks,' they said! I guess she won't be troubled no great with 'em up to the old place!" When they reached the door of the lonely house and stopped to unlock it, and the cat came to purr loudly, and rub against them, a deserted pussy, indeed, but fat with young robins, Sylvia whispered that this was a beautiful place to live in, and she never should wish to go home.

4   The companions followed the shady woodroad, the cow taking slow steps, and the child very fast ones. The cow stopped long at the brook to drink, as if the pasture were not half swamp, and Sylvia stood still and waited, letting her bare feet cool themselves in the shoal water, while the great twilight moths struck softly against her. She waded on through the brook as the cow moved away, and listened to the thrushes with a heart that beat fast with pleasure. There was a stirring in the great boughs overhead. They were full of little birds and beasts that seemed to be wide-awake, and going about their world, or else saying goodnight to each other in sleepy twitters. Sylvia herself felt sleepy as she walked along. However, it was not much farther to the house, and the air was soft and sweet. She was not often in the woods so late as this, and it made her feel as if she were a part of the gray shadows and the moving leaves. She was just thinking how long it seemed since she first came to the farm a year ago, and wondering if everything went on in the noisy town just the same as when she was there; the thought of the great red-faced boy who used to chase and frighten her made her hurry along the path to escape from the shadow of the trees.

5   Suddenly this little woods-girl is horror-stricken to hear a clear whistle not very far away. Not a bird's whistle, which would have a sort of friendliness, but a boy's whistle, determined, and somewhat aggres-

sive. Sylvia left the cow to whatever sad fate might await her, and stepped discreetly aside into the bushes, but she was just too late. The enemy had discovered her, and called out in a very cheerful and persuasive tone, "Halloa, little girl, how far is it to the road?" and trembling Sylvia answered almost inaudibly, "A good ways."

6   She did not dare to look boldly at the tall young man, who carried a gun over his shoulder, but she came out of her bush and again followed the cow, while he walked alongside.

7   "I've been hunting for some birds," the stranger said kindly, "and I have lost my way, and need a friend very much. Don't be afraid," he added gallantly. "Speak up and tell me what your name is, and whether you think I can spend the night at your house, and go out gunning early in the morning."

8   Sylvia was more alarmed than before. Would not her grandmother consider her much to blame? But who could have foreseen such an accident as this? It did not appear to be her fault, and she hung her head as if the stem of it were broken, but managed to answer, "Sylvy," with much effort when her companion again asked her name.

9   Mrs. Tilley was standing in the doorway when the trio came into view. The cow gave a loud moo by way of explanation.

10  "Yes, you'd better speak up for yourself, you old trial! Where'd she tuck herself away this time, Sylvy?" Sylvia kept an awed silence; she knew by instinct that her grandmother did not comprehend the gravity of the situation. She must be mistaking the stranger for one of the farmer-lads of the region.

11  The young man stood his gun beside the door, and dropped a heavy game-bag beside it; then he bade Mrs. Tilley good-evening, and repeated his wayfarer's story, and asked if he could have a night's lodging.

12  "Put me anywhere you like," he said. "I must be off early in the morning, before day; but I am very hungry, indeed. You can give me some milk at any rate, that's plain."

13  "Dear sakes, yes," responded the hostess, whose long slumbering hospitality seemed to be easily awakened. "You might fare better if you went out the main road a mile or so, but you're welcome to what we've got. I'll milk right off, and you make yourself at home. You can sleep on husks or feathers," she proffered graciously. "I raised them all myself. There's good pasturing for geese just below here towards the ma'sh. Now step round and set a plate for the gentleman, Sylvy!" And Sylvia promptly stepped. She was glad to have something to do, and she was hungry herself.

14  It was a surprise to find so clean and comfortable a little dwelling in this New England wilderness. The young man had known the horrors of its most primitive housekeeping, and the dreary squalor of that level of society which does not rebel at the companionship of hens. This was the best thrift of an old-fashioned farmstead, though on such a small scale that it seemed like a hermitage. He listened eagerly to the

old woman's quaint talk, he watched Sylvia's pale face and shining gray eyes with ever growing enthusiasm, and insisted that this was the best supper he had eaten for a month; then, afterward, the new-made friends sat down in the doorway together while the moon came up.

15   Soon it would be berry-time, and Sylvia was a great help at picking. The cow was a good milker, though a plaguy thing to keep track of, the hostess gossiped frankly, adding presently that she had buried four children, so that Sylvia's mother, and a son (who might be dead) in California were all the children she had left. "Dan, my boy, was a great hand to go gunning," she explained sadly, "I never wanted for pa'tridges or gray squer'ls while he was to home. He's been a great wand'rer, I expect, and he's no hand to write letters. There, I don't blame him, I'd ha' seen the world myself if it had been so I could."

16   "Sylvia takes after him," the grandmother continued affectionately, after a minute's pause. "There ain't a foot o' ground she don't know her way over, and the wild creatur's counts her one o' themselves. Squer'ls she'll tame to come an' feed right out o' her hands, and all sorts o' birds. Last winter she got the jay-birds to bangeing[1] here, and I believe she'd 'a' scanted herself of her own meals to have plenty to throw out amongst 'em, if I hadn't kep' watch. Anything but crows, I tell her, I'm willin' to help support, — though Dan he went an' tamed one o' them that did seem to have reason same as folks. It was round here a good spell after he went away. Dan an' his father they didn't hitch, — but he never held up his head ag'in after Dan dared him an' gone off."

17   The guest did not notice this hint of family sorrows in his eager interest in something else.

18   "So Sylvy knows all about birds, does she?" he exclaimed, as he looked round at the little girl who sat, very demure but increasingly sleepy, in the moonlight. "I am making a collection of birds myself. I have been at it ever since I was a boy." (Mrs. Tilley smiled.) "There are two or three very rare ones I have been hunting for these five years. I mean to get them on my own ground if they can be found."

19   "Do you cage 'em up?" asked Mrs. Tilley doubtfully, in response to this enthusiastic announcement.

20   "Oh, no, they're stuffed and preserved, dozens and dozens of them," said the ornithologist, "and I have shot or snared every one myself. I caught a glimpse of a white heron three miles from here on Saturday, and I have followed it in this direction. They have never been found in this district at all. The little white heron, it is," and he turned again to look at Sylvia with the hope of discovering that the rare bird was one of her acquaintances.

21   But Sylvia was watching a hop-toad in the narrow footpath.

---

1. Scrounging.

22   "You would know the heron if you saw it," the stranger continued eagerly. "A queer tall white bird with soft feathers and long thin legs. And it would have a nest perhaps in the top of a high tree, made of sticks, something like a hawk's nest."

23   Sylvia's heart gave a wild beat; she knew that strange white bird, and had once stolen softly near where it stood in some bright green swamp grass, away over at the other side of the woods. There was an open place where the sunshine always seemed strangely yellow and hot, where tall, nodding rushes grew, and her grandmother had warned her that she might sink in the soft black mud underneath and never be heard of more. Not far beyond were the salt marshes and beyond those was the sea, the sea which Sylvia wondered and dreamed about, but never had looked upon, though its great voice could often be heard above the noise of the woods on stormy nights.

24   "I can't think of anything I should like so much as to find that heron's nest," the handsome stranger was saying. "I would give ten dollars to anybody who could show it to me," he added desperately, "and I mean to spend my whole vacation hunting for it if need be. Perhaps it was only migrating, or had been chased out of its own region by some bird of prey."

25   Mrs. Tilley gave amazed attention to all this, but Sylvia still watched the toad, not divining, as she might have done at some calmer time, that the creature wished to get to its hole under the doorstep, and was much hindered by the unusual spectators at that hour of the evening. No amount of thought, that night, could decide how many wished-for treasures the ten dollars, so lightly spoken of, would buy.

26   The next day the young sportsman hovered about the woods, and Sylvia kept him company, having lost her first fear of the friendly lad, who proved to be most kind and sympathetic. He told her many things about the birds and what they knew and where they lived and what they did with themselves. And he gave her a jack-knife, which she thought as great a treasure as if she were a desert-islander. All day long he did not once make her troubled or afraid except when he brought down some unsuspecting singing creature from its bough. Sylvia would have liked him vastly better without his gun; she could not understand why he killed the very birds he seemed to like so much. But as the day waned, Sylvia still watched the young man with loving admiration. She had never seen anybody so charming and delightful; the woman's heart, asleep in the child, was vaguely thrilled by a dream of love. Some premonition of that great power stirred and swayed these young foresters who traversed the solemn woodlands with soft-footed silent care. They stopped to listen to a bird's song; they pressed forward again eagerly, parting the branches, — speaking to each other rarely and in whispers; the young man going first and Sylvia following, fascinated, a few steps behind, with her gray eyes dark with excitement.

27  She grieved because the longed-for white heron was elusive, but she did not lead the guest, she only followed, and there was no such thing as speaking first. The sound of her own unquestioned voice would have terrified her, — it was hard enough to answer yes or no when there was need of that. At last evening began to fall, and they drove the cow home together, and Sylvia smiled with pleasure when they came to the place where she heard the whistle and was afraid only the night before.

## 2

28  Half a mile from home, at the farther edge of the woods, where the land was highest, a great pine-tree stood, the last of its generation. Whether it was left for a boundary mark, or for what reason, no one could say; the woodchoppers who had felled its mates were dead and gone long ago, and a whole forest of sturdy trees, pines and oaks and maples, had grown again. But the stately head of this old pine towered above them all and made a landmark for sea and shore miles and miles away. Sylvia knew it well. She had always believed that whoever climbed to the top of it could see the ocean; and the little girl had often laid her hand on the great rough trunk and looked up wistfully at those dark boughs that the wind always stirred, no matter how hot and still the air might be below. Now she thought of the tree with a new excitement, for why, if one climbed it at break of day, could not one see all the world, and easily discover whence the white heron flew, and mark the place and find the hidden nest?

29  What a spirit of adventure, what wild ambition! What fancied triumph and delight and glory for the later morning when she could make known the secret! It was almost too real and too great for the childish heart to bear.

30  All night the door of the little house stood open, and the whippoorwills came and sang upon the very step. The young sportsman and his old hostess were sound asleep, but Sylvia's great design kept her broad awake and watching. She forgot to think of sleep. The short summer night seemed as long as the winter darkness, and at last when the whippoorwills ceased, and she was afraid the morning would after all come too soon, she stole out of the house and followed the pasture path through the woods, hastening toward the open ground beyond, listening with a sense of comfort and companionship to the drowsy twitter of a half-awakened bird, whose perch she had jarred in passing. Alas, if the great wave of human interest which flooded for the first time this dull little life should sweep away the satisfactions of an existence heart to heart with nature and the dumb life of the forest!

31  There was the huge tree asleep yet in the paling moonlight, and small and hopeful Sylvia began with utmost bravery to mount to the

top of it, with tingling, eager blood coursing the channels of her whole frame, with her bare feet and fingers, that pinched and held like bird's claws to the monstrous ladder reaching up, up, almost to the sky itself. First she must mount the white oak tree that grew alongside, where she was almost lost among the dark branches and the green leaves heavy and wet with dew; a bird fluttered off its nest, and a red squirrel ran to and fro and scolded pettishly at the harmless housebreaker. Sylvia felt her way easily. She had often climbed there, and knew that higher still one of the oak's upper branches chafed against the pine trunk, just where its lower boughs were set close together. There, when she made the dangerous pass from one tree to the other, the great enterprise would really begin.

32   She crept out along the swaying oak limb at last, and took the daring step across into the old pine-tree. The way was harder than she thought; she must reach far and hold fast, the sharp dry twigs caught and held her and scratched her like angry talons, the pitch made her thin little fingers clumsy and stiff as she went round and round the tree's great stem, higher and higher upward. The sparrows and robins in the woods below were beginning to wake and twitter to the dawn, yet it seemed much lighter there aloft in the pine-tree, and the child knew that she must hurry if her project were to be of any use.

33   The tree seemed to lengthen itself out as she went up, and to reach farther and farther upward. It was like a great main-mast to the voyaging earth; it must truly have been amazed that morning through all its ponderous frame as it felt this determined spark of human spirit creeping and climbing from higher branch to branch. Who knows how steadily the least twigs held themselves to advantage this light, weak creature on her way! The old pine must have loved his new dependent. More than all the hawks, and bats, and moths, and even the sweet-voiced thrushes, was the brave, beating heart of the solitary gray-eyed child. And the tree stood still and held away the winds that June morning while the dawn grew bright in the east.

34   Sylvia's face was like a pale star, if one had seen it from the ground when the last thorny bough was past, and she stood trembling and tired, but wholly triumphant, high in the tree-top. Yes, there was the sea with the dawning sun making a golden dazzle over it, and toward that glorious east flew two hawks with slow-moving pinions. How low they looked in the air from that height when before one had only seen them far up, and dark against the blue sky. Their gray feathers were soft as moths; they seemed only a little way from the tree, and Sylvia felt as if she too could go flying away among the clouds. Westward, the woodlands and farms reached miles and miles into the distance; here and there were church steeples, and white villages; truly it was a vast and awesome world.

35   The birds sang louder and louder. At last the sun came up bewilderingly bright. Sylvia could see the white sails of ships out at sea, and the clouds that were purple and rose-colored and yellow at first began

to fade away. Where was the white heron's nest in the sea of green branches, and was this wonderful sight and pageant of the world the only reward for having climbed to such a giddy height? Now look down again, Sylvia, where the green marsh is set among the shining birches and dark hemlocks; there where you saw the white heron once you will see him again; look, look! a white spot of him like a single floating feather comes up from the dead hemlock and grows larger, and rises, and comes close at last, and goes by the landmark pine with steady sweep of wing and outstretched slender neck and crested head. And wait! wait! do not move a foot or a finger, little girl, do not send an arrow of light and consciousness from your two eager eyes, for the heron has perched on a pine bough not far beyond yours, and cries back to his mate on the nest, and plumes his feathers for the new day!

36   The child gives a long sigh a minute later when a company of shouting catbirds comes also to the tree, and vexed by their fluttering and lawlessness the solemn heron goes away. She knows his secret now, the wild, light, slender bird that floats and wavers, and goes back like an arrow presently to his home in the green world beneath. Then Sylvia, well satisfied, makes her perilous way down again, not daring to look far below the branch she stands on, ready to cry sometimes because her fingers ache and her lamed feet slip. Wondering over and over again what the stranger would say to her, and what he would think when she told him how to find his way straight to the heron's nest.

37   "Sylvy, Sylvy!" called the busy old grandmother again and again, but nobody answered, and the small husk bed was empty, and Sylvia had disappeared.

38   The guest waked from a dream, and remembering the day's pleasure hurried to dress himself that it might sooner begin. He was sure from the way the shy little girl looked once or twice yesterday that she had at least seen the white heron, and now she must really be persuaded to tell. Here she comes now, paler than ever, and her worn old frock is torn and tattered, and smeared with pine pitch. The grandmother and the sportsman stand in the door together and question her, and the splendid moment has come to speak of the dead hemlock-tree by the green marsh.

39   But Sylvia does not speak after all, though the old grandmother fretfully rebukes her, and the young man's kind appealing eyes are looking straight in her own. He can make them rich with money; he has promised it, and they are poor now. He is so well worth making happy, and he waits to hear the story she can tell.

40   No, she must keep silence! What is it that suddenly forbids her and makes her dumb? Has she been nine years growing, and now, when the great world for the first time puts out a hand to her, must she thrust it aside for a bird's sake? The murmur of the pine's green branches is in her ears, and she remembers how the white heron came

flying through the golden air and how they watched the sea and the morning together, and Sylvia cannot speak; she cannot tell the heron's secret and give its life away.

41 Dear loyalty, that suffered a sharp pang as the guest went away disappointed later in the day, that could have served and followed him and loved him as a dog loves! Many a night Sylvia heard the echo of his whistle haunting the pasture path as she came home with the loitering cow. She forgot even her sorrow at the sharp report of his gun and the piteous sight of thrushes and sparrows dropping silent to the ground, their songs hushed and their pretty feathers stained and wet with blood. Were the birds better friends than their hunter might have been, — who can tell? Whatever treasures were lost to her, woodlands and summer-time, remember! Bring your gifts and graces and tell your secrets to this lonely country child!

(1886)

# Charlotte Perkins Gilman (1860–1935)

Born in Hartford, Connecticut, and the great-niece of Harriet Beecher Stowe, Charlotte Perkins was brought up by her mother after her father deserted the family. Soon after the birth of her daughter in 1885, she suffered a nervous breakdown — and escaped her first marriage by moving to California where she later remarried and established herself as a lecturer and feminist writer. Faced with inoperable cancer, in 1935 she committed suicide.

## The Yellow Wallpaper

1. It is very seldom that mere ordinary people like John and myself secure ancestral halls for the summer.
2. A colonial mansion, a hereditary estate, I would say a haunted house, and reach the height of romantic felicity — but that would be asking too much of fate!
3. Still I will proudly declare that there is something queer about it.
4. Else, why should it be let so cheaply? And why have stood so long untenanted?
5. John laughs at me, of course, but one expects that in marriage.
6. John is practical in the extreme. He has no patience with faith, an intense horror of superstition, and he scoffs openly at any talk of things not to be felt and seen and put down in figures.
7. John is a physician, and *perhaps* — (I would not say it to a living soul, of course, but this is dead paper and a great relief to my mind) — *perhaps* that is one reason I do not get well faster.
8. You see he does not believe I am sick!
9. And what can one do?
10. If a physician of high standing, and one's own husband, assures friends and relatives that there is really nothing the matter with one but temporary nervous depression — a slight hysterical tendency — what is one to do?
11. My brother is also a physician, and also of high standing, and he says the same thing.
12. So I take phosphates or phosphites — whichever it is, and tonics, and journeys, and air, and exercise, and am absolutely forbidden to "work" until I am well again.
13. Personally, I disagree with their ideas.

14   Personally, I believe that congenial work, with excitement and change, would do me good.

15   But what is one to do?

16   I did write for a while in spite of them; but it *does* exhaust me a good deal — having to be so sly about it, or else meet with heavy opposition.

17   I sometimes fancy that in my condition if I had less opposition and more society and stimulus — but John says the very worst thing I can do is think about my condition, and I confess it always makes me feel bad.

18   So I will let it alone and talk about the house.

19   The most beautiful place! It is quite alone, standing well back from the road, quite three miles from the village. It makes me think of English places that you read about, for there are hedges and walls and gates that lock, and lots of separate little houses for the gardeners and people.

20   There is a *delicious* garden! I never saw such a garden — large and shady, full of box-bordered paths, and lined with long grape-covered arbors with seats under them.

21   There were greenhouses, too, but they are all broken now.

22   There was some legal trouble, I believe, something about the heirs and coheirs; anyhow, the place has been empty for years.

23   That spoils my ghostliness, I am afraid, but I don't care — there is something strange about the house — I can feel it.

24   I even said so to John one moonlight evening, but he said what I felt was a *draught*, and shut the window.

25   I get unreasonably angry with John sometimes. I'm sure I never used to be so sensitive. I think it is due to this nervous condition.

26   But John says if I feel so, I shall neglect proper self-control; so I take pains to control myself — before him, at least, and that makes me very tired.

27   I don't like our room a bit. I wanted one downstairs that opened on the piazza and had roses all over the window, and such pretty old-fashioned chintz hangings! But John would not hear of it.

28   He said there was only one window and not room for two beds, and no near room for him if he took another.

29   He is very careful and loving, and hardly lets me stir without special direction.

30   I have a schedule prescription for each hour in the day; he takes all care from me, and I feel basely ungrateful not to value it more.

31   He said we came here solely on my account, that I was to have perfect rest and all the air I could get. "Your exercise depends on your strength, my dear," said he, "and your food somewhat on your appetite; but air you can absorb all the time." So we took the nursery at the top of the house.

32   It is a big, airy room, the whole floor nearly, with windows that look all ways, and air and sunshine galore. It was nursery first and

then playroom and gymnasium, I should judge; for the windows are barred for little children, and there are rings and things in the walls.

33  The paint and paper look as if a boys' school had used it. It is stripped off — the paper — in great patches all around the head of my bed, about as far as I can reach, and in a great place on the other side of the room low down. I never saw a worse paper in my life.

34  One of those sprawling flamboyant patterns committing every artistic sin.

35  It is dull enough to confuse the eye in following, pronounced enough to constantly irritate and provoke study, and when you follow the lame uncertain curves for a little distance they suddenly commit suicide — plunge off at outrageous angles, destroy themselves in unheard of contradictions.

36  The color is repellent, almost revolting; a smouldering unclean yellow, strangely faded by the slow-turning sunlight.

37  It is a dull yet lurid orange in some places, a sickly sulphur tint in others.

38  No wonder the children hated it! I should hate it myself if I had to live in this room long.

39  There comes John, and I must put this away, — he hates to have me write a word.

40  We have been here two weeks, and I haven't felt like writing before, since that first day.

41  I am sitting by the window now, up in this atrocious nursery, and there is nothing to hinder my writing as much as I please, save lack of strength.

42  John is away all day, and even some nights when his cases are serious.

43  I am glad my case is not serious!

44  But these nervous troubles are dreadfully depressing.

45  John does not know how much I really suffer. He knows there is no *reason* to suffer, and that satisfies him.

46  Of course it is only nervousness. It does weigh on me so not to do my duty in any way!

47  I meant to be such a help to John, such a real rest and comfort, and here I am a comparative burden already!

48  Nobody would believe what an effort it is to do what little I am able, — to dress and entertain, and order things.

49  It is fortunate Mary is so good with the baby. Such a dear baby!

50  And yet I *cannot* be with him, it makes me so nervous.

51  I suppose John never was nervous in his life. He laughs at me so about this wallpaper!

52  At first he meant to repaper the room, but afterwards he said that I was letting it get the better of me, and that nothing was worse for a nervous patient than to give way to such fancies.

53   He said that after the wallpaper was changed it would be the heavy bedstead, and then the barred windows, and then that gate at the head of the stairs, and so on.

54   "You know the place is doing you good," he said, "and really, dear, I don't care to renovate the house just for a three months' rental."

55   "Then do let us go downstairs," I said, "there are such pretty rooms there."

56   Then he took me in his arms and called me a blessed little goose, and said he would go down to the cellar, if I wished, and have it whitewashed into the bargain.

57   But he is right enough about the beds and windows and things.

58   It is as airy and comfortable room as any one need wish, and, of course, I would not be so silly as to make him uncomfortable just for a whim.

59   I'm really getting quite fond of the big room, all but that horrid paper.

60   Out of one window I can see the garden, those mysterious deep-shaded arbors, the riotous old-fashioned flowers, and bushes and gnarly trees.

61   Out of another I get a lovely view of the bay and a little private wharf belonging to the estate. There is a beautiful shaded lane that runs down there from the house. I always fancy I see people walking in these numerous paths and arbors, but John has cautioned me not to give way to fancy in the least. He says that with my imaginative power and habit of story-making, a nervous weakness like mine is sure to lead to all manner of excited fancies, and that I ought to use my will and good sense to check the tendency. So I try.

62   I think sometimes that if I were only well enough to write a little it would relieve the press of ideas and rest me.

63   But I find I get pretty tired when I try.

64   It is so discouraging not to have any advice and companionship about my work. When I get really well, John says we will ask Cousin Henry and Julia down for a long visit; but he says he would as soon put fireworks in my pillow-case as to let me have those stimulating people about now.

65   I wish I could get well faster.

66   But I must not think about that. This paper looks to me as if it *knew* what a vicious influence it had!

67   There is a recurrent spot where the pattern lolls like a broken neck and two bulbous eyes stare at you upside down.

68   I get positively angry with the impertinence of it and the everlastingness. Up and down and sideways they crawl, and those absurd, unblinking eyes are everywhere. There is one place where two breadths didn't match, and the eyes go all up and down the line, one a little higher than the other.

69   I never saw so much expression in an inanimate thing before, and we all know how much expression they have! I used to lie awake as

a child and get more entertainment and terror out of blank walls and plain furniture than most children could find in a toy-store.

I remember what a kindly wink the knobs of our big, old bureau used to have, and there was one chair that always seemed like a strong friend.

I used to feel that if any of the other things looked too fierce I could always hop into that chair and be safe.

The furniture in this room is no worse than inharmonious, however, for we had to bring it all from downstairs. I suppose when this was used as a playroom they had to take the nursery things out, and no wonder! I never saw such ravages as the children have made here.

The wallpaper, as I said before, is torn off in spots, and it sticketh closer than a brother — they must have had perseverance as well as hatred.

Then the floor is scratched and gouged and splintered, the plaster itself is dug out here and there, and this great heavy bed, which is all we found in the room, looks as if it had been through the wars.

But I don't mind it a bit — only the paper.

There comes John's sister. Such a dear girl as she is, and so careful of me! I must not let her find me writing.

She is a perfect and enthusiastic housekeeper, and hopes for no better profession. I verily believe she thinks it is the writing which made me sick!

But I can write when she is out, and see her a long way off from these windows.

There is one that commands the road, a lovely shaded winding road, and one that just looks off over the country. A lovely country, too, full of great elms and velvet meadows.

This wallpaper has a kind of sub-pattern in a different shade, a particularly irritating one, for you can only see it in certain lights, and not clearly then.

But in the places where it isn't faded and where the sun is just so — I can see a strange, provoking, formless sort of figure, that seems to skulk about behind that silly and conspicuous front design.

There's sister on the stairs!

Well, the Fourth of July is over! The people are all gone and I am tired out. John thought it might do me good to see a little company, so we just had Mother and Nellie and the children down for the week.

Of course I didn't do a thing. Jennie sees to everything now.

But it tired me all the same.

John says if I don't pick up faster he shall send me to Weir Mitchell in the fall.

But I don't want to go there at all. I had a friend who was in his hands once, and she says he is just like John and my brother, only more so!

Besides, it is such an undertaking to go so far.

89  I don't feel as if it was worth while to turn my hand over for anything, and I'm getting dreadfully fretful and querulous.
90  I cry at nothing, and cry most of the time.
91  Of course I don't when John is here, or anybody else, but when I am alone.
92  And I am alone a good deal just now. John is kept in town very often by serious cases, and Jennie is good and lets me alone when I want her to.
93  So I walk a little in the garden or down that lovely lane, sit on the porch under the roses, and lie down up here a good deal.
94  I'm getting really fond of the room in spite of the wallpaper. Perhaps *because* of the wallpaper.
95  It dwells in my mind so!
96  I lie here on this great immovable bed — it is nailed down, I believe — and follow that pattern about by the hour. It is as good as gymnastics, I assure you. I start, we'll say, at the bottom, down in the corner over there where it has not been touched, and I determine for the thousandth time that I *will* follow that pointless pattern to some sort of a conclusion.
97  I know a little of the principle of design, and I know this thing was not arranged on any laws of radiation, or alternation, or repetition, or symmetry, or anything else that I ever heard of.
98  It is repeated, of course, by the breadths, but not otherwise.
99  Looked at in one way each breadth stands alone, the bloated curves and flourishes — a kind of "debased Romanesque" with *delirium tremens* — go waddling up and down in isolated columns of fatuity.
100  But, on the other hand, they connect diagonally, and the sprawling outlines run off in great slanting waves of optic horror, like a lot of wallowing seaweeds in full chase.
101  The whole thing goes horizontally too, at least it seems so, and I exhaust myself in trying to distinguish the order of its going in that direction.
102  They have used a horizontal breadth for a frieze, and that adds wonderfully to the confusion.
103  There is one end of the room where it is almost intact, and there, when the crosslights fade and the low sun shines directly upon it, I can almost fancy radiation after all, — the interminable grotesques seem to form around a common center and rush off in headlong plunges of equal distraction.
104  It makes me tired to follow it. I will take a nap I guess.
105  I don't know why I should write this.
106  I don't want to.
107  I don't feel able.
108  And I know John would think it absurd. But I *must* say what I feel and think in some way — it is such a relief!
109  But the effort is getting to be greater than the relief.
110  Half the time now I am awfully lazy, and lie down ever so much.

111  John says I mustn't lose my strength, and has me take cod liver oil and lots of tonics and things, to say nothing of ale and wine and rare meat.

112  Dear John! He loves me dearly, and hates to have me sick. I tried to have a real earnest reasonable talk with him the other day, and tell him how I wish he would let me go and make a visit to Cousin Henry and Julia.

113  But he said I wasn't able to go, nor able to stand it after I got there; and I did not make out a very good case for myself, for I was crying before I had finished.

114  It is getting to be a great effort for me to think straight. Just this nervous weakness I suppose.

115  And dear John gathered me in his arms, and just carried me upstairs and laid me on the bed, and sat by me and read to me till it tired my head.

116  He said I was his darling and his comfort and all he had, and that I must take care of myself for his sake, and keep well.

117  He says no one but myself can help me out of it, that I must use my will and self-control and not let any silly fancies run away with me.

118  There's one comfort, the baby is well and happy, and does not have to occupy this nursery with the horrid wallpaper.

119  If we had not used it, that blessed child would have! What a fortunate escape! Why, I wouldn't have a child of mine, an impressionable little thing, live in such a room for worlds.

120  I never thought of it before, but it is lucky that John kept me here after all, I can stand it so much easier than a baby, you see.

121  Of course I never mention it to him any more — I am too wise — but keep watch of it all the same.

122  There are things in that paper that nobody knows but me, or ever will.

123  Behind that outside pattern the dim shapes get clearer every day.

124  It is always the same shape, only very numerous.

125  And it is like a woman stooping down and creeping about behind that pattern. I don't like it a bit. I wonder — I begin to think — I wish John would take me away from here!

126  It is so hard to talk with John about my case, because he is so wise, and because he loves me so.

127  But I tried it last night.

128  It was moonlight. The moon shines all around just as the sun does.

129  I hate to see it sometimes, it creeps so slowly, and always comes in by one window or another.

130  John was asleep and I hated to waken him, so I kept still and watched the moonlight on that undulating wallpaper till I felt creepy.

131  The faint figure behind seemed to shake the pattern, just as if she wanted to get out.

132  I got up softly and went to feel and see if the paper *did* move, and when I came back John was awake.

133  "What is it, little girl?" he said. "Don't go walking about like that — you'll get cold."

134     I thought it was a good time to talk, so I told him that I really was not gaining here, and that I wished he would take me away.

135     "Why darling!" said he, "our lease will be up in three weeks, and I can't see how to leave before.

136     "The repairs are not done at home, and I cannot possibly leave town just now. Of course if you were in any danger, I could and would, but you really are better, dear, and I know. You are gaining flesh and color, your appetite is better, I feel really much easier about you."

137     "I don't weigh a bit more," said I, "nor as much; and my appetite may be better in the evening when you are here, but it is worse in the morning when you are away!"

138     "Bless her little heart!" said he with a big hug, "she shall be as sick as she pleases! But now let's improve the shining hours by going to sleep, and talk about it in the morning!"

139     "And you won't go away?" I asked gloomily.

140     "Why, how can I, dear? It is only three weeks more and then we will take a nice little trip of a few days while Jennie is getting the house ready. Really dear you are better!"

141     "Better in body perhaps —" I began, and stopped short, for he sat straight up and looked at me with such a stern, reproachful look that I could not say another word.

142     "My darling," said he, "I beg of you, for my sake and for our child's sake, as well as for your own, that you will never one instant let that idea enter your mind! There is nothing so dangerous, so fascinating, to a temperament like yours. It is a false and foolish fancy. Can you not trust me as a physician when I tell you so?"

143     So of course I said no more on that score, and we went to sleep before long. He thought I was asleep first, but I wasn't, and lay there for hours trying to decide whether that front pattern and the back pattern really did move together or separately.

144 On a pattern like this, by daylight, there is a lack of sequence, a defiance of law, that is a constant irritant to a normal mind.

145     The color is hideous enough, and reliable enough, and infuriating enough, but the pattern is torturing.

146     You think you have mastered it, but just as you get well underway in following, it turns a back-somersault and there you are. It slaps you in the face, knocks you down, and tramples upon you. It is like a bad dream.

147     The outside pattern is a florid arabesque, reminding one of a fungus. If you can imagine a toadstool in joints, an interminable string of toadstools, budding and sprouting in endless convolutions — why, that is something like it.

148     That is, sometimes!

149     There is one marked peculiarity about this paper, a thing nobody seems to notice but myself, and that is that it changes as the light changes.

150     When the sun shoots through the east window — I always watch for that first long, straight ray — it changes so quickly that I never can quite believe it.

151 That is why I watch it always.

152 By moonlight — the moon shines in all night when there is a moon — I wouldn't know it was the same paper.

153 At night any kind of light, in twilight, candle light, lamplight, and worst of all by moonlight, it becomes bars! The outside pattern I mean, and the woman behind it is as plain as can be.

154 I didn't realize for a long time what the thing was that showed behind, that dim sub-pattern, but now I am quite sure it is a woman.

155 By daylight she is subdued, quiet. I fancy it is the pattern that keeps her so still. It is so puzzling. It keeps me quiet by the hour.

156 I lie down ever so much now. John says it is good for me, and to sleep all I can.

157 Indeed he started the habit by making me lie down for an hour after each meal.

158 It is a very bad habit I am convinced, for you see I don't sleep.

159 And that cultivates deceit, for I don't tell them I'm awake — O no!

160 The fact is I am getting a little afraid of John.

161 He seems very queer sometimes, and even Jennie has an inexplicable look.

162 It strikes me occasionally, just as a scientific hypothesis, — that perhaps it is the paper!

163 I have watched John when he did not know I was looking, and come into the room suddenly on the most innocent excuses, and I've caught him several times *looking at the paper*! And Jennie too. I caught Jennie with her hand on it once.

164 She didn't know I was in the room, and when I asked her in a quiet, a very quiet voice, with the most restrained manner possible, what she was doing with the paper — she turned around as if she had been caught stealing, and looked quite angry — asked me why I should frighten her so!

165 Then she said that the paper stained everything it touched, that she had found yellow smooches on all my clothes and John's and she wished we would be more careful!

166 Did not that sound innocent? But I know she was studying that pattern, and I am determined that nobody shall find it out but myself!

167 Life is very much more exciting now than it used to be. You see I have something more to expect, to look forward to, to watch. I really do eat better, and am more quiet than I was.

168 John is so pleased to see me improve! He laughed a little the other day, and said I seemed to be flourishing in spite of my wallpaper.

169 I turned it off with a laugh. I had no intention of telling him it was *because* of the wallpaper — he would make fun of me. He might even want to take me away.

170 I don't want to leave now until I have found it out. There is a week more, and I think that will be enough.

171 I'm feeling ever so much better! I don't sleep much at night, for it is so interesting to watch developments; but I sleep a good deal in the daytime.

172 In the daytime it is tiresome and perplexing.

173 There are always new shoots on the fungus, and new shades of yellow all over it. I cannot keep count of them, though I have tried conscientiously.

174 It is the strangest yellow, that wallpaper! It makes me think of all the yellow things I ever saw — not beautiful ones like buttercups, but old foul, bad yellow things.

175 But there is something else about that paper — the smell! I noticed it the moment we came into the room, but with so much air and sun it was not bad. Now we have had a week of fog and rain, and whether the windows are open or not, the smell is here.

176 It creeps all over the house.

177 I find it hovering in the dining-room, skulking in the parlor, hiding in the hall, lying in wait for me on the stairs.

178 It gets into my hair.

179 Even when I go to ride, if I turn my head suddenly and surprise it — there is that smell!

180 Such a peculiar odor, too! I have spent hours in trying to analyze it, to find what it smelled like.

181 It is not bad — at first, and very gentle, but quite the subtlest, most enduring odor I ever met.

182 In this damp weather it is awful, I wake up in the night and find it hanging over me.

183 It used to disturb me at first. I thought seriously of burning the house — to reach the smell.

184 But now I am used to it. The only thing I can think of that it is like is the *color* of the paper! A yellow smell.

185 There is a very funny mark on this wall, low down, near the mopboard. A streak that runs round the room. It goes behind every piece of furniture, except the bed, a long, straight, even *smooch*, as if it had been rubbed over and over.

186 I wonder how it was done and who did it, and what they did it for. Round and round and round — round and round and round — it makes me dizzy!

187 I really have discovered something at last.

188 Through watching so much at night, when it changes so, I have finally found out.

189 The front pattern *does* move — and no wonder! The woman behind shakes it!

190 Sometimes I think there are a great many women behind, and sometimes only one, and she crawls around fast, and her crawling shakes it all over.

Then in the very bright spots she keeps still, and in the very shady spots she just takes hold of the bars and shakes them hard.

And she is all the time trying to climb through. But nobody could climb through that pattern — it strangles so; I think that is why it has so many heads.

They get through, and then the pattern strangles them off and turns them upside down, and makes their eyes white!

If those heads were covered or taken off it would not be half so bad.

I think that woman gets out in the daytime!

And I'll tell you why — privately — I've seen her!

I can see her out of every one of my windows!

It is the same woman, I know, for she is always creeping, and most women do not creep by daylight.

I see her on that long road under the trees, creeping along, and when a carriage comes she hides under the blackberry vines.

I don't blame her a bit. It must be very humiliating to be caught creeping by daylight!

I always lock the door when I creep by daylight. I can't do it at night, for I know John would suspect something at once.

And John is so queer now, that I don't want to irritate him. I wish he would take another room! Besides, I don't want anybody to get that woman out at night but myself.

I often wonder if I could see her out of all the windows at once.

But, turn as fast as I can, I can only see out of one at a time.

And though I always see her, she *may* be able to creep faster than I can turn!

I have watched her sometimes away off in the open country, creeping as fast as a cloud shadow in a high wind.

If only that top pattern could be gotten off from the under one! I mean to try it, little by little.

I have found out another funny thing, but I shan't tell it this time! It does not do to trust people too much.

There are only two more days to get this paper off, and I believe John is beginning to notice. I don't like the look in his eyes.

And I heard him ask Jennie a lot of professional questions about me. She had a very good report to give.

She said I slept a good deal in the daytime.

John knows I don't sleep very well at night, for all I'm so quiet!

He asked me all sorts of questions, too, and pretended to be very loving and kind.

As if I couldn't see through him!

Still, I don't wonder he acts so, sleeping under this paper for three months.

It only interests me, but I feel sure John and Jennie are secretly affected by it.

217 Hurrah! This is the last day, but it is enough. John had to stay in town over night, and won't be out until this evening.

218 Jennie wanted to sleep with me — the sly thing! but I told her I should undoubtedly rest better for a night all alone.

219 That was clever, for really I wasn't alone a bit! As soon as it was moonlight and that poor thing began to crawl and shake the pattern, I got up and ran to help her.

220 I pulled and she shook, I shook and she pulled, and before morning we had peeled off yards of that paper.

221 A strip about as high as my head and half around the room.

222 And then when the sun came and that awful pattern began to laugh at me, I declared I would finish it to-day!

223 We go away to-morrow, and they are moving all my furniture down again to leave things as they were before.

224 Jennie looked at the wall in amazement, but I told her merrily that I did it out of pure spite at the vicious thing.

225 She laughed and said she wouldn't mind doing it herself, but I must not get tired.

226 How she betrayed herself that time!

227 But I am here, and no person touches this paper but me, — not *alive*!

228 She tried to get me out of the room — it was too patent! But I said it was so quiet and empty and clean now that I believed I would lie down again and sleep all I could; and not to wake me even for dinner — I would call when I woke.

229 So now she is gone, and the servants are gone, and the things are gone, and there is nothing left but the great bedstead nailed down, with the canvas mattress we found on it.

230 We shall sleep downstairs to-night, and take the boat home to-morrow.

231 I quite enjoy the room, now it is bare again.

232 How those children did tear about here!

233 This bedstead is fairly gnawed!

234 But I must get to work.

235 I have locked the door and thrown the key down into the front path.

236 I don't want to go out, and I don't want to have anybody come in, till John comes.

237 I want to astonish him.

238 I've got a rope up here that even Jennie did not find. If that woman does get out, and tries to get away, I can tie her!

239 But I forgot I could not reach far without anything to stand on!

240 This bed will *not* move!

241 I tried to lift and push it until I was lame, and then I got so angry I bit off a little piece at one corner — but it hurt my teeth.

242 Then I peeled off all the paper I could reach standing on the floor. It sticks horribly and the pattern just enjoys it! All those strangled

heads and bulbous eyes and waddling fungus growths just shriek with derision!

243 I am getting angry enough to do something desperate. To jump out of the window would be admirable exercise, but the bars are too strong even to try.

244 Besides I wouldn't do it. Of course not. I know well enough that a step like that is improper and might be misconstrued.

245 I don't like to *look* out of the windows even — there are so many of those creeping women, and they creep so fast.

246 I wonder if they all come out of that wallpaper as I did?

247 But I am securely fastened now by my well-hidden rope — you don't get *me* out in the road there!

248 I suppose I shall have to get back behind the pattern when it comes night, and that is hard!

249 It is so pleasant to be out in this great room and creep around as I please!

250 I don't want to go outside. I won't, even if Jennie asks me to.

251 For outside you have to creep on the ground, and everything is green instead of yellow.

252 But here I can creep smoothly on the floor, and my shoulder just fits in that long smooch around the wall, so I cannot lose my way.

253 Why there's John at the door!

254 It is no use, young man, you can't open it!

255 How he does call and pound!

256 Now he's crying for an axe.

257 It would be a shame to break down that beautiful door!

258 "John dear!" said I in the gentlest voice, "the key is down by the front steps, under a plantain leaf!"

259 That silenced him for a few moments.

260 Then he said — very quietly indeed, "Open the door, my darling!"

261 "I can't," said I. "The key is down by the front door under a plantain leaf!"

262 And then I said it again, several times, very gently and slowly, and said it so often that he had to go to see, and he got it of course, and came in. He stopped short by the door.

263 "What is the matter?" he cried. "For God's sake, what are you doing?"

264 I kept on creeping just the same, but I looked at him over my shoulder.

265 "I've got out at last," said I, "in spite of you and Jane. And I've pulled off most of the paper, so you can't put me back!"

266 Now why should that man have fainted? But he did, and right across my path by the wall, so that I had to creep over him every time!

(1892)

# James Joyce (1882–1941)

With his innovative narrative methods and linguistic experimentation, Joyce changed the form of fiction. He not only devised new ways of shaping character and action, but also articulated the Irish consciousness of his era.

## The Boarding House[1]

1 Mrs. Mooney was a butcher's daughter. She was a woman who was quite able to keep things to herself: a determined woman. She had married her father's foreman, and opened a butcher's shop near Spring Gardens. But as soon as his father-in-law was dead Mr. Mooney began to go to the devil. He drank, plundered the till, ran headlong into debt. It was no use making him take the pledge: he was sure to break out again a few days after. By fighting his wife in the presence of customers and by buying bad meat he ruined his business. One night he went for his wife with the cleaver, and she had to sleep in a neighbour's house.

2 After that they lived apart. She went to the priest and got a separation from him, with care of the children. She would give him neither money nor food nor house-room; and so he was obliged to enlist himself as a sheriff's man. He was a shabby stooped little drunkard with a white face and a white moustache and white eyebrows, pencilled above his little eyes, which were pink-veined and raw; and all day long he sat in the bailiff's room, waiting to be put on a job. Mrs. Mooney, who had taken what remained of her money out of the butcher business and set up a boarding house in Hardwicke Street, was a big imposing woman. Her house had a floating population made up of tourists from Liverpool and the Isle of Man and, occasionally, *artistes* from the music halls. Its resident population was made up of clerks from the city. She governed the house cunningly and firmly, knew when to give credit, when to be stern and when to let things pass. All the resident young men spoke of her as *The Madam*.

---

1. From Joyce's collection of short stories, *Dubliners* (1914). Place names all refer to the city of Dublin, Ireland.

3   Mrs. Mooney's young men paid fifteen shillings a week for board and lodgings (beer or stout at dinner excluded). They shared in common tastes and occupations and for this reason they were very chummy with one another. They discussed with one another the chances of favourites and outsiders. Jack Mooney, the Madam's son, who was clerk to a commission agent in Fleet Street, had the reputation of being a hard case. He was fond of using soldiers' obscenities: usually he came home in the small hours. When he met his friends he had always a good one to tell them and he was always sure to be on to a good thing — that is to say, a likely horse or a likely *artiste*. He was also handy with the mits[2] and sang comic songs. On Sunday night there would often be a reunion in Mrs. Mooney's front drawingroom. The music-hall *artistes* would oblige; and Sheridan played waltzes and polkas and vamped accompaniments. Polly Mooney, the Madam's daughter, would also sing. She sang:

> *I'm a ... naughty girl.*
> *You needn't sham:*
> *You know I am.*

4   Polly was a slim girl of nineteen; she had light soft hair and a small full mouth. Her eyes, which were grey with a shade of green through them, had a habit of glancing upwards when she spoke with anyone, which made her look like a little perverse madonna. Mrs. Mooney had first sent her daughter to be a typist in a corn-factor's[3] office, but as a disreputable sheriff's man used to come every other day to the office, asking to be allowed to say a word to his daughter, she had taken her daughter home again and set her to do housework. As Polly was very lively, the intention was to give her the run of the young men. Besides, young men like to feel that there is a young woman not very far away. Polly, of course, flirted with the young men, but Mrs. Mooney, who was a shrewd judge, knew that the young men were only passing the time away: none of them meant business. Things went on so for a long time, and Mrs. Mooney began to think of sending Polly back to typewriting, when she noticed that something was going on between Polly and one of the young men. She watched the pair and kept her own counsel.

5   Polly knew that she was being watched, but still her mother's persistent silence could not be misunderstood. There had been no open complicity between mother and daughter, no open understanding, but though people in the house began to talk of the affair, still Mrs. Mooney did not intervene. Polly began to grow a little strange in her manner and the young man was evidently perturbed. At last, when she judged it to be the right moment, Mrs. Mooney intervened. She dealt

---

2. A variant of "mitts" or "mittens." "Handy with the mits" is a colloquialism meaning "ready with his fists."
3. Corn-merchant.

with moral problems as a cleaver deals with meat: and in this case she had made up her mind.

It was a bright Sunday morning of early summer, promising heat, but with a fresh breeze blowing. All the windows of the boarding house were open and the lace curtains ballooned gently towards the street beneath the raised sashes. The belfry of George's Church sent out constant peals and worshippers, singly or in groups, traversed the little circus[4] before the church, revealing their purpose by their self-contained demeanour no less than by the little volumes in their gloved hands. Breakfast was over in the boarding house, and the table of the breakfast-room was covered with plates on which lay yellow streaks of eggs with morsels of bacon-fat and bacon-rind. Mrs. Mooney sat in the straw armchair and watched the servant Mary remove the breakfast things. She made Mary collect the crusts and pieces of broken bread to help to make Tuesday's bread pudding. When the table was cleared, the broken bread collected, the sugar and butter safe under lock and key, she began to reconstruct the interview which she had had the night before with Polly. Things were as she had suspected: she had been frank in her questions and Polly had been frank in her answers. Both had been somewhat awkward, of course. She had been made awkward by her not wishing to receive the news in too cavalier a fashion or to seem to have connived, and Polly had been made awkward not merely because allusions of that kind always made her awkward, but also because she did not wish it to be thought that in her wise innocence she had divined the intention behind her mother's tolerance.

Mrs. Mooney glanced instinctively at the little gilt clock on the mantelpiece as soon as she had become aware through her reverie that the bells of George's Church had stopped ringing. It was seventeen minutes past eleven: she would have lots of time to have the matter out with Mr. Doran and then catch short twelve[5] at Marlborough Street. She was sure she would win. To begin with, she had all the weight of social opinion on her side: she was an outraged mother. She had allowed him to live beneath her roof, assuming that he was a man of honour, and he had simply abused her hospitality. He was thirty-four or thirty-five years of age, so that youth could not be pleaded as his excuse; nor could ignorance be his excuse, since he was a man who had seen something of the world. He had simply taken advantage of Polly's youth and inexperience: that was evident. The question was: What reparation would he make?

There must be reparation made in such case. It is all very well for the man: he can go his ways as if nothing had happened, having had his moment of pleasure, but the girl has to bear the brunt. Some

---

4. Semicircular street.
5. The shortest Sunday Mass, lasting only fifteen or twenty minutes.

mothers would be content to patch up such an affair for a sum of money; she had known cases of it. But she would not do so. For her only one reparation could make up for the loss of her daughter's honour: marriage.

9   She counted all her cards again before sending Mary up to Mr. Doran's room to say that she wished to speak with him. She felt sure she would win. He was a serious young man, not rakish or loud-voiced like the others. If it had been Mr. Sheridan or Mr. Meade or Bantam Lyons, her task would have been much harder. She did not think he would face publicity. All the lodgers in the house knew something of the affair; details had been invented by some. Besides, he had been employed for thirteen years in a great Catholic wine-merchant's office, and publicity would mean for him, perhaps, the loss of his sit.[6] Whereas if he agreed all might be well. She knew he had a good screw[7] for one thing, and she suspected he had a bit of stuff put by.

10   Nearly the half-hour! She stood up and surveyed herself in the pier-glass. The decisive expression on her great florid face satisfied her, and she thought of some mothers she knew who could not get their daughters off their hands.

11   Mr. Doran was very anxious indeed this Sunday morning. He had made two attempts to shave, but his hand had been so unsteady that he had been obliged to desist. Three days' reddish beard fringed his jaws, and every two or three minutes a mist gathered on his glasses so that he had to take them off and polish them with his pocket-handkerchief. The recollection of his confession of the night before was a cause of acute pain to him; the priest had drawn out every ridiculous detail of the affair, and in the end had so magnified his sin that he was almost thankful at being afforded a loophole of reparation. The harm was done. What could he do now but marry her or run away? He could not brazen it out. The affair would be sure to be talked of, and his employer would be certain to hear of it. Dublin is such a small city: everyone knows everyone else's business. He felt his heart leap warmly in his throat as he heard in his excited imagination old Mr. Leonard calling out in his rasping voice: *"Send Mr. Doran here, please."*

12   All his long years of service gone for nothing! All his industry and diligence thrown away! As a young man he had sown his wild oats, of course; he had boasted of his free-thinking and denied the existence of God to his companions in public-houses. But that was all passed and done with ... nearly. He still bought a copy of *Reynolds Newspaper*[8] every week, but he attended to his religious duties, and for nine-tenths of the year lived a regular life. He had money enough to settle

---

6. Situation, i.e., his job.

7. Salary.

8. A popular newspaper perceived as expressing radical political views.

down on; it was not that. But the family would look down on her. First of all there was her disreputable father, and then her mother's boarding house was beginning to get a certain fame. He had a notion that he was being had. He could imagine his friends talking of the affair and laughing. She *was* a little vulgar; sometimes she said "*I seen*" and "*If I had've known*." But what would grammar matter if he really loved her? He could not make up his mind whether to like her or despise her for what she had done. Of course he had done it too. His instinct urged him to remain free, not to marry. Once you are married you are done for, it said.

13   While he was sitting helplessly on the side of the bed in shirt and trousers, she tapped lightly at his door and entered. She told him all, that she had made a clean breast of it to her mother and that her mother would speak to him that morning. She cried and threw her arms around his neck, saying:

14   "O, Bob! Bob! What am I to do? What am I to do at all?"

15   She would put an end to herself, she said.

16   He comforted her feebly, telling her not to cry, that it would be all right, never fear. He felt against his shirt the agitation of her bosom.

17   It was not altogether his fault that it had happened. He remembered well, with the curious patient memory of the celibate, the first casual caresses her dress, her breath, her fingers had given him. Then late one night as he was undressing for bed she had tapped at his door, timidly. She wanted to relight her candle at his, for hers had been blown out by a gust. It was her bath night. She wore a loose open combing-jacket of printed flannel. Her white instep shone in the opening of her furry slippers and the blood glowed warmly behind her perfumed skin. From her hands and wrists too as she lit and steadied her candle a faint perfume arose.

18   On nights when he came in very late it was she who warmed up his dinner. He scarcely knew what he was eating feeling her beside him alone, at night, in the sleeping house. And her thoughtfulness! If the night was anyway cold or wet or windy there was sure to be a little tumbler of punch ready for him. Perhaps they could be happy together. ...

19   They used to go upstairs together on tiptoe, each with a candle, and on the third landing exchange reluctant good nights. They used to kiss. He remembered well her eyes, the touch of her hand and his delirium. ...

20   But delirium passes. He echoed her phrase, applying it to himself: "*What am I to do?*" The instinct of the celibate warned him to hold back. But the sin was there; even his sense of honour told him that reparation must be made for such a sin.

21   While he was sitting with her on the side of the bed Mary came to the door and said that the missus wanted to see him in the parlour. He stood up to put on his coat and waistcoat, more helpless than ever. When he was dressed he went over to her to comfort her. It would be

all right, never fear. He left her crying on the bed and moaning softly: "O my God!"

22    Going down the stairs his glasses became so dimmed with moisture that he had to take them off and polish them. He longed to ascend through the roof and fly away to another country where he would never hear again of his trouble, and yet a force pushed him downstairs step by step. The implacable faces of his employer and of the Madam stared upon his discomfiture. On the last flight of stairs he passed Jack Mooney who was coming up from the pantry nursing two bottles of *Bass*.[9] They saluted coldly; and the lover's eyes rested for a second or two on a thick bulldog face and a pair of thick short arms. When he reached the foot of the staircase he glanced up and saw Jack regarding him from the door of the return-room.

23    Suddenly he remembered the night when one of the music-hall *artistes*, a little blond Londoner, had made a rather free allusion to Polly. The reunion had been almost broken up on account of Jack's violence. Everyone tried to quiet him. The music-hall *artiste*, a little paler than usual, kept smiling and saying that there was no harm meant; but Jack kept shouting at him that if any fellow tried that sort of game on with *his* sister he'd bloody well put his teeth down his throat, so he would.

24    Polly sat for a little time on the side of the bed, crying. Then she dried her eyes and went over to the looking-glass. She dipped the end of the towel in the water-jug and refreshed her eyes with the cool water. She looked at herself in profile and readjusted a hairpin above her ear. Then she went back to the bed again and sat at the foot. She regarded the pillows for a long time and the sight of them awakened in her mind secret amiable memories. She rested the nape of her neck against the cool iron bed-rail and fell into a reverie. There was no longer any perturbation visible on her face.

25    She waited on patiently, almost cheerfully, without alarm, her memories gradually giving place to hopes and visions of the future. Her hopes and visions were so intricate that she no longer saw the white pillows on which her gaze was fixed or remembered that she was waiting for anything.

26    At last she heard her mother calling. She started to her feet and ran to the banisters.

— Polly! Polly!

— Yes, mamma?

— Come down, dear. Mr. Doran wants to speak to you.

Then she remembered what she had been waiting for.

(*1914*)

---

9. A brand of beer.

# D.H. Lawrence (1885-1930)

*Lawrence's centrality as a modern literary figure is due largely to his attempts to free British fiction from the fetters of puritanism and class. He was a prolific and controversial author of fiction, poetry, plays, and literary criticism. The emotional relations of Lawrence's fictional characters are often intensely unsettling.*

## You Touched Me

1   The Pottery House was a square, ugly, brick house girt in by the wall that enclosed the whole grounds of the pottery itself. To be sure, a privet hedge partly masked the house and its ground from the pottery-yard and works: but only partly. Through the hedge could be seen the desolate yard, and the many-windowed, factory-like pottery, over the hedge could be seen the chimneys and the out-houses. But inside the hedge, a pleasant garden and lawn sloped down to a willow pool, which had once supplied the works.

2   The Pottery itself was now closed, the great doors of the yard permanently shut. No more the great crates with yellow straw showing through stood in stacks by the packing-shed. No more the drays drawn by great horses rolled down the hill with a high load. No more the pottery-lasses in their clay-coloured overalls, their faces and hair splashed with grey fine mud, shrieked and larked with the men. All that was over.

3   "We like it much better — oh, much better — quieter," said Matilda Rockley.

4   "Oh, yes," assented Emmie Rockley, her sister.

5   "I'm sure you do," agreed the visitor.

6   But whether the two Rockley girls really like it better, or whether they only imagined they did, is a question. Certainly their lives were much more grey and dreary now that the grey clay had ceased to spatter its mud and silt its dust over the premises. They did not quite realise how they missed the shrieking, shouting lasses, whom they had known all their lives and disliked so much.

7   Matilda and Emmie were already old maids. In a thorough industrial district, it is not easy for the girls who have expectations above the common to find husbands. The ugly industrial town was full of

men, young men who were ready to marry. But they were all colliers or pottery-hands, mere workmen. The Rockley girls would have about ten thousand pounds each when their father died: ten thousand pounds' worth of profitable house-property. It was not to be sneezed at: they felt so themselves, and refrained from sneezing away such a fortune on any mere member of the proletariat. Consequently, bank-clerks or non-conformist clergymen or even school-teachers having failed to come forward, Matilda had begun to give up all idea of ever leaving the Pottery House.

8   Matilda was a tall, thin, graceful, fair girl, with a rather large nose. She was the Mary to Emmie's Martha: that is, Matilda loved painting and music, and read a good many novels, whilst Emmie looked after the housekeeping. Emmie was shorter, plumper than her sister, and she had no accomplishments. She looked up to Matilda, whose mind was naturally refined and sensible.

9   In their quiet, melancholy way, the two girls were happy. Their mother was dead. Their father was ill also. He was an intelligent man who had had some education, but preferred to remain as if he were one with the rest of the working people. He had a passion for music and played the violin pretty well. But now he was getting old, he was very ill, dying of a kidney disease. He had been rather a heavy whisky-drinker.

10   This quiet household, with one servant-maid, lived on year after year in the Pottery House. Friends came in, the girls went out, the father drank himself more and more ill. Outside in the street there was a continual racket of the colliers and their dogs and children. But inside the pottery wall was a deserted quiet.

11   In all this ointment there was one little fly. Ted Rockley, the father of the girls, had had four daughters, and no son. As his girls grew, he felt angry at finding himself always in a household of women. He went off to London and adopted a boy out of a Charity Institution. Emmie was fourteen years old, and Matilda sixteen, when their father arrived home with his prodigy, the boy of six, Hadrian.

12   Hadrian was just an ordinary boy from a Charity Home, with ordinary brownish hair and ordinary bluish eyes and of ordinary rather Cockney speech. The Rockley girls — there were three at home at the time of his arrival — had resented his being sprung on them. He, with his watchful, charity-institution instinct, knew this at once. Though he was only six years old, Hadrian had a subtle, jeering look on his face when he regarded the three young women. They insisted he should address them as Cousin: Cousin Flora, Cousin Matilda, Cousin Emmie. He complied, but there seemed a mockery in his tone.

13   The girls, however, were kind-hearted by nature. Flora married and left home. Hadrian did very much as he pleased with Matilda and Emmie, though they had certain strictnesses. He grew up in the Pottery House and about the Pottery premises, went to an elementary school, and was invariably called Hadrian Rockley. He regarded

Cousin Matilda and Cousin Emmie with a certain laconic indifference, was quiet and reticent in his ways. The girls called him sly, but that was unjust. He was merely cautious, and without frankness. His uncle, Ted Rockley, understood him tacitly, their natures were somewhat akin. Hadrian and the elderly man had a real but unemotional regard for one another.

14   When he was thirteen years old the boy was sent to a High School in the County town. He did not like it. His Cousin Matilda had longed to make a little gentleman of him, but he refused to be made. He would give a little contemptuous curve to his lip, and take on a shy, charity-boy grin, when refinement was thrust upon him. He played truant from the High School, sold his books, his cap with its badge, even his very scarf and pocket-handkerchief, to his school-fellows, and went raking off heaven knows where with the money. So he spent two very unsatisfactory years.

15   When he was fifteen he announced that he wanted to leave England to go to the Colonies. He had kept touch with the Home. The Rockleys knew that, when Hadrian made a declaration, in his quiet, half-jeering manner, it was worse than useless to oppose him. So at last the boy departed, going to Canada under the protection of the Institution to which he had belonged. He said good-bye to the Rockleys, without a word of thanks, and parted, it seemed, without a pang. Matilda and Emmie wept often to think of how he left them: even on their father's face a queer look came. But Hadrian wrote fairly regularly from Canada. He had entered some electricity works near Montreal, and was doing well.

16   At last, however, the war came. In his turn, Hadrian joined up and came to Europe. The Rockleys saw nothing of him. They lived on, just the same, in the Pottery House. Ted Rockley was dying of a sort of dropsy, and in his heart he wanted to see the boy. When the Armistice was signed, Hadrian had a long leave, and wrote that he was coming home to the Pottery House.

17   The girls were terribly fluttered. To tell the truth, they were a little afraid of Hadrian. Matilda, tall and thin, was frail in her health, both girls were worn with nursing their father. To have Hadrian, a young man of twenty-one, in the house with them, after he had left them so coldly five years before, was a trying circumstance.

18   They were in a flutter. Emmie persuaded her father to have his bed made finally in the morning-room downstairs, whilst his room upstairs was prepared for Hadrian. This was done, and preparations were going on for the arrival, when, at ten o'clock in the morning, the young man suddenly turned up, quite unexpectedly. Cousin Emmie, with her hair bobbed up in absurd little bobs round her forehead, was busily polishing the stair-rods, while Cousin Matilda was in the kitchen washing the drawing-room ornaments in a lather, her sleeves rolled back on her thin arms, and her head tied up oddly and coquettishly in a duster.

19    Cousin Matilda blushed deep with mortification when the self-possessed young man walked in with his kit-bag, and put his cap on the sewing-machine. He was little and self-confident, with a curious neatness about him that still suggested the Charity Institution. His face was brown, he had a small moustache, he was vigorous enough in his smallness.

20    "*Well*, it is Hadrian!" exclaimed Cousin Matilda, wringing the lather off her hand. "We didn't expect you till to-morrow."

21    "I got off Monday night," said Hadrian, glancing round the room.

22    "Fancy!" said Cousin Matilda. Then, having dried her hands, she went forward, held out her hand, and said:

23    "How are you?"

24    "Quite well, thank you," said Hadrian.

25    "You're quite a man," said Cousin Matilda.

26    Hadrian glanced at her. She did not look her best: so thin, so large-nosed, with that pink-and-white checked duster tied round her head. She felt her disadvantage. But she had had a good deal of suffering and sorrow, she did not mind any more.

27    The servant entered — one that did not know Hadrian.

28    "Come and see my father," said Cousin Matilda.

29    In the hall they roused Cousin Emmie like a partridge from cover. She was on the stairs pushing the bright stair-rods into place. Instinctively her hand went to the little knobs, her front hair bobbed on her forehead.

30    "Why!" she exclaimed, crossly. "What have you come today for?"

31    "I got off a day earlier," said Hadrian, and his man's voice so deep and unexpected was like a blow to Cousin Emmie.

32    "Well, you've caught us in the midst of it," she said, with resentment. Then all three went into the middle room.

33    Mr. Rockley was dressed — that is, he had on his trousers and socks — but he was resting on the bed, propped up just under the window, from whence he could see his beloved and resplendent garden, where tulips and apple trees were ablaze. He did not look as ill as he was, for the water puffed him up, and his face kept its colour. His stomach was much swollen.

34    He glanced round swiftly, turning his eyes without turning his head. He was the wreck of a handsome, well-built man.

35    Seeing Hadrian, a queer, unwilling smile went over his face. The young man greeted him sheepishly.

36    "You wouldn't make a life-guardsman," he said. "Do you want something to eat?"

37    Hadrian looked around — as if for the meal.

38    "I don't mind," he said.

39    "What shall you have — egg and bacon?" asked Emmie shortly.

40    "Yes, I don't mind," said Hadrian.

41    The sisters went down to the kitchen, and sent the servant to finish the stairs.

"Isn't he *altered*?" said Matilda, *sotto voce*.

"Isn't he!" said Cousin Emmie. "What a little man!"

They both made a grimace, and laughed nervously.

"Get the frying-pan," said Emmie to Matilda.

"But he's as cocky as ever," said Matilda, narrowing her eyes and shaking her head knowingly, as she handed the frying-pan.

"Mannie!" said Emmie sarcastically. Hadrian's new-fledged, cocksure manliness evidently found no favour in her eyes.

"Oh, he's not bad," said Matilda. "You don't want to be prejudiced against him."

"I'm not prejudiced against him. I think he's all right for looks," said Emmie, "but there's too much of the little mannie about him."

"Fancy catching us like this," said Matilda.

"They've no thought for anything," said Emmie with contempt. "You go up and get dressed, our Matilda. I don't care about him. I can see to things, and you can talk to him. I shan't."

"He'll talk to my father," said Matilda, meaningful.

"*Sly* — !" exclaimed Emmie, with a grimace.

The sisters believed that Hadrian had come hoping to get something out of their father — hoping for a legacy. And they were not at all sure he would not get it.

Matilda went upstairs to change. She had thought it all out how she would receive Hadrian, and impress him. And he had caught her with her head tied up in a duster, and her thin arms in a basin of lather. But she did not care. She now dressed herself most scrupulously, carefully folded her long, beautiful, blonde hair, touched her pallor with a little rouge, and put her long string of exquisite crystal beads over her soft green dress. Now she looked elegant, like a heroine in a magazine illustration, and almost as unreal.

She found Hadrian and her father talking away. The young man was short of speech as a rule, but he could find tongue with his "uncle." They were both sipping a glass of brandy, and smoking, and chatting like a pair of old cronies. Hadrian was telling about Canada. He was going back there when his leave was up.

"You wouldn't like to stop in England, then?" said Mr. Rockley.

"No, I wouldn't stop in England," said Hadrian.

"How's that? There's plenty of electricians here," said Mr. Rockley.

"Yes. But there's too much difference between the men and the employers over here — too much of that for me," said Hadrian.

The sick man looked at him narrowly, with oddly smiling eyes.

"That's it, is it?" he replied.

Matilda heard and understood. "So that's your big idea, is it, my little man," she said to herself. She had always said of Hadrian that he had no proper *respect* for anybody or anything, that he was sly and *common*. She went down to the kitchen for a *sotto voce* confab with Emmie.

"He thinks a rare lot of himself!" she whispered.

65 "He's somebody, he is!" said Emmie with contempt.

66 "He thinks there's too much difference between masters and men over here," said Matilda.

67 "Is it any different in Canada?" asked Emmie.

68 "Oh yes — democratic," replied Matilda. "He thinks they're all on a level over there."

69 "Ay, well, he's over here now," said Emmie dryly, "so he can keep his place."

70 As they talked they saw the young man sauntering down the garden, looking casually at the flowers. He had his hands in his pockets, and his soldier's cap neatly on his head. He looked quite at his ease, as if in possession. The two women, fluttered, watched him through the window.

71 "We know what he's come for," said Emmie, churlishly. Matilda looked a long time at the neat khaki figure. It had something of the charity-box about it still; but now it was a man's figure, laconic, charged with plebeian energy. She thought of a derisive passion in his voice as he had declaimed against the propertied classes, to her father.

72 "You don't know, Emmie. Perhaps he's not come for that," she rebuked her sister. They were both thinking of the money.

73 They were still watching the young soldier. He stood away at the bottom of the garden, with his back to them, his hands in his pockets, looking into the water of the willow pond. Matilda's dark blue eyes had a strange, full look in them, the lids, with the faint blue veins showing, dropped rather low. She carried her head light and high, but she had a look of pain. The young man at the bottom of the garden turned and looked up the path. Perhaps he saw them through the window. Matilda moved into shadow.

74 That afternoon their father seemed weak or ill. He was easily exhausted. The doctor came, and told Matilda that the sick man might die at any moment — but then he might not. They must be prepared.

75 So the day passed, and the next. Hadrian made himself at home. He went about in the morning in his brownish jersey and his khaki trousers, collarless, his bare neck showing. He explored the pottery premises, as if he had some secret purpose in so doing, he talked with Mr. Rockley, when the sick man had strength. The two girls were always angry when the two men sat talking together like cronies. Yet it was chiefly a kind of politics they talked.

76 On the second day after Hadrian's arrival, Matilda sat with her father in the evening. She was drawing a picture which she wanted to copy. It was very still, Hadrian was gone out somewhere, no one knew where, and Emmie was busy. Mr. Rockley reclined on his bed, looking out in silence over his evening-sunny garden.

77 "If anything happens to me, Matilda," he said, "you won't sell this house — you'll stop here — "

78   Matilda's eyes took their slightly haggard look as she stared at her father.
79   "Well, we couldn't do anything else," she said.
80   "You don't know what you might do," he said. "Everything is left to you and Emmie, equally. You do as you like with it — only don't sell this house, don't part with it."
81   "No," she said.
82   "And give Hadrian my watch and chain, and a hundred pounds out of what's in the bank — and help him if he ever wants helping. I haven't put his name in the will."
83   "Your watch and chain, and a hundred pounds — yes. But you'll be here when he goes back to Canada, father."
84   "You never know what'll happen," said her father.
85   Matilda sat and watched him, with her full, haggard eyes, for a long time, as if tranced. She saw that he knew he must go soon — she saw like a clairvoyant.
86   Later on she told Emmie what her father had said about the watch and chain and the money.
87   "What right has *he*" — *he* — meaning Hadrian — "to my father's watch and chain — what has it to do with him? Let him have the money, and get off," said Emmie. She loved her father.
88   That night Matilda sat late in her room. Her heart was anxious and breaking, her mind seemed entranced. She was too much entranced even to weep, and all the time she thought of her father, only her father. At last she felt she must go to him.
89   It was near midnight. She went along the passage and to his room. There was a faint light from the moon outside. She listened at his door. Then she softly opened and entered. The room was faintly dark. She heard a movement on the bed.
90   "Are you asleep?" she said softly, advancing to the side of the bed.
91   "Are you asleep?" she repeated gently, as she stood at the side of the bed. And she reached her hand in the darkness to touch his forehead. Delicately, her fingers met the nose and the eyebrows, she laid her fine, delicate hand on his brow. It seemed fresh and smooth — very fresh and smooth. A sort of surprise stirred her, in her entranced state. But it could not waken her. Gently, she leaned over the bed and stirred her fingers over the low-growing hair on his brow.
92   "Can't you sleep to-night?" she said.
93   There was a quick stirring in the bed. "Yes, I can," a voice answered. It was Hadrian's voice. She started away. Instantly she was wakened from her late-at-night trance. She remembered that her father was downstairs, that Hadrian had his room. She stood in the darkness as if stung.
94   "Is it you, Hadrian?" she said. "I thought it was my father." She was so startled, so shocked, that she could not move. The young man gave an uncomfortable laugh, and turned in his bed.

95   At last she got out of the room. When she was back in her own room, in the light, and her door was closed, she stood holding up her hand that had touched him, as if it were hurt. She was almost too shocked, she could not endure.

96   "Well," said her calm and weary mind, "it was only a mistake, why take any notice of it."

97   But she could not reason her feelings so easily. She suffered, feeling herself in a false position. Her right hand, which she had laid so gently on his face, on his fresh skin, ached now, as if it were really injured. She could not forgive Hadrian for the mistake: it made her dislike him deeply.

98   Hadrian too slept badly. He had been awakened by the opening of the door, and had not realised what the question meant. But the soft, straying tenderness of her hand on his face startled something out of his soul. He was a charity boy, aloof and more or less at bay. The fragile exquisiteness of her caress startled him most, revealed unknown things to him.

99   In the morning she could feel the consciousness in his eyes, when she came downstairs. She tried to bear herself as if nothing at all had happened, and she succeeded. She had the calm self-control, self-indifference, of one who has suffered and borne her suffering. She looked at him from her darkish, almost drugged blue eyes, she met the spark of consciousness in his eyes, and quenched it. And with her long, fine hand she put the sugar in his coffee.

100   But she could not control him as she thought she could. He had a keen memory stinging his mind, a new set of sensations working in his consciousness. Something new was alert in him. At the back of his reticent, guarded mind he kept his secret alive and vivid. She was at his mercy, for he was unscrupulous, his standard was not her standard.

101   He looked at her curiously. She was not beautiful, her nose was too large, her chin was too small, her neck was too thin. But her skin was clear and fine, she had a high-bred sensitiveness. This queer, brave, high-bred quality she shared with her father. The charity boy could see it in her tapering fingers, which were white and ringed. The same glamour that he knew in the elderly man he now saw in the woman. And he wanted to possess himself of it, he wanted to make himself master of it. As he went about through the old pottery-yard, his secretive mind schemed and worked. To be master of that strange soft delicacy such as he had felt in her hand upon his face — this was what he set himself towards. He was secretly plotting.

102   He watched Matilda as she went about, and she became aware of his attention, as of some shadow following her. But her pride made her ignore it. When he sauntered near her, his hands in his pockets, she received him with that same commonplace kindliness which mastered him more than any contempt. Her superior breeding seemed to control him. She made herself feel towards him exactly as she had

always felt: he was a young boy who lived in the house with them, but was a stranger. Only, she dared not remember his face under her hand. When she remembered that, she was bewildered. Her hand had offended her, she wanted to cut it off. And she wanted, fiercely, to cut off the memory in him. She assumed she had done so.

103   One day, when he sat talking with his "uncle," he looked straight into the eyes of the sick man, and said:
104   "But I shouldn't like to live and die here in Rawsley."
105   "No — well — you needn't," said the sick man.
106   "Do you think Cousin Matilda likes it?"
107   "I should think so."
108   "I don't call it much of a life," said the youth. "How much older is she than me, Uncle?"
109   The sick man looked at the young soldier.
110   "A good bit," he said.
111   "Over thirty?" said Hadrian.
112   "Well, not much. She's thirty-two."
113   Hadrian considered a while.
114   "She doesn't look it," he said.
115   Again the sick father looked at him.
116   "Do you think she'd like to leave here?" said Hadrian.
117   "Nay, I don't know," replied the father, restive.
118   Hadrian sat still, having his own thoughts. Then in a small, quiet voice, as if he were speaking from inside himself, he said:
119   "I'd marry her if you wanted me to."
120   The sick man raised his eyes suddenly and stared. He stared for a long time. The youth looked inscrutably out of the window.
121   "*You!*" said the sick man, mocking, with some contempt. Hadrian turned and met his eyes. The two men had an inexplicable understanding.
122   "If you wasn't against it," said Hadrian.
123   "Nay," said the father, turning aside, "I don't think I'm against it. I've never thought of it. But — but Emmie's the youngest."
124   He had flushed, and looked suddenly more alive. Secretly he loved the boy.
125   "You might ask her," said Hadrian.
126   The elder man considered.
127   "Hadn't you better ask her yourself?" he said.
128   "She'd take more notice of you," said Hadrian.
129   They were both silent. Then Emmie came in.
130   For two days Mr. Rockley was excited and thoughtful. Hadrian went about quietly, secretly, unquestioning. At last the father and daughter were alone together. It was very early morning, the father had been in much pain. As the pain abated, he lay still thinking.
131   "Matilda!" he said suddenly, looking at his daughter.
132   "Yes, I'm here," she said.
133   "Ay! I want you to do something — "

134  She rose in anticipation.
135  "Nay, sit still. I want you to marry Hadrian — "
136  She thought he was raving. She rose, bewildered and frightened.
137  "Nay, sit you still, sit you still. You hear what I tell you."
138  "But you don't know what you're saying, father."
139  "Ay, I know well enough. I want you to marry Hadrian, I tell you."
140  She was dumbfounded. He was a man of few words.
141  "You'll do what I tell you," he said.
142  She looked at him slowly.
143  "What put such an idea in your mind?" she said proudly.
144  "He did."
145  Matilda almost looked her father down, her pride was so offended.
146  "Why, it's disgraceful," she said.
147  "Why?"
148  She watched him slowly.
149  "What do you ask me for?" she said. "It's disgusting."
150  "The lad's sound enough," he said testily.
151  "You'd better tell him to clear out," she said coldly.
152  He turned and looked out of the window. She sat flushed and erect for a long time. At length her father turned to her, looking really malevolent.
153  "If you won't," he said, "you're a fool, and I'll make you pay for your foolishness, do you see?"
154  Suddenly a cold fear gripped her. She could not believe her senses. She was terrified and bewildered. She stared at her father, believing him to be delirious, or mad, or drunk. What could she do?
155  "I tell you," he said. "I'll send for Whittle to-morrow if you don't. You shall neither of you have anything of mine."
156  Whittle was the solicitor. She understood her father well enough: he would send for his solicitor, and make a will leaving all his property to Hadrian: neither she nor Emmie should have anything. It was too much. She rose and went out of the room, up to her own room, where she locked herself in.
157  She did not come out for some hours. At last, late at night, she confided in Emmie.
158  "The sliving demon, he wants the money," said Emmie. "My father's out of his mind."
159  The thought that Hadrian merely wanted the money was another blow to Matilda. She did not love the impossible youth — but she had not yet learned to think of him as a thing of evil. He now became hideous to her mind.
160  Emmie had a little scene with her father the next day.
161  "You don't mean what you said to our Matilda yesterday, do you, father?" she asked aggressively.
162  "Yes," he replied.
163  "What, that you'll alter your will?"
164  "Yes."
165  "You won't," said his angry daughter.

166 But he looked at her with a malevolent little smile.
167 "Annie!" he shouted. "Annie!"
168 He had still power to make his voice carry. The servant maid came in from the kitchen.
169 "Put your things on, and go down to Whittle's office, and say I want to see Mr. Whittle as soon as he can, and will he bring a will-form."
170 The sick man lay back a while — he could not lie down. His daughter sat as if she had been struck. Then she left the room.
171 Hadrian was pottering about in the garden. She went straight down to him.
172 "Here," she said. "You'd better get off. You'd better take your things and go from here, quick."
173 Hadrian looked slowly at the infuriated girl.
174 "Who says so?" he asked.
175 "*We* say so — get off, you've done enough mischief and damage."
176 "Does Uncle say so?"
177 "Yes, he does."
178 "I'll go and ask him."
179 But like a fury Emmie barred his way.
180 "No, you needn't. You needn't ask him nothing at all. We don't want you, so you can go."
181 "Uncle's boss here."
182 "A man that's dying, and you crawling round and working on him for his money! — you're not fit to live."
183 "Oh!" he said. "Who says I'm working for his money?"
184 "I say. But my father told our Matilda, and *she* knows what you are. *She* knows what you're after. So you might as well clear out, for all you'll get — guttersnipe!"
185 He turned his back on her, to think. It had not occurred to him that they would think he was after the money. He *did* want the money — badly. He badly wanted to be an employer himself, not one of the employed. But he knew, in his subtle, calculating way, that it was not for the money he wanted Matilda. He wanted both the money and Matilda. But he told himself the two desires were separate, not one. He could not do with Matilda, *without* the money. But he did not want her *for* the money.
186 When he got this clear in his mind, he sought for an opportunity to tell it her, lurking and watching. But she avoided him. In the evening the lawyer came. Mr. Rockley seemed to have a new access of strength — a will was drawn up, making the previous arrangements wholly conditional. The old will held good, if Matilda would consent to marry Hadrian. If she refused then at the end of six months the whole property passed to Hadrian.
187 Mr. Rockley told this to the young man, with malevolent satisfaction. He seemed to have a strange desire, quite unreasonable, for revenge upon the women who had surrounded him for so long, and served him so carefully.
188 "Tell her in front of me," said Hadrian.

189   So Mr. Rockley sent for his daughters.

190   At last they came, pale, mute, stubborn. Matilda seemed to have retired far off, Emmie seemed like a fighter ready to fight to the death. The sick man reclined on the bed, his eyes bright, his puffed hand trembling. But his face had again some of its old, bright handsomeness. Hadrian sat quiet, a little aside: the indomitable, dangerous charity boy.

191   "There's the will," said their father, pointing them to the paper.

192   The two women sat mute and immovable, they took no notice.

193   "Either you marry Hadrian, or he has everything," said the father with satisfaction.

194   "Then let him have everything," said Matilda coldly.

195   "He's not! He's not!" cried Emmie fiercely. "He's not going to have it. The guttersnipe!"

196   An amused look came on her father's face.

197   "You hear that, Hadrian," he said.

198   "I didn't offer to marry Cousin Matilda for the money," said Hadrian, flushing and moving on his seat.

199   Matilda looked at him slowly, with her dark blue, drugged eyes. He seemed a strange monster to her.

200   "Why, you liar, you know you did," cried Emmie.

201   The sick man laughed. Matilda continued to gaze strangely at the young man.

202   "She knows I didn't," said Hadrian.

203   He too had his courage, as a rat has indomitable courage in the end. Hadrian had some of the neatness, the reserve, the underground quality of the rat. But he had perhaps the ultimate courage, the most unquenched courage of all.

204   Emmie looked at her sister.

205   "Oh, well," she said. "Matilda — don't you bother. Let him have everything, we can look after ourselves."

206   "I know he'll take everything," said Matilda, abstractedly.

207   Hadrian did not answer. He knew in fact that if Matilda refused him he would take everything, and go off with it.

208   "A clever little mannie — !" said Emmie, with a jeering grimace.

209   The father laughed noiselessly to himself. But he was tired. ...

210   "Go on, then," he said. "Go on, let me be quiet."

211   Emmie turned and looked at him.

212   "You deserve what you've got," she said to her father bluntly.

213   "Go on," he answered mildly. "Go on."

214   Another night passed — a night nurse sat up with Mr. Rockley. Another day came. Hadrian was there as ever, in his woollen jersey and coarse khaki trousers and bare neck. Matilda went about, frail and distant, Emmie black-browed in spite of her blondness. They were all quiet, for they did not intend the mystified servant to learn anything.

215   Mr. Rockley had very bad attacks of pain, he could not breathe. The end seemed near. They all went about quiet and stoical, all unyielding. Hadrian pondered within himself. If he did not marry Matilda he

would go to Canada with twenty thousand pounds. This was itself a very satisfactory prospect. If Matilda consented he would have nothing — she would have her own money.

216  Emmie was the one to act. She went off in search of the solicitor and brought him home with her. There was an interview, and Whittle tried to frighten the youth into withdrawal — but without avail. The clergyman and relatives were summoned — but Hadrian stared at them and took no notice. It made him angry, however.

217  He wanted to catch Matilda alone. Many days went by, and he was not successful: she avoided him. At last, lurking, he surprised her one day as she came to pick gooseberries, and he cut off her retreat. He came to the point at once.

218  "You don't want me, then?" he said, in his subtle, insinuating voice.

219  "I don't want to speak to you," she said, averting her face.

220  "You put your hand on me, though," he said. "You shouldn't have done that, and then I should never have thought of it. You shouldn't have touched me."

221  "If you were anything decent, you'd know that was a mistake, and forget it," she said.

222  "I know it was a mistake — but I shan't forget it. If you wake a man up, he can't go to sleep again because he's told to."

223  "If you had any decent feeling in you, you'd have gone away," she replied.

224  "I didn't want to," he replied.

225  She looked away into the distance. At last she asked:

226  "What do you persecute me for, if it isn't for the money? I'm old enough to be your mother. In a way I've been your mother."

227  "Doesn't matter," he said. "You've been no mother to me. Let us marry and go to Canada — you might as well — you've touched me."

228  She was white and trembling. Suddenly she flushed with anger.

229  "It's so *indecent*," she said.

230  "How?" he retorted. "You touched me."

231  But she walked away from him. She felt as if he had trapped her. He was angry and depressed, he felt again despised.

232  That same evening she went into her father's room.

233  "Yes," she said suddenly. "I'll marry him."

234  Her father looked up at her. He was in pain, and very ill.

235  "You like him now, do you?" he said, with a faint smile.

236  She looked down into his face, and saw death not far off. She turned and went coldly out of the room.

237  The solicitor was sent for, preparations were hastily made. In all the interval Matilda did not speak to Hadrian, never answered him if he addressed her. He approached her in the morning.

238  "You've come round to it, then?" he said, giving her a pleasant look from his twinkling, almost kindly eyes. She looked down at him and turned aside. She looked down on him both literally and figuratively. Still he persisted, and triumphed.

239 Emmie raved and wept, the secret flew abroad. But Matilda was silent and unmoved. Hadrian was quiet and satisfied, and nipped with fear also. But he held out against his fear. Mr. Rockley was very ill, but unchanged.

240 On the third day the marriage took place, Matilda and Hadrian drove straight home from the registrar, and went straight into the room of the dying man. His face lit up with a clear twinkling smile.

241 "Hadrian — you've got her?" he said, a little hoarsely.

242 "Yes," said Hadrian, who was pale round the gills.

243 "Ay, my lad, I'm glad you're mine," replied the dying man. Then he turned his eyes closely on Matilda.

244 "Let's look at you, Matilda," he said. Then his voice went strange and unrecognisable. "Kiss me," he said.

245 She stooped and kissed him. She had never kissed him before, not since she was a tiny kid. But she was quiet, very still.

246 "Kiss him," the dying man said.

247 Obediently, Matilda put forward her mouth and kissed the young husband.

248 "That's right! That's right!" murmured the dying man.

(1922)

# Katherine Mansfield (1888–1923)

New Zealand–born but very much a London literary figure, Mansfield is admired for her discipline as a short-story writer. Her sharply observed human portraits and her ability to penetrate the surface realities of life can be found in her five volumes of short stories, three published during her lifetime and two published posthumously.

## The Fly

1. "Y'are very snug in here," piped old Mr. Woodifield and he peered out of the great, green-leather armchair by his friend the boss's desk as a baby peers out of its pram. His talk was over; it was time for him to be off. But he did not want to go. Since he had retired, since his ... stroke, the wife and the girls kept him boxed up in the house every day of the week except Tuesday. On Tuesday he was dressed and brushed and allowed to cut back to the City for the day. Though what he did there the wife and the girls couldn't imagine. Made a nuisance of himself to his friends, they supposed. ... Well, perhaps so. All the same, we cling to our last pleasures as the tree clings to its last leaves. So there sat old Woodifield, smoking a cigar and staring almost greedily at the boss, who rolled in his office chair, stout, rosy, five years older than he, and still going strong, still at the helm. It did one good to see him.

2. Wistfully, admiringly, the old voice added, "It's snug in here, upon my word!"

3. "Yes, it's comfortable enough," agreed the boss, and he flipped the *Financial Times* with a paper-knife. As a matter of fact he was proud of his room; he liked to have it admired, especially by old Woodifield. It gave him a feeling of deep, solid satisfaction to be planted there in the midst of it in full view of that frail old figure in the muffler.

4. "I've had it done up lately," he explained, as he had explained for the past — how many? — weeks. "New carpet," and he pointed to the bright red carpet with a pattern of large white rings. "New furniture," and he nodded towards the massive bookcase and the table with legs like twisted treacle. "Electric heating!" He waved almost exultantly towards the five transparent, pearly sausages glowing so softly in the tilted copper pan.

5   But he did not draw old Woodifield's attention to the photograph over the table of a grave-looking boy in uniform standing in one of those spectral photographers' parks with photographers' storm-clouds behind him. It was not new. It had been there for over six years.

6   "There was something I wanted to tell you," said old Woodifield, and his eyes grew dim remembering. "Now what was it? I had it in my mind when I started out this morning." His hands began to tremble, and patches of red showed above his beard.

7   Poor old chap, he's on his last pins, thought the boss. And, feeling kindly, he winked at the old man, and said jokingly, "I tell you what. I've got a little drop of something here that'll do you good before you go out into the cold again. It's beautiful stuff. It wouldn't hurt a child." He took a key off his watch-chain, unlocked a cupboard below his desk, and drew forth a dark, squat bottle. "That's the medicine," said he. "And the man from whom I got it told me on the strict Q.T. it came from the cellars at Windsor Castle."

8   Old Woodifield's mouth fell open at the sight. He couldn't have looked more surprised if the boss had produced a rabbit.

9   "It's whisky, ain't it?" he piped feebly.

10  The boss turned the bottle and lovingly showed him the label. Whisky it was.

11  "D'you know," said he, peering up at the boss wonderingly, "they won't let me touch it at home." And he looked as though he was going to cry.

12  "Ah, that's where we know a bit more than the ladies," cried the boss, swooping across for two tumblers that stood on the table with the water-bottle, and pouring a generous finger into each. "Drink it down. It'll do you good. And don't put any water with it. It's sacrilege to tamper with stuff like this. Ah!" He tossed off his, pulled out his handkerchief, hastily wiped his moustaches, and cocked an eye at old Woodifield, who was rolling his in his chaps.[1]

13  The old man swallowed, was silent a moment, and then said faintly, "It's nutty!"

14  But it warmed him; it crept into his chill old brain — he remembered.

15  "That was it," he said, heaving himself out of his chair. "I thought you'd like to know. The girls were in Belgium last week having a look at poor Reggie's grave, and they happened to come across your boy's. They're quite near each other, it seems."

16  Old Woodifield paused, but the boss made no reply. Only a quiver in his eyelids showed that he heard.

17  "The girls were delighted with the way the place is kept," piped the old voice. "Beautifully looked after. Couldn't be better if they were at home. You've not been across, have yer?"

---

1. Mouth or jaws.

18 "No, no!" For various reasons the boss had not been across.

19 "There's miles of it," quavered old Woodifield, "and it's all as neat as a garden. Flowers growing on all the graves. Nice broad paths." It was plain from his voice how much he liked a nice broad path.

20 The pause came again. Then the old man brightened wonderfully.

21 "D'you know what the hotel made the girls pay for a pot of jam?" he piped. "Ten francs! Robbery, I call it. It was a little pot, so Gertrude says, no bigger than a half-crown. And she hadn't taken more than a spoonful when they charged her ten francs. Gertrude brought the pot away with her to teach 'em a lesson. Quite right, too; it's trading on our feelings. They think because we're over there having a look round we're ready to pay anything. That's what it is." And he turned towards the door.

22 "Quite right, quite right!" cried the boss, though what was quite right he hadn't the least idea. He came round by his desk, followed the shuffling footsteps to the door, and saw the old fellow out. Woodifield was gone.

23 For a long moment the boss stayed, staring at nothing, while the grey-haired office messenger, watching him, dodged in and out of his cubby-hole like a dog that expects to be taken for a run. Then: "I'll see nobody for half an hour, Macey," said the boss. "Understand? Nobody at all."

24 "Very good, sir."

25 The door shut, the firm heavy steps recrossed the bright carpet, the fat body plumped down in the spring chair, and leaning forward, the boss covered his face with his hands. He wanted, he intended, he had arranged to weep. ...

26 It had been a terrible shock to him when old Woodifield sprang that remark upon him about the boy's grave. It was exactly as though the earth had opened and he had seen the boy lying there with Woodifield's girls staring down at him. For it was strange. Although over six years had passed away, the boss never thought of the boy except as lying unchanged, unblemished in his uniform, asleep for ever. "My son!" groaned the boss. But no tears came yet. In the past, in the first months and even years after the boy's death, he had only to say those words to be overcome by such grief that nothing short of a violent fit of weeping could relieve him. Time, he had declared then, he had told everybody, could make no difference. Other men perhaps might recover, might live their loss down, but not he. How was it possible? His boy was an only son. Ever since his birth the boss had worked at building up this business for him; it had no other meaning if it was not for the boy. Life itself had come to have no other meaning. How on earth could he have slaved, denied himself, kept going all those years without the promise for ever before him of the boy's stepping into his shoes and carrying on where he left off?

27 And that promise had been so near being fulfilled. The boy had been in the office learning the ropes for a year before the war. Every

morning they had started off together; they had come back by the same train. And what congratulations he had received as the boy's father! No wonder; he had taken to it marvellously. As to his popularity with the staff, every man jack of them down to old Macey couldn't make enough of the boy. And he wasn't in the least spoilt. No, he was just his bright natural self, with the right word for everybody, with that boyish look and his habit of saying, "Simply splendid!"

28    But all that was over and done with as though it never had been. The day had come when Macey had handed him the telegram that brought the whole place crashing about his head. "Deeply regret to inform you ..." And he had left the office a broken man, with his life in ruins.

29    Six years ago, six years. ... How quickly time passed! It might have happened yesterday. The boss took his hands from his face; he was puzzled. Something seemed to be wrong with him. He wasn't feeling as he wanted to feel. He decided to get up and have a look at the boy's photograph. But it wasn't a favourite photograph of his; the expression was unnatural. It was cold, even stern-looking. The boy had never looked like that.

30    At that moment the boss noticed that a fly had fallen into his broad inkpot, and was trying feebly but desperately to clamber out again. Help! Help! said those struggling legs. But the sides of the inkpot were wet and slippery; it fell back again and began to swim. The boss took up a pen, picked the fly out of the ink, and shook it on a piece of blotting-paper. For a fraction of a second it lay still on the dark patch that oozed round it. Then the front legs waved, took hold, and, pulling its small, sodden body up, it began the immense task of cleaning the ink from its wings. Over and under, over and under, went a leg along a wing as the stone goes over and under the scythe. Then there was a pause, while the fly, seeming to stand on the tips of its toes, tried to expand first one wing and then the other. It succeeded at last, and, sitting down, it began, like a minute cat, to clean its face. Now one could imagine that the little front legs rubbed against each other lightly, joyfully. The horrible danger was over; it had escaped; it was ready for life again.

31    But just then the boss had an idea. He plunged his pen back into the ink, leaned his thick wrist on the blotting-paper, and as the fly tried its wings down came a great heavy blot. What would it make of that? What indeed! The little beggar seemed absolutely cowed, stunned, and afraid to move because of what would happen next. But then, as if painfully, it dragged itself forward. The front legs waved, caught hold, and, more slowly this time, the task began from the beginning.

32    He's a plucky little devil, thought the boss, and he felt a real admiration for the fly's courage. That was the way to tackle things; that was the right spirit. Never say die; it was only a question of ... But the fly had again finished its laborious task, and the boss had just time to

refill his pen, to shake fair and square on the new-cleaned body yet another dark drop. What about it this time? A painful moment of suspense followed. But behold, the front legs were again waving; the boss felt a rush of relief. He leaned over the fly and said to it tenderly, "You artful little b ..." And he actually had the brilliant notion of breathing on it to help the drying process. All the same, there was something timid and weak about its efforts now, and the boss decided that this time should be the last, as he dipped the pen deep into the inkpot.

33   It was. The last blot fell on the soaked blotting-paper, and the draggled fly lay in it and did not stir. The back legs were stuck to the body; the front legs were not to be seen.

34   "Come on," said the boss. "Look sharp!" And he stirred it with his pen — in vain. Nothing happened or was likely to happen. The fly was dead.

35   The boss lifted the corpse on the end of the paper-knife and flung it into the waste-paper basket. But such a grinding feeling of wretchedness seized him that he felt positively frightened. He started forward and pressed the bell for Macey.

36   "Bring me some fresh blotting-paper," he said sternly, "and look sharp about it." And while the old dog padded away he fell to wondering what it was he had been thinking about before. What was it? It was ... He took out his handkerchief and passed it inside his collar. For the life of him he could not remember.

(1922)

# Ethel Wilson (1888–1980)

A novelist as well as a short-story writer, Ethel Wilson moved to Vancouver in 1898. "We Have to Sit Opposite," included in Mrs. Golightly and Other Stories (1961), builds on the image of opposition suggested by its title and demonstrates the importance of place in Wilson's work. Her best-known novel, Swamp Angel (1954), is set in British Columbia.

## We Have to Sit Opposite

1   Even in the confusion of entering the carriage at Salzburg, Mrs. Montrose and her cousin Mrs. Forrester noticed the man with the blue tooth. He occupied a corner beside the window. His wife sat next to him. Next to her sat their daughter of perhaps seventeen. People poured into the train. A look passed between Mrs. Montrose and Mrs. Forrester. The look said, "These people seem to have filled up the carriage pretty well, but we'd better take these seats while we can as the train is so full. At least we can have seats together." The porter, in his porter's tyrannical way, piled their suitcases onto the empty rack above the heads of the man with the blue tooth, and his wife, and his daughter, and departed. The opposite rack was full of baskets, bags, and miscellaneous parcels. The train started. Here they were. Mrs. Montrose and Mrs. Forrester smiled at each other as they settled down below the rack which was filled with miscellaneous articles. Clinging vines that they were, they felt adventurous and successful. They had travelled alone from Vienna to Salzburg, leaving in Vienna their doctor husbands to continue attending the clinics of Dr. Bauer and Dr. Hirsch. And now, after a week in Salzburg, they were happily on their way to rejoin their husbands, who had flown to Munich.

2   Both Mrs. Montrose and Mrs. Forrester were tall, slight and fair. They were dressed with dark elegance. They knew that their small hats were smart, suitable and becoming, and they rejoiced in the simplicity and distinction of their own costumes. The selection of these and other costumes, and of these and other hats in Vienna had, they regretted, taken from the study of art, music and history a great deal of valuable time. Mrs. Montrose and Mrs. Forrester were sincerely fond of art, music and history and longed almost passionately to spend their days in the Albertina Gallery and the Kunsthistorische

Museum. But the modest shops and shop windows of the craftsmen of Vienna had rather diverted the two young women from the study of art and history, and it was easy to lay the blame for this on the museums and art galleries, which, in truth, closed their doors at very odd times. After each day's enchanting pursuits and disappointments, Mrs. Montrose and Mrs. Forrester hastened in a fatigued state to the café where they had arranged to meet their husbands who by this time had finished their daily sessions with Dr. Bauer and Dr. Hirsch.

3   This was perhaps the best part of the day, to sit together happily in the sunshine, toying with the good Viennese coffee or a glass of wine, gazing and being gazed upon, and giving up their senses to the music that flowed under the chestnut trees. (Ah Vienna, they thought, Vienna, Vienna.)

4   No, perhaps the evenings had been the best time when after their frugal pension dinner they hastened out to hear opera or symphony or wild atavistic gypsy music. All was past now. They had been very happy. They were fortunate. Were they too fortunate?

5   Mrs. Montrose and Mrs. Forrester were in benevolent good spirits as they looked round the railway carriage and prepared to take their seats and settle down for the journey to Munich to meet their husbands. In their window corner, opposite the man with the blue tooth, was a large hamper. "*Do* you mind?" asked Mrs. Montrose, smiling sweetly at the man, his wife, and his daughter. She prepared to lift the hamper on which the charming view from the carriage window was of course wasted, intending to move it along the seat, and take its place. The man, his wife, and his daughter had never taken their eyes off Mrs. Montrose and Mrs. Forrester since they had entered the carriage.

6   "*If* you please," said the man loudly and slowly in German English, "*if* you please, that place belongs to my wife or to my daughter. For the moment they sit beside me, but I keep that place for my wife or my daughter. That seat is therefore reserved. It is our seat. You may of course use the two remaining seats."

7   "I'm sorry," said Mrs. Montrose, feeling snubbed, and she and Mrs. Forrester sat down side by side on the two remaining seats opposite the German family. Beside them the hamper looked out of the window at the charming view. Their gaiety and self-esteem evaporated. The train rocked along.

8   The three continued to stare at the two young women. Suddenly the mother leaned toward her daughter. She put up her hand to her mouth and whispered behind her hand, her eyes remaining fixed on Mrs. Montrose. The daughter nodded. She also stared at Mrs. Montrose. Mrs. Montrose flushed. The mother sat upright again, still looking at Mrs. Montrose, who felt very uncomfortable, and very much annoyed at blushing.

9   The man ceased staring at the two young women. He looked up at the rack above him, which contained their suitcases.

10     "Those are your suitcases," he asked, or rather announced.

11     "Yes," said Mrs. Montrose and Mrs. Forrester without smiles.

12     "They are large," said the man in a didactic manner, "they are too large. They are too large to be put on racks. A little motion, a very little motion, and they might fall. If they fall they will injure myself, my wife, or my daughter. It is better," he continued instructively, "that if they fall, they should fall upon your heads, not upon our heads. That is logical. They are not my suitcases. They are your suitcases. You admit it. Please to move your suitcases to the opposite rack, where, if they fall, they will fall upon your own heads." And he continued to sit there motionless. So did his wife. So did his daughter.

13     Mrs. Montrose and Mrs. Forrester looked at the suitcases in dismay. "Oh," said Mrs. Forrester, "they are so heavy to move. If you feel like that, please won't you sit on this side of the carriage, and we will move across, under our own suitcases, though I can assure you they will not fall. Or perhaps you will help us?"

14     "We prefer this side of the carriage," said the man with the blue tooth. "We have sat here because we prefer this side of the carriage. It is logical that you should move your suitcases. It is not logical that my wife, my daughter and I should give up our seats in this carriage, or remove your suitcases."

15     Mrs. Montrose and Mrs. Forrester looked at each other with rage in their hearts. All their self-satisfaction was gone. They got up and tugged and tugged as the train rocked along. They leaned resentfully across the erectly sitting man, and his wife and his daughter. They experienced with exasperation the realization that they had better make the best of it. The train, they knew, was crowded. They had to remain in this carriage with this disagreeable family. With much pulling and straining they hauled down the heavy suitcases. Violently they removed the parcels of the German family and lifted their own suitcases onto the rack above their heads, disposing them clumsily on the rack. Panting a little (they disliked panting), they settled down again side by side with high colour and loosened wisps of hair. They controlled their features so as to appear serene and unaware of the existence of anyone else in the railway carriage, but their hearts were full of black hate.

16     The family exchanged whispered remarks, and then resumed their scrutiny of the two young women, whose elegance had by this time a sort of tipsy quality. The girl leaned toward her mother. She whispered behind her hand to her mother, who nodded. Both of them stared at Mrs. Forrester. Then they laughed.

17     "Heavens!" thought the affronted Mrs. Forrester, "this is outrageous! Why can't Alice and I whisper behind our hands to each other about those people and make them feel simply awful! But they wouldn't feel awful. Well, we can't, just because we've been properly brought up, and it would be too childish. And perhaps they don't even know

they're rude. They're just being natural." She breathed in frustration, and composed herself again.

18   Suddenly the man with the blue tooth spoke. "Are you English?" he said loudly.

19   "Yes — well — no," said Mrs. Forrester.

20   "No — well — yes," said Mrs. Montrose, simultaneously.

21   A derisive look came over the man's face. "You must know what you are," he said, "either you are English or you are not English. Are you, or are you not?"

22   "No," said Mrs. Montrose and Mrs. Forrester, speaking primly. Their chins were high, their eyes flashed, and they were ready for discreet battle.

23   "Then you are Americans?" said the man in the same bullying manner.

24   "No," said Mrs. Montrose and Mrs. Forrester.

25   "You can't deceive *me*, you know," said the man with the blue tooth, "I know well the English language. You *say* you are not English. You *say* you are not American. What, then, may I ask, are you? You must be something."

26   "We are Canadians," said Mrs. Forrester, furious at this catechism.

27   "*Canadians*," said the man.

28   "Yes, Canadians," said Mrs. Montrose.

29   "This," murmured Mrs. Forrester to Mrs. Montrose, "is more than I can bear!"

30   "What did you say?" said the man, leaning forward quickly, his hands on his knees.

31   "I spoke to my friend," said Mrs. Forrester coldly, "I spoke about my bear."

32   "Yes," said Mrs. Montrose, "she spoke about her bear."

33   "Your bear? Have you a bear? But you cannot have a bear!" said the man with some surprise.

34   "In Canada I have a bear. I have two bears," said Mrs. Forrester conceitedly.

35   "That is true," said Mrs. Montrose nodding, "she has two bears. I myself have five bears. My father has seven bears. That is nothing. It is the custom."

36   "What do you do with your bears?" asked the man.

37   "We eat them," said Mrs. Forrester.

38   "Yes," said Mrs. Montrose, "we eat them. It is the custom."

39   The man turned and spoke briefly to his wife and daughter, whose eyes opened wider than ever.

40   Mrs. Montrose and Mrs. Forrester felt pleased. This was better.

41   The man with the blue tooth became really interested. "Are you married?" he asked Mrs. Forrester.

42   "Yes," she replied. (We'll see what he'll say next, then we'll see what we can do.)

43 "And you?" he enquired of Mrs. Montrose. Mrs. Montrose seemed uncertain. "Well, yes, in a way, I suppose," she said.

44 The man with the blue tooth scrutinized Mrs. Montrose for a moment. "*Then*," he said, as though he had at last found her out, "if you are married, where is your husband?"

45 Mrs. Montrose took out her pocket handkerchief. She buried her face in her hands, covering her eyes with her handkerchief. She shook. Evidently she sobbed.

46 "Now you see what you've done!" said Mrs. Forrester. "You shouldn't ask questions like that. Just look at what you've done."

47 The three gazed fascinated at Mrs. Montrose. "Is he dead or what is he?" asked the man of Mrs. Forrester, making the words almost quietly with his mouth.

48 "Sh!!" said Mrs. Forrester very loudly indeed. The three jumped a little. So did Mrs. Montrose.

49 There was a silence while Mrs. Montrose wiped her eyes. She looked over the heads opposite. The wife leaned toward her husband and addressed him timidly behind her hand. He nodded, and spoke to Mrs. Forrester.

50 "Well," he said, "at least you admit that *you* have a husband. If you have a husband then, where is he?"

51 "Oh, I don't know," said Mrs. Forrester lightly.

52 "No, she doesn't know," said Mrs. Montrose.

53 The three on the opposite seat went into a conference. Mrs. Montrose and Mrs. Forrester did not dare to look at each other. They were enjoying themselves. Their self-esteem had returned. They had impressed. Unfavourably, it is true. But still they had impressed.

54 The man with the blue tooth pulled himself together. He reasserted himself. Across his waistcoat hung a watch chain. He took his watch out of his pocket and looked at the time. Then to the surprise of Mrs. Montrose and Mrs. Forrester he took another watch out of the pocket at the other end of the chain. "You see," he said proudly, "I have two watches."

55 Mrs. Montrose and Mrs. Forrester were surprised, but they had themselves well in hand.

56 Mrs. Montrose looked at the watches disparagingly. "My husband has six watches," she said.

57 "Yes, that is true," nodded Mrs. Forrester, "her husband *has* got six watches, but my husband, like you, unfortunately has only two watches."

58 The man put his watches back. Decidedly the battle was going in favour of the two young women. How horrid of us, he was so pleased with his watches, thought Mrs. Montrose. Isn't it true that horridness just breeds horridness. We're getting horrider every minute. She regarded the man, his wife and his daughter with distaste but with pity.

59 "You *say*," said the man, who always spoke as though their statements were open to doubt, which of course they were, "that you come from Canada. Do you come from Winnipeg? I know about Winnipeg."

60 "No," said Mrs. Montrose, and she spoke this time quite truthfully, "I come from Vancouver." Mrs. Forrester remained silent.

61 "And you, where do you come from?" persisted the man in a hectoring tone, addressing Mrs. Forrester. Mrs. Forrester remained silent, she had almost decided to answer no more questions.

62 "Oh, do not tell, please do not tell," begged Mrs. Montrose in an anguished way.

63 "No," said Mrs. Forrester importantly, "I shall not tell. Rest assured. I shall not tell."

64 "Why will she not tell?" demanded the man. He was tortured by curiosity. So was his wife. So was his daughter.

65 "Sh!!" said Mrs. Montrose very loudly.

66 The man seemed ill at ease. By this time nothing existed in the world for him, or for his wife, or for his daughter but these two Canadian women who ate bears.

67 "How is it," asked the man, "that you no longer buy my trousers?"

68 "I beg your pardon?" faltered Mrs. Montrose. For a moment she lost ground.

69 "I said," replied the man, "why is it that you no longer buy my trousers?"

70 The ladies did not answer. They could not think of a good answer to that one.

71 "I," said the man, "am a manufacturer of trousers. I make the most beautiful trousers in Germany. Indeed in the world." (You do not so, thought Mrs. Forrester, picturing her husband's good London legs.) "For three years I receive orders from Winnipeg for my trousers. And now, since two years, yes, since 1929, I receive no more orders for my trousers. Why is that?" he asked, like a belligerent.

72 "Shall we tell him?" asked Mrs. Forrester, looking at Mrs. Montrose. Neither of them knew why he had received no more orders for his trousers, but they did not wish to say so. "Shall we tell him?" asked Mrs. Forrester.

73 "You tell him," said Mrs. Montrose.

74 "No, *you* tell him," said Mrs. Forrester.

75 "I do not like to tell him," said Mrs. Montrose, "I'd rather you told him."

76 The man with the blue tooth looked from one to the other.

77 "Very well. I shall tell him," said Mrs. Forrester. "The fact is," she said, looking downward, "that in Canada men no longer wear trousers."

78 "What are you saying? That is not true, never can that be true!" said the man in some confusion.

79  "Yes," said Mrs. Montrose, corroborating sombrely. "Yes, indeed that is true. When they go abroad they wear trousers, but in Canada, no. It is a new custom."

80  "It is the climate," said Mrs. Forrester.

81  "Yes, that is the reason, it is the climate," agreed Mrs. Montrose.

82  "But in Canada," argued the man with the blue tooth, "your climate is cold. Everyone knows your climate is cold."

83  "In the Arctic regions, yes, it is really intensely cold, we all find it so. But not in Winnipeg. Winnipeg is very salubrious." (That's a good one, thought Mrs. Montrose.)

84  The man turned and spoke rapidly to his wife. She also turned, and looked askance at her daughter. The expressions of the man, his wife, and his daughter were a blend of pleasure and shock. The two liars were delighted.

85  At last the man could not help asking, "But they *must* wear something! It is not logical."

86  "Oh, it's logical, all right!" said Mrs. Forrester.

87  "But what *do* they wear?" persisted the man.

88  "I never looked to see," said Mrs. Montrose. "*I* did, I looked," said Mrs. Forrester.

89  "Well?" asked the man.

90  "Oh, they just wear kilts," said Mrs. Forrester.

91  "Kilts? What are kilts? I do not know kilts," said the man.

92  "I would rather not tell you," said Mrs. Forrester primly.

93  "Oh," said the man.

94  Mrs. Montrose took out her vanity case, and inspected herself, powder puff in hand.

95  "I do not allow my wife and daughter to paint their faces so," said the man with the blue tooth.

96  "No?" said Mrs. Montrose.

97  "It is not good that women should paint their faces so. Good women do not do that. It is a pity."

98  (Oh, Alice, thought Mrs. Forrester in a fury, he shall not dare!) "It is a pity," she hissed, "that in your country there are no good dentists!"

99  "Be careful, be careful," whispered Mrs. Montrose.

100  "What do you mean?" demanded the man with the blue tooth.

101  (She will go too far, I know she will, thought Mrs. Montrose, alarmed, putting out her hand.)

102  "In our country," said the rash Mrs. Forrester "anyone needing attention is taken straight to the State Dentist by the Police. This is done for aesthetic reasons. It is logical."

103  "I am going to sleep," said Mrs. Montrose very loudly, and she shut her eyes tight.

104  "So am I," said Mrs. Forrester, in a great hurry, and she shut her eyes too. This had been hard work but good fun for Mrs. Montrose and Mrs. Forrester. They felt, though, that they had gone a bit too far.

It might be as well if they slept, or pretended to sleep, until they reached Munich. They felt that outside their closed eyes was something frightening. The voice of the man with the blue tooth was saying, "I wish to tell you, I wish to tell you ..." but Mrs. Montrose was in a deep sleep, and so was Mrs. Forrester. They sat with their eyes tightly closed, beside the hamper which still occupied the seat with the view by the darkening window. Mrs. Montrose had the inside corner, and so by reason of nestling down in the corner, and by reason of having an even and sensible temperament, she really and truly fell asleep at last.

105 Not so Mrs. Forrester. Her eyes were tightly closed, but her mind was greatly disturbed. Why had they permitted themselves to be baited? She pondered on the collective mentality that occupied the seat near to them (knees almost touching), and its results which now filled the atmosphere of the carriage so unpleasantly. She had met this mentality before, but had not been closely confined with it, as now. What of a world in which this mentality might ever become dominant? Then one would be confined with it without appeal or relief. The thought was shocking. She felt unreasonably agitated. She felt rather a fool, too, with her eyes shut tightly. But, if she opened them, she would have to look somewhere, presumably at the family, so it seemed safer to keep them closed. The train sped on. After what seemed to her a very long time, she peeped. The wife and daughter were busy. The husband sat back, hands on knees, chin raised, expectant, eyes closed. His wife respectfully undid his tie, his collar, and his top shirt button. By this time the daughter had opened the hamper, and had taken from it a bottle and a clean napkin. These she handed to her mother. The wife moistened the napkin from the bottle and proceeded to wash her husband, his face, his ears, round the back of his neck, and inside his shirt collar, with great care. "Like a cat," thought Mrs. Forrester, who had forgotten to shut her eyes.

106 The man with the blue tooth lowered his raised chin and caught her. "You see," he said loudly, "you see, wives should look properly after their husbands, instead of travelling alone and ..." But Mrs. Forrester was fast asleep again. The whole absurd encounter had begun to hold an element of terror. They had been tempted into folly. She knew — as she screwed up her closed eyes — that they were implicated in fear and folly.

107 The two young women took care to sleep until the train reached Munich. Then they both woke up.

108 Many people slept until they reached Munich. Then they all began to wake up.

(1945)

# William Faulkner (1897–1962)

Faulkner spent most of his life in his native Mississippi. Having left school without graduating, he joined the Royal Canadian Air Force in 1918, lived in New Orleans for a short time in the twenties, and clerked in a New York bookstore for a few months, before publishing The Marble Faun (1924), a book of poems. Many of his works focus on the fictional Yoknapatawpha County and its characters and families. He won the Nobel Prize for literature in 1950.

## A Rose for Emily

1   When Miss Emily Grierson died, our whole town went to her funeral: the men through a sort of respectful affection for a fallen monument, the women mostly out of curiosity to see the inside of her house, which no one save an old man-servant — a combined gardener and cook — had seen in at least ten years.

2   It was a big, squarish frame house that had once been white, decorated with cupolas and spires and scrolled balconies in the heavily lightsome style of the seventies, set on what had once been our most select street. But garages and cotton gins had encroached and obliterated even the august names of that neighborhood; only Miss Emily's house was left, lifting its stubborn and coquettish decay above the cotton wagons and the gasoline pumps — an eyesore among eyesores. And now Miss Emily had gone to join the representatives of those august names where they lay in the cedar-bemused cemetery among the ranked and anonymous graves of Union and Confederate soldiers who fell at the battle of Jefferson.

3   Alive, Miss Emily had been a tradition, a duty, and a care; a sort of hereditary obligation upon the town, dating from that day in 1894 when Colonel Sartoris, the mayor — he who fathered the edict that no Negro woman should appear on the streets without an apron — remitted her taxes, the dispensation dating from the death of her father on into perpetuity. Not that Miss Emily would have accepted charity. Colonel Sartoris invented an involved tale to the effect that Miss Emily's father had loaned money to the town, which the town, as a matter of business, preferred this way of repaying. Only a man of Colonel Sartoris' generation and thought could have invented it, and only a woman could have believed it.

4   When the next generation, with its more modern ideas, became mayors and aldermen, this arrangement created some little dissatisfaction. On the first of the year they mailed her a tax notice. February came, and there was no reply. They wrote her a formal letter, asking her to call at the sheriff's office at her convenience. A week later the mayor wrote her himself, offering to call or to send his car for her, and received in reply a note on paper of an archaic shape, in a thin, flowing calligraphy in faded ink, to the effect that she no longer went out at all. The tax notice was also enclosed, without comment.

5   They called a special meeting of the Board of Aldermen. A deputation waited upon her, knocked at the door through which no visitor had passed since she ceased giving her china-painting lessons eight or ten years earlier. They were admitted by the old Negro into a dim hall from which a stairway mounted into still more shadow. It smelled of dust and disuse — a close, dank smell. The Negro led them into the parlor. It was furnished in heavy, leather-covered furniture. When the Negro opened the blinds of one window, they could see that the leather was cracked; and when they sat down, a faint dust rose sluggishly about their thighs, spinning with slow motes in the single sun-ray. On a tarnished gilt easel before the fireplace stood a crayon portrait of Miss Emily's father.

6   They rose when she entered — a small, fat woman in black, with a thin gold chain descending to her waist and vanishing into her belt, leaning on an ebony cane with a tarnished gold head. Her skeleton was small and spare; perhaps that was why what would have been merely plumpness in another was obesity in her. She looked bloated, like a body long submerged in motionless water, and of that pallid hue. Her eyes, lost in the fatty ridges of her face, looked like two small pieces of coal pressed into a lump of dough as they moved from one face to another while the visitors stated their errand.

7   She did not ask them to sit. She just stood in the door and listened quietly until the spokesman came to a stumbling halt. They could hear the invisible watch ticking at the end of the gold chain.

8   Her voice was dry and cold. "I have no taxes in Jefferson. Colonel Sartoris explained it to me. Perhaps one of you can gain access to the city records and satisfy yourselves."

9   "But we have. We are the city authorities, Miss Emily. Didn't you get a notice from the sheriff, signed by him?"

10   "I received a paper, yes," Miss Emily said. "Perhaps he considers himself the sheriff ... I have no taxes in Jefferson."

11   "But there is nothing on the books to show that, you see. We must go by the — "

12   "See Colonel Sartoris. I have no taxes in Jefferson."

13   "But, Miss Emily — "

14   "See Colonel Sartoris." (Colonel Sartoris had been dead almost ten years.) "I have no taxes in Jefferson. Tobe!" The Negro appeared. "Show these gentlemen out."

## II

15  So she vanquished them, horse and foot, just as she had vanquished their fathers thirty years before about the smell. That was two years after her father's death and a short time after her sweetheart — the one we believed would marry her — had deserted her. After her father's death she went out very little; after her sweetheart went away, people hardly saw her at all. A few of the ladies had the temerity to call, but were not received, and the only sign of life about the place was the Negro man — a young man then — going in and out with a market basket.

16  "Just as if a man — any man — could keep a kitchen properly," the ladies said; so they were not surprised when the smell developed. It was another link between the gross, teeming world and the high and mighty Griersons.

17  A neighbor, a woman, complained to the mayor, Judge Stevens, eighty years old.

18  "But what will you have me do about it, madam?" he said.

19  "Why, send her word to stop it," the woman said. "Isn't there a law?"

20  "I'm sure that won't be necessary," Judge Stevens said. "It's probably just a snake or a rat that nigger of hers killed in the yard. I'll speak to him about it."

21  The next day he received two more complaints, one from a man who came in diffident deprecation. "We really must do something about it, Judge. I'd be the last one in the world to bother Miss Emily, but we've got to do something." That night the Board of Aldermen met — three graybeards and one younger man, a member of the rising generation.

22  "It's simple enough," he said. "Send her word to have her place cleaned up. Give her a certain time to do it in, and if she don't ..."

23  "Dammit, sir," Judge Stevens said, "will you accuse a lady to her face of smelling bad?"

24  So the next night, after midnight, four men crossed Miss Emily's lawn and slunk about the house like burglars, sniffing along the base of the brickwork and at the cellar openings while one of them performed a regular sowing motion with his hand out of a sack slung from his shoulder. They broke open the cellar door and sprinkled lime there, and in all the outbuildings. As they recrossed the lawn, a window that had been dark was lighted and Miss Emily sat in it, the light behind her, and her upright torso motionless as that of an idol. They crept quietly across the lawn and into the shadow of the locusts that lined the street. After a week or two the smell went away.

25  That was when people had begun to feel really sorry for her. People in our town, remembering how old lady Wyatt, her great-aunt, had gone completely crazy at last, believed that the Griersons held themselves a little too high for what they really were. None of the young

men were quite good enough for Miss Emily and such. We had long thought of them as a tableau, Miss Emily a slender figure in white in the background, her father a spraddled[1] silhouette in the foreground, his back to her and clutching a horsewhip, the two of them framed by the back-flung front door. So when she got to be thirty and was still single, we were not pleased exactly, but vindicated; even with insanity in the family she wouldn't have turned down all of her chances if they had really materialized.

26 When her father died, it got about that the house was all that was left to her; and in a way, people were glad. At last they could pity Miss Emily. Being left alone, and a pauper, she had become humanized. Now she too would know the old thrill and the old despair of a penny more or less.

27 The day after his death all the ladies prepared to call at the house and offer condolence and aid, as is our custom. Miss Emily met them at the door, dressed as usual and with no trace of grief on her face. She told them that her father was not dead. She did that for three days, with the ministers calling on her, and the doctors, trying to persuade her to let them dispose of the body. Just as they were about to resort to law and force, she broke down, and they buried her father quickly.

28 We did not say she was crazy then. We believed she had to do that. We remembered all the young men her father had driven away, and we know that with nothing left, she would have to cling to that which had robbed her, as people will.

## III

29 She was sick for a long time. When we saw her again, her hair was cut short, making her look like a girl, with a vague resemblance to those angels in colored church windows — sort of tragic and serene.

30 The town had just let the contracts for paving and sidewalks, and in the summer after her father's death they began the work. The construction company came with niggers and mules and machinery, and a foreman named Homer Barron, a Yankee — a big, dark, ready man, with a big voice and eyes lighter than his face. The little boys would follow in groups to hear him cuss the niggers, and the niggers singing in time to the rise and fall of picks. Pretty soon he knew everybody in town. Whenever you heard a lot of laughing anywhere about the square, Homer Barron would be in the center of the group. Presently we began to see him and Miss Emily on Sunday afternoons driving in the yellow-wheeled buggy and the matched team of bays from the livery stable.

---

1. Sprawled.

31    At first we were glad that Miss Emily would have an interest, because the ladies all said, "Of course a Grierson would not think seriously of a Northerner, a day laborer." But there were still others, older people, who said that even grief could not cause a real lady to forget *noblesse oblige* — without calling it *noblesse oblige*. They just said, "Poor Emily. Her kinsfolk should come to her." She had some kin in Alabama; but years ago her father had fallen out with them over the estate of old lady Wyatt, the crazy woman, and there was no communication between the two families. They had not even been represented at the funeral.

32    And as soon as the old people said, "Poor Emily," the whispering began. "Do you suppose it's really so?" they said to one another. "Of course it is. What else could ..." This behind their hands; rustling of craned silk and satin behind jalousies closed upon the sun of Sunday afternoon as the thin, swift clop-clop-clop of the matched team passed: "Poor Emily."

33    She carried her head high enough — even when we believed that she was fallen. It was as if she demanded more than ever the recognition of her dignity as the last Grierson; as if it had wanted that touch of earthiness to reaffirm her imperviousness. Like when she bought the rat poison, the arsenic. That was over a year after they had begun to say "Poor Emily," and while two female cousins were visiting her.

34    "I want some poison," she said to the druggist. She was over thirty then, still a slight woman, though thinner than usual, with cold, haughty black eyes in a face the flesh of which was strained across the temples and about the eye-sockets as you imagine a lighthouse-keeper's face ought to look. "I want some poison," she said.

35    "Yes, Miss Emily. What kind? For rats and such? I'd recom — "

36    "I want the best you have. I don't care what kind."

37    The druggist named several. "They'll kill anything up to an elephant. But what you want is — "

38    "Arsenic," Miss Emily said. "Is that a good one?"

39    "Is ... arsenic? Yes, ma'am. But what you want — "

40    "I want arsenic."

41    The druggist looked down at her. She looked back at him, erect, her face like a strained flag. "Why, of course," the druggist said. "If that's what you want. But the law requires you to tell what you are going to use it for."

42    Miss Emily just stared at him, her head tilted back in order to look him eye for eye, until he looked away and went and got the arsenic and wrapped it up. The Negro delivery boy brought her the package; the druggist didn't come back. When she opened the package at home there was written on the box, under the skull and bones: "For rats."

IV

43    So the next day we all said, "She will kill herself"; and we said it would be the best thing. When she had first begun to be seen with Homer

Barron, we had said, "She will marry him." Then we said, "She will persuade him yet," because Homer himself had remarked — he liked men, and it was known that he drank with the younger men in the Elks' Club — that he was not a marrying man. Later we said, "Poor Emily" behind the jalousies as they passed on Sunday afternoon in the glittering buggy, Miss Emily with her head high and Homer Barron with his hat cocked and a cigar in his teeth, reins and whip in a yellow glove.

44   Then some of the ladies began to say that it was a disgrace to the town and a bad example to the young people. The men did not want to interfere, but at last the ladies forced the Baptist minister — Miss Emily's people were Episcopal — to call upon her. He would never divulge what happened during the interview, but he refused to go back again. The next Sunday they again drove about the streets, and the following day the minister's wife wrote to Miss Emily's relations in Alabama.

45   So she had blood-kin under her roof again and we sat back to watch developments. At first nothing happened. Then we were sure that they were to be married. We learned that Miss Emily had been to the jeweler's and ordered a man's toilet set in silver, with the letters H.B. on each piece. Two days later we learned that she had bought a complete outfit of men's clothing, including a nightshirt, and we said, "They are married." We were really glad. We were glad because the two female cousins were even more Grierson than Miss Emily had been.

46   So we were surprised when Homer Barron — the streets had been finished some time since — was gone. We were a little disappointed that there was not a public blowing-off, but we believed that he had gone on to prepare for Miss Emily's coming, or to give her a chance to get rid of the cousins. (By that time it was a cabal, and we were all Miss Emily's allies to help circumvent the cousins.) Sure enough, after another week they departed. And, as we had expected all along, within three days Homer Barron was back in town. A neighbor saw the Negro man admit him at the kitchen door at dusk one evening.

47   And that was the last we saw of Homer Barron. And of Miss Emily for some time. The Negro man went in and out with the market basket, but the front door remained closed. Now and then we would see her at a window for a moment, as the men did that night when they sprinkled the lime, but for almost six months she did not appear on the streets. Then we knew that this was to be expected too; as if that quality of her father which had thwarted her woman's life so many times had been too virulent and too furious to die.

48   When we next saw Miss Emily, she had grown fat and her hair was turning gray. During the next few years it grew grayer and grayer until it attained an even pepper-and-salt iron-gray, when it ceased turning. Up to the day of her death at seventy-four it was still that vigorous iron-gray, like the hair of an active man.

49   From that time on her front door remained closed, save for a period of six or seven years, when she was about forty, during which she gave

lessons in china-painting. She fitted up a studio in one of the downstairs rooms, where the daughters and granddaughters of Colonel Sartoris' contemporaries were sent to her with the same regularity and in the same spirit that they were sent to church on Sundays with a twenty-five-cent piece for the collection plate. Meanwhile her taxes had been remitted.

50    Then the newer generation became the backbone and the spirit of the town, and the painting pupils grew up and fell away and did not send their children to her with boxes of color and tedious brushes and pictures cut from the ladies' magazines. The front door closed upon the last one and remained closed for good. When the town got free postal delivery, Miss Emily alone refused to let them fasten the metal numbers above her door and attach a mailbox to it. She would not listen to them.

51    Daily, monthly, yearly we watched the Negro grow grayer and more stooped, going in and out with the market basket. Each December we sent her a tax notice, which would be returned by the post office a week later, unclaimed. Now and then we would see her in one of the downstairs windows — she had evidently shut up the top floor of the house — like the carven torso of an idol in a niche, looking or not looking at us, we could never tell which. Thus she passed from generation to generation — dear, inescapable, impervious, tranquil, and perverse.

52    And so she died. Fell ill in the house filled with dust and shadows, with only a doddering Negro man to wait on her. We did not even know she was sick; we had long since given up trying to get any information from the Negro. He talked to no one, probably not even to her, for his voice had grown harsh and rusty, as if from disuse.

53    She died in one of the downstairs rooms, in a heavy walnut bed with a curtain, her gray head propped on a pillow yellow and mouldy with age and lack of sunlight.

V

54    The Negro met the first of the ladies at the front door and let them in, with their hushed, sibilant voices and their quick, curious glances, and then he disappeared. He walked right through the house and out the back and was not seen again.

55    The two female cousins came at once. They held the funeral on the second day, with the town coming to look at Miss Emily beneath a mass of bought flowers, with the crayon face of her father musing profoundly above the bier and the ladies sibilant and macabre; and the very old men — some in their brushed Confederate uniforms — on the porch and the lawn, talking of Miss Emily as if she had been a contemporary of theirs, believing that they had danced with her and courted her perhaps, confusing time with its mathematical progres-

sion, as the old do, to whom all the past is not a diminishing road but, instead, a huge meadow which no winter ever quite touches, divided from them now by the narrow bottle-neck of the most recent decade of years.

Already we knew that there was one room in that region above stairs which no one had seen in forty years, and which would have to be forced. They waited until Miss Emily was decently in the ground before they opened it.

The violence of breaking down the door seemed to fill this room with pervading dust. A thin, acrid pall as of the tomb seemed to lie everywhere upon this room decked and furnished as for a bridal: upon the valance curtains of faded rose color, upon the rose-shaded lights, upon the dressing table, upon the delicate array of crystal and the man's toilet things backed with tarnished silver, silver so tarnished that the monogram was obscured. Among them lay a collar and tie, as if they had just been removed, which, lifted, left upon the surface a pale crescent in the dust. Upon a chair hung the suit, carefully folded; beneath it the two mute shoes and the discarded socks.

The man himself lay in the bed.

For a long while we just stood there, looking down at the profound and fleshless grin. The body had apparently once lain in the attitude of an embrace, but now the long sleep that outlasts love, that conquers even the grimace of love, had cuckolded him. What was left of him, rotted beneath what was left of the nightshirt, had become inextricable from the bed in which he lay; and upon him and upon the pillow beside him lay that even coating of the patient and biding dust.

Then we noticed that in the second pillow was the indentation of a head. One of us lifted something from it, and leaning forward, that faint and invisible dust dry and acrid in the nostrils, we saw a long strand of iron-gray hair.

*(1930)*

# Ernest Hemingway (1899–1961)

Hemingway's terse and economical style, his code of self-realization through action, and his often disillusioned characters are largely related to his experiences and observations of two world wars and the Spanish Civil War. One of the most influential American writers of this century, he received a Nobel Prize for literature in 1954.

## In Another Country

In the fall the war was always there, but we did not go to it any more. It was cold in the fall in Milan and the dark came very early. Then the electric lights came on, and it was pleasant along the streets looking in the windows. There was much game hanging outside the shops, and the snow powdered in the fur of the foxes and the wind blew their tails. The deer hung stiff and heavy and empty, and small birds blew in the wind and the wind turned their feathers. It was a cold fall and the wind came down from the mountains.

We were all at the hospital every afternoon, and there were different ways of walking across the town through the dusk to the hospital. Two of the ways were alongside canals, but they were long. Always, though, you crossed a bridge across a canal to enter the hospital. There was a choice of three bridges. On one of them a woman sold roasted chestnuts. It was warm, standing in front of her charcoal fire, and the chestnuts were warm afterward in your pocket. The hospital was very old and very beautiful, and you entered through a gate and walked across a courtyard and out a gate on the other side. There were usually funerals starting from the courtyard. Beyond the old hospital were the new brick pavilions, and there we met every afternoon and were all very polite and interested in what was the matter, and sat in the machines that were to make so much difference.

The doctor came up to the machine where I was sitting and said: "What did you like best to do before the war? Did you practise a sport?"

I said: "Yes, football."

"Good," he said. "You will be able to play football again better than ever."

My knee did not bend and the leg dropped straight from the knee to the ankle without a calf, and the machine was to bend the knee and make it move as in riding a tricycle. But it did not bend yet, and instead the machine lurched when it came to the bending part. The doctor said: "That will all pass. You are a fortunate young man. You will play football again like a champion."

7   In the next machine was a major who had a little hand like a baby's. He winked at me when the doctor examined his hand, which was between two leather straps that bounced up and down and flapped the stiff fingers, and said: "And will I play football, captain-doctor?" He had been a very great fencer, and before the war the greatest fencer in Italy.

8   The doctor went to his office in a back room and brought a photograph which showed a hand that had been withered almost as small as the major's, before it had taken a machine course, and after was a little larger. The major held the photograph with his good hand and looked at it very carefully. "A wound?" he asked.

9   "An industrial accident," the doctor said.

10  "Very interesting, very interesting," the major said, and handed it back to the doctor.

11  "You have confidence?"

12  "No," said the major.

13  There were three boys who came each day who were about the same age I was. They were all three from Milan, and one of them was to be a lawyer, and one was to be a painter, and one had intended to be a soldier, and after we were finished with the machines, sometimes we walked back together to the Café Cova, which was next door to the Scala.[1] We walked the short way through the communist quarter because we were four together. The people hated us because we were officers, and from a wine-shop someone called out, *"A basso gli ufficiali!"*[2] as we passed. Another boy who walked with us sometimes and made us five wore a black silk handkerchief across his face because he had no nose then and his face was to be rebuilt. He had gone out to the front from the military academy and been wounded within an hour after he had gone into the front line for the first time. They rebuilt his face, but he came from a very old family and they could never get the nose exactly right. He went to South America and worked in a bank. But this was a long time ago, and then we did not any of us know how it was going to be afterward. We only knew then that there was always the war, but that we were not going to it any more.

14  We all had the same medals, except the boy with the black silk bandage across his face, and he had not been at the front long enough to get any medals. The tall boy with a very pale face who was to be a lawyer had been a lieutenant of Arditi[3] and had three medals of the

---

1. La Scala Opera House.
2. Down with officers!
3. A group of volunteers with the Italian army during World War I who were renowned for their daring.

sort we each had only one of. He had lived a very long time with death and was a little detached. We were all a little detached, and there was nothing that held us together except that we met every afternoon at the hospital. Although, as we walked to the Cova through the tough part of town, walking in the dark, with light and singing coming out of the wine-shops, and sometimes having to walk into the street when the men and women would crowd together on the sidewalk so that we would have had to jostle them to get by, we felt held together by there being something that had happened that they, the people who disliked us, did not understand.

15   We ourselves all understood the Cova, where it was rich and warm and not too brightly lighted, and noisy and smoky at certain hours, and there were always girls at the tables and the illustrated papers on a rack on the wall. The girls at the Cova were very patriotic, and I found that the most patriotic people in Italy were the café girls — and I believe they are still patriotic.

16   The boys at first were very polite about my medals and asked me what I had done to get them. I showed them the papers, which were written in beautiful language and full of *fratellanza* and *abnegazione*,[4] but which really said, with the adjectives removed, that I had been given the medals because I was an American. After that their manner changed a little toward me, although I was their friend against outsiders. I was a friend, but I was never really one of them after they had read the citations, because it had been different with them and they had done very different things to get their medals. I had been wounded, it was true; but we all knew that being wounded, after all, was really an accident. I was never ashamed of the ribbons, though, and sometimes, after the cocktail hour, I would imagine myself having done all the things they had done to get their medals; but walking home at night through the empty streets with the cold wind and all the shops closed, trying to keep near the street lights, I knew that I would never have done such things, and I was very much afraid to die, and often lay in bed at night by myself, afraid to die and wondering how I would be when I went back to the front again.

17   The three with the medals were like hunting-hawks; and I was not a hawk, although I might seem a hawk to those who had never hunted; they, the three, knew better and so we drifted apart. But I stayed good friends with the boy who had been wounded his first day at the front, because he would never be accepted either, and I liked him because I thought perhaps he would not have turned out to be a hawk either.

18   The major, who had been the great fencer, did not believe in bravery, and spent much time while we sat in the machines correcting my grammar. He had complimented me on how I spoke Italian, and

---

4. Brotherhood and self-denial.

we talked together very easily. One day I had said that Italian seemed such an easy language to me that I could not take a great interest in it; everything was so easy to say. "Ah, yes," the major said. "Why, then, do you not take up the use of grammar?" So we took up the use of grammar, and soon Italian was such a difficult language that I was afraid to talk to him until I had the grammar straight in my mind.

19    The major came very regularly to the hospital. I do not think he ever missed a day, although I am sure he did not believe in the machines. There was a time when none of us believed in the machines, and one day the major said it was all nonsense. The machines were new then and it was we who were to prove them. It was an idiotic idea, he said, "a theory, like another." I had not learned my grammar, and he said I was a stupid impossible disgrace, and he was a fool to have bothered with me. He was a small man and he sat straight up in his chair with his right hand thrust into the machine and looked straight ahead at the wall while the straps thumped up and down with his fingers in them.

20    "What will you do when the war is over if it is over?" he asked me. "Speak grammatically!"
21    "I will go to the States."
22    "Are you married?"
23    "No, but I hope to be."
24    "The more of a fool you are," he said. He seemed very angry. "A man must not marry."
25    "Why, Signor Maggiore?"
26    "Don't call me 'Signor Maggiore.'"
27    "Why must not a man marry?"
28    "He cannot marry. He cannot marry," he said angrily. "If he is to lose everything, he should not place himself in a position to lose that. He should not place himself in a position to lose. He should find things he cannot lose."
29    He spoke very angrily and bitterly, and looked straight ahead while he talked.
30    "But why should he necessarily lose it?"
31    "He'll lose it," the major said. He was looking at the wall. Then he looked down at the machine and jerked his little hand out from between the straps and slapped it hard against his thigh. "He'll lose it," he almost shouted. "Don't argue with me!" Then he called to the attendant who ran the machines. "Come and turn this damned thing off."
32    He went back into the other room for the light treatment and the massage. Then I heard him ask the doctor if he might use his telephone and he shut the door. When he came back into the room, I was sitting in another machine. He was wearing his cape and had his cap on, and he came directly toward my machine and put his arm on my shoulder.

33 "I am so sorry," he said, and patted me on the shoulder with his good hand. "I would not be rude. My wife has just died. You must forgive me."

34 "Oh — " I said, feeling sick for him. "I am *so* sorry."

35 He stood there biting his lower lip. "It is very difficult," he said. "I cannot resign myself."

36 He looked straight past me and out through the window. Then he began to cry. "I am utterly unable to resign myself," he said and choked. And then crying, his head up looking at nothing, carrying himself straight and soldierly, with tears on his cheeks and biting his lips, he walked past the machines and out the door.

37 The doctor told me that the major's wife, who was very young and whom he had not married until he was definitely invalided out of the war, had died of pneumonia. She had been sick only a few days. No one expected her to die. The major did not come to the hospital for three days. Then he came at the usual hour, wearing a black band on the sleeve of his uniform. When he came back, there were large framed photographs around the wall, of all sorts of wounds before and after they had been cured by the machines. In front of the machine the major used were three photographs of hands like his that were completely restored. I do not know where the doctor got them. I always understood we were the first to use the machines. The photographs did not make much difference to the major because he only looked out of the window.

(1927)

# Langston Hughes (1902–1967)

A central figure of the Harlem Renaissance, Langston Hughes was an American poet, short-story writer, novelist, dramatist, children's writer, editor, and translator. Irony and humour characterize his work, which in large measure reflects the urban African-American culture of his time.

## On the Road

1 He was not interested in snow. When he got off the freight, one early evening during the depression, Sargeant never even noticed the snow. But he must have felt it seeping down his neck, cold, wet, sopping in his shoes. But if you had asked him, he wouldn't have known it was snowing. Sargeant didn't see the snow, not even under the bright lights of the main street, falling white and flaky against the night. He was too hungry, too sleepy, too tired.

2 The Reverend Mr. Dorset, however, saw the snow when he switched on his porch light, opened the front door of his parsonage, and found standing there before him a big black man with snow on his face, a human piece of night with snow on his face — obviously unemployed.

3 Said the Reverend Mr. Dorset before Sargeant even realized he'd opened his mouth: "I'm sorry. No! Go right on down this street four blocks and turn to your left, walk up seven and you'll see the Relief Shelter. I'm sorry. No!" He shut the door.

4 Sargeant wanted to tell the holy man that he had already been to the Relief Shelter, been to hundreds of relief shelters during the depression years, the beds were always gone and supper was over, the place was full, and they drew the color line anyhow. But the minister said, "No," and shut the door. Evidently he didn't want to hear about it. And he *had* a door to shut.

5 The big black man turned away. And even yet he didn't see the snow, walking right into it. Maybe he sensed it, cold, wet, sticking to his jaws, wet on his black hands, sopping in his shoes. He stopped and stood on the sidewalk hunched over — hungry, sleepy, cold — looking up and down. Then he looked right where he was — in front of a church. Of course! A church! Sure, right next to a parsonage, certainly a church.

6 It had *two* doors.

7   Broad white steps in the night all snowy white. Two high arched doors with slender stone pillars on either side. And way up, a round lacy window with a stone crucifix in the middle and Christ on the crucifix in stone. All this was pale in the street light, solid and stony pale in the snow.

8   Sargeant blinked. When he looked up, the snow fell into his eyes. For the first time that night he *saw* the snow. He shook his head. He shook the snow from his coat sleeves, felt hungry, felt lost, felt not lost, felt cold. He walked up the steps of the church. He knocked at the door. No answer. He tried the handle. Locked. He put his shoulder against the door and his long black body slanted like a ramrod. He pushed. With loud rhythmic grunts, like the grunts in a chain-gang song, he pushed against the door.

9   "I'm tired … Huh! … Hongry … Uh! … I'm sleepy … Huh! I'm cold … I got to sleep somewheres," Sargeant said. "This is a church, ain't it? Well, uh!"

10  He pushed against the door.

11  Suddenly, with an undue cracking and screaking, the door began to give way to the tall black Negro who pushed ferociously against it.

12  By now two or three white people had stopped in the street, and Sargeant was vaguely aware of some of them yelling at him concerning the door. Three or four more came running, yelling at him.

13  "Hey!" they said. "Hey!"

14  "Uh-huh," answered the big tall Negro, "I know it's a white folks' church, but I got to sleep somewhere." He gave another lunge at the door. "Huh!"

15  And the door broke open.

16  But just when the door gave way, two white cops arrived in a car, ran up the steps with their clubs, and grabbed Sargeant. But Sargeant for once had no intention of being pulled or pushed away from the door.

17  Sargeant grabbed, but not for anything so weak as a broken door. He grabbed for one of the tall stone pillars beside the door, grabbed at it and caught it. And held it. The cops pulled and Sargeant pulled. Most of the people in the street got behind the cops and helped them pull.

18  "A big black unemployed Negro holding onto our church!" thought the people. "The idea!"

19  The cops began to beat Sargeant over the head, and nobody protested. But he held on.

20  And then the church fell down.

21  Gradually, the big stone front of the church fell down, the walls and the rafters, the crucifix and the Christ. Then the whole thing fell down, covering the cops and the people with bricks and stones and debris. The whole church fell down in the snow.

22  Sargeant got out from under the church and went walking on up the street with the stone pillar on his shoulder. He was under the

impression that he had buried the parsonage and the Reverend Mr. Dorset who said, "No!" So he laughed, and threw the pillar six blocks up the street and went on.

23   Sargeant thought he was alone, but listening to the *crunch, crunch, crunch* on the snow of his own footsteps, he heard other footsteps, too, doubling his own. He looked around, and there was Christ walking beside him, the same Christ that had been on the cross on the church — still stone with a rough surface, walking along beside him just like he was broken off the cross when the church fell down.

24   "Well, I'll be dogged," said Sargeant. "This here's the first time I ever seed you off the cross."

25   "Yes," said Christ, crunching his feet in the snow. "You had to pull the church down to get me off the cross."

26   "You glad?" said Sargeant.
27   "I sure am," said Christ.
28   They both laughed.
29   "I'm a hell of a fellow, ain't I?" said Sargeant. "Done pulled the church down!"

30   "You did a good job," said Christ. "They have kept me nailed on a cross for nearly two thousand years."

31   "Whee-ee-e!" said Sargeant. "I know you are glad to get off."
32   "I sure am," said Christ.
33   They walked on in the snow. Sargeant looked at the man of stone.
34   "And you have been up there two thousand years?"
35   "I sure have," said Christ.
36   "Well, if I had a little cash," said Sargeant, "I'd show you around a bit."

37   "I been around," said Christ.
38   "Yeah, but that was a long time ago."
39   "All the same," said Christ, "I've been around."
40   They walked on in the snow until they came to the railroad yards. Sargeant was tired, sweating and tired.

41   "Where you goin'?" Sargeant said, stopping by the tracks. He looked at Christ. Sargeant said, "I'm just a bum on the road. How about you? Where you goin'?"

42   "God knows," Christ said, "but I'm leavin' here."
43   They saw the red and green lights of the railroad yard half veiled by the snow that fell out of the night. Away down the track they saw a fire in a hobo jungle.

44   "I can go there and sleep," Sargeant said.
45   "You can?"
46   "Sure," said Sargeant. "That place ain't got no doors."
47   Outside the town, along the tracks, there were barren trees and bushes below the embankment, snow-gray in the dark. And down among the trees and bushes there were makeshift houses made out of boxes and tin and old pieces of wood and canvas. You couldn't see them in the dark, but you knew they were there if you'd ever been on

the road, if you had ever lived with the homeless and hungry in a depression.

48  "I'm side-tracking," Sargeant said. "I'm tired."
49  "I'm gonna make it on to Kansas City," said Christ.
50  "O.K.," Sargeant said. "So long!"
51  He went down into the hobo jungle and found himself a place to sleep. He never did see Christ no more. About 6:00 A.M. a freight train came by. Sargeant scrambled out of the jungle with a dozen or so more hobos and ran along the track, grabbing at the freight. It was dawn, early dawn, cold and gray.
52  "Wonder where Christ is by now?" Sargeant thought. "He musta gone on way on down the road. He didn't sleep in this jungle."
53  Sargeant grabbed the train and started to pull himself up into a moving coal car, over the edge of a wheeling coal car. But strangely enough, the car was full of cops. The nearest cop rapped Sargeant soundly across the knuckles with his night stick. Wham! Rapped his big black hands for clinging to the top of the car. Wham! But Sargeant did not turn loose. He clung on and tried to pull himself into the car. He hollered at the top of his voice, "Damn it, lemme in this car!"
54  "Shut up," barked the cop. "You crazy coon!" He rapped Sargeant across the knuckles and punched him in the stomach. "You ain't out in no jungle now. This ain't no train. You in jail."
55  Wham! across his bare black fingers clinging to the bars of his cell. Wham! between the steel bars low down against his shins.
56  Suddenly Sargeant realized that he really was in jail. He wasn't on no train. The blood of the night before had dried on his face, his head hurt terribly, and a cop outside in the corridor was hitting him across the knuckles for holding onto the door, yelling and shaking the cell door.
57  "They musta took me to jail for breaking down the door last night," Sargeant thought, "that church door."
58  Sargeant went over and sat on a wooden bench against the cold stone wall. He was emptier than ever. His clothes were wet, clammy cold wet, and shoes sloppy with snow water. It was just about dawn. There he was, locked up behind a cell door, nursing his bruised fingers.
59  The bruised fingers were his, but not the *door*.
60  Not the *club*, but the fingers.
61  "You wait," mumbled Sargeant, black against the jail wall. "I'm gonna break down this door, too."
62  "Shut up — or I'll paste you one," said the cop.
63  "I'm gonna break down this door," yelled Sargeant as he stood up in his cell.
64  Then he must have been talking to himself because he said, "I wonder where Christ's gone? I wonder if he's gone to Kansas City?"

(1935)

# Tillie Olsen (b. 1913)

Nebraska-born Tillie Olsen worked at a number of jobs, engaged in labour union activities, and raised four children before writing the stories collected in Tell Me a Riddle (1961). Her fiction is charged with her lifelong political and social concerns.

## I Stand Here Ironing

1. I stand here ironing, and what you asked me moves tormented back and forth with the iron.

2. "I wish you would manage the time to come in and talk with me about your daughter. I'm sure you can help me understand her. She's a youngster who needs help and whom I'm deeply interested in helping."

3. "Who needs help." Even if I came, what good would it do? You think because I am her mother I have a key, or that in some way you could use me as a key? She has lived for nineteen years. There is all that life that has happened outside of me, beyond me.

4. And when is there time to remember, to sift, to weigh, to estimate, to total? I will start and there will be an interruption and I will have to gather it all together again. Or I will become engulfed with all I did or did not do, with what should have been and what cannot be helped.

5. She was a beautiful baby. The first and only one of our five that was beautiful at birth. You do not guess how new and uneasy her tenancy in her now-loveliness. You did not know her all those years she was thought homely, or see her poring over her baby pictures, making me tell her over and over how beautiful she had been — and would be, I would tell her — and was now, to the seeing eye. But the seeing eyes were few or nonexistent. Including mine.

6. I nursed her. They feel that's important nowadays. I nursed all the children, but with her, with all the fierce rigidity of first motherhood, I did like the books then said. Though her cries battered me to trembling and my breasts ached with swollenness, I waited till the clock decreed.

7. Why do I put that first? I do not even know if it matters, or if it explains anything.

8   She was a beautiful baby. She blew shining bubbles of sound. She loved motion, loved light, loved color and music and textures. She would lie on the floor in her blue overalls patting the surface so hard in ecstasy her hands and feet would blur. She was a miracle to me, but when she was eight months old I had to leave her daytimes with the woman downstairs to whom she was no miracle at all, for I worked or looked for work and for Emily's father, who "could no longer endure" (he wrote in his good-bye note) "sharing want with us."

9   I was nineteen. It was the pre-relief, pre-WPA[1] world of the depression. I would start running as soon as I got off the streetcar, running up the stairs, the place smelling sour, and awake or asleep to startle awake, when she saw me she would break into a clogged weeping that could not be comforted, a weeping I can hear yet.

10  After a while I found a job hashing at night so I could be with her days, and it was better. But it came to where I had to bring her to his family and leave her.

11  It took a long time to raise the money for her fare back. Then she got chicken pox and I had to wait longer. When she finally came, I hardly knew her, walking quick and nervous like her father, looking like her father, thin, and dressed in a shoddy red that yellowed her skin and glared at the pockmarks. All the baby loveliness gone.

12  She was two. Old enough for nursery school they said, and I did not know then what I know now — the fatigue of the long day, and the lacerations of group life in nurseries that are only parking places for children.

13  Except that it would have made no difference if I had known. It was the only place there was. It was the only way we could be together, the only way I could hold a job.

14  And even without knowing, I knew. I knew the teacher that was evil because all these years it has curdled into my memory, the little boy hunched over in the corner, her rasp, "why aren't you outside, because Alvin hits you? that's no reason, go out, scaredy." I knew Emily hated it even if she did not clutch and implore "don't go Mommy" like the other children, mornings.

15  She always had a reason why we should stay home. Momma, you look sick, Momma. I feel sick, Momma, the teachers aren't there today, they're sick. Momma, we can't go, there was a fire there last night. Momma, it's a holiday today, no school, they told me.

16  But never a direct protest, never rebellion. I think of our others in their three-, four-year-oldness — the explosions, the tempers, the denunciations, the demands — and I feel suddenly ill. I put the iron down. What in me demanded that goodness in her? And what was the cost, the cost to her of such goodness?

---

1. Work Progress Administration, an agency created during the Great Depression in the United States to make work for the unemployed.

17   The old man living in the back once said in his gentle way: "You should smile at Emily more when you look at her." What *was* in my face when I looked at her? I loved her. There were all the acts of love.

18   It was only with the others I remembered what he said, and it was the face of joy, and not of care or tightness or worry I turned to them — too late for Emily. She does not smile easily, let alone almost always as her brothers and sisters do. Her face is closed and sombre, but when she wants, how fluid. You must have seen it in her pantomimes, you spoke of her rare gift for comedy on the stage that rouses a laughter out of the audience so dear they applaud and applaud and do not want to let her go.

19   Where does it come from, that comedy? There was none of it in her when she came back to me that second time, after I had had to send her away again. She had a new daddy now to learn to love, and I think perhaps it was a better time.

20   Except when we left her alone nights, telling ourselves she was old enough.

21   "Can't you go some other time, Mommy, like tomorrow?" she would ask. "Will it be just a little while you'll be gone? Do you promise?"

22   The time we came back, the front door open, the clock on the floor in the hall. She rigid awake. "It wasn't just a little while. I didn't cry. Three times I called you, just three times, and then I ran downstairs to open the door so you could come faster. The clock talked loud. I threw it away, it scared me what it talked."

23   She said the clock talked loud again that night I went to the hospital to have Susan. She was delirious with fever that comes before red measles, but she was fully conscious all week I was gone and the week after we were home when she would not come near the new baby or me.

24   She did not get well. She stayed skeleton thin, not wanting to eat, and night after night she had nightmares. She would call for me, and I would rouse from exhaustion to sleepily call back: "You're all right, darling, go to sleep, it's just a dream," and if she still called, in a sterner voice, "now go to sleep, Emily, there's nothing to hurt you." Twice, only twice, when I had to get up for Susan anyhow, I went to sit with her.

25   Now when it is too late (as if she would let me hold and comfort her like I do the others) I get up and go to her at once at her moan or restless stirring. "Are you awake, Emily? Can I get you something?" And the answer is always the same: "No, I'm all right, go back to sleep, Mother."

26   They persuaded me at the clinic to send her away to a convalescent home in the country where "she can have the kind of food and care you can't manage for her, and you'll be free to concentrate on the new baby." They still send children to that place. I see pictures on the society page of sleek young women planning affairs to raise money for it,

or dancing at the affairs, or decorating Easter eggs or filling Christmas stockings for the children.

27   They never have a picture of the children so I do not know if the girls still wear those gigantic red bows and the ravaged looks on the every other Sunday when parents come to visit "unless otherwise notified" — as we were notified the first six weeks.

28   Oh it is a handsome place, green lawns and tall trees and fluted flower beds. High up on the balconies of each cottage the children stand, the girls in their red bows and white dresses, the boys in white suits and giant red ties. The parents stand below shrieking up to be heard and the children shriek down to be heard, and between them the invisible wall "Not To Be Contaminated by Parental Germs or Physical Affection."

29   There was a tiny girl who always stood hand in hand with Emily. Her parents never came. One visit she was gone. "They moved her to Rose College," Emily shouted in explanation. "They don't like you to love anybody here."

30   She wrote once a week, the labored writing of a seven-year-old. "I am fine. How is the baby. If I write my leter nicly I will have a star. Love." There was never a star. We wrote every other day, letters she could never hold or keep but only hear read once. "We simply do not have room for children to keep any personal possessions," they patiently explained when we pieced one Sunday's shrieking together to plead how much it would mean to Emily, who loved so to keep things, to be allowed to keep her letters and cards.

31   Each visit she looked frailer. "She isn't eating," they told us.

32   (They had runny eggs for breakfast or mush with lumps, Emily said later. I'd hold it in my mouth and not swallow. Nothing ever tasted good, just when they had chicken.)

33   It took us eight months to get her released home, and only the fact that she gained back so little of her seven lost pounds convinced the social worker.

34   I used to try to hold and love her after she came back, but her body would stay stiff, and after a while she'd push away. She ate little. Food sickened her; and I think much of life too. Oh she had physical lightness and brightness, twinkling on skates, bouncing like a ball up and down up and down over the jump rope, skimming over the hill; but these were momentary.

35   She fretted about her appearance, thin and dark and foreign-looking at a time when every little girl was supposed to look or thought she should look a chubby blonde replica of Shirley Temple. The doorbell sometimes rang for her, but no one seemed to come and play in the house or be a best friend. Maybe because we moved so much.

36   There was a boy she loved painfully through two school semesters. Months later she told me how she had taken pennies from my purse to buy him candy. "Licorice was his favorite and I brought him some

every day, but he still liked Jennifer better'n me. Why, Mommy?" The kind of question for which there is no answer.

School was a worry to her. She was not glib or quick in a world where glibness and quickness were easily confused with ability to learn. To her overworked and exasperated teachers she was an over-conscientious "slow learner" who kept trying to catch up and was absent entirely too often.

I let her be absent, though sometimes the illness was imaginary. How different from my now-strictness about attendance with the others. I wasn't working. We had a new baby, I was home anyhow. Sometimes, after Susan grew old enough, I would keep her home from school, too, to have them all together.

Mostly Emily had asthma, and her breathing, harsh and labored, would fill the house with a curiously tranquil sound. I would bring her the two old dresser mirrors and her boxes of collections to her bed. She would select beads and single earrings, bottle tops and shells, dried flowers and pebbles, old postcards and scraps, all sorts of oddments; then she and Susan would play kingdom, setting up landscapes and furniture, peopling them with action.

Those were the only times of peaceful companionship between her and Susan. I have edged away from it, that poisonous feeling between them, that terrible balancing of hurts and needs I had to do between the two, and did so badly, those earlier years.

Oh there are conflicts between the others too, each one human, needing, demanding, hurting, taking — but only between Emily and Susan, no, Emily toward Susan that corroding resentment. It seems so obvious on the surface, yet it is not obvious. Susan, the second child, Susan, golden- and curly-haired and chubby, quick and articulate and assured, everything in appearance and manner Emily was not; Susan, not able to resist Emily's precious things, losing or sometimes clumsily breaking them; Susan telling jokes and riddles to company for applause while Emily sat silent (to say to me later: that was *my* riddle, Mother, I told it to Susan); Susan, who for all the five years' difference in age was just a year behind Emily in developing physically.

I am glad for that slow physical development that widened the difference between her and her contemporaries, though she suffered over it. She was too vulnerable for that terrible world of youthful competition, of preening and parading, of constant measuring of yourself against every other, of envy, "If I had that copper hair," "If I had that skin. ..." She tormented herself enough about not looking like the others, there was enough of that unsureness, the having to be conscious of words before you speak, the constant caring — what are they thinking of me? without having it all magnified by the merciless physical drives.

Ronnie is calling. He is wet and I change him. It is rare there is such a cry now. That time of motherhood is almost behind me when the ear is not one's own but must always be racked and listening for the child cry, the child call. We sit for a while and I hold him, looking out over the city spread in charcoal with its soft aisles of light. "*Shoogily*," he breathes and curls closer. I carry him back to bed, asleep. *Shoogily*. A funny word, a family word, inherited from Emily, invented by her to say: *comfort*.

44     In this and other ways she leaves her seal, I say aloud. And startle at my saying it. What do I mean? What did I start to gather together, to try and make coherent? I was at the terrible, growing years. War years. I do not remember them well. I was working, there were four smaller ones now, there was not time for her. She had to help be a mother, a housekeeper, a shopper. She had to set her seal. Mornings of crisis and near hysteria trying to get lunches packed, hair combed, coats and shoes found, everyone to school or Child Care on time, the baby ready for transportation. And always the paper scribbled on by a smaller one, the book looked at by Susan then mislaid, the homework not done. Running out to that huge school where she was one, she was lost, she was a drop; suffering over the unpreparedness, stammering and unsure in her classes.

45     There was so little time left at night after the kids were bedded down. She would struggle over books, always eating (it was those years she developed her enormous appetite that is legendary in our family) and I would be ironing, or preparing food for the next day, or writing V-mail[2] to Bill, or tending the baby. Sometimes, to make me laugh, or out of her despair, she would imitate happenings or types at school.

46     I think I said once: "Why don't you do something like this in the school amateur show?" One morning she phoned me at work, hardly understandable through the weeping: "Mother, I did it. I won, I won: they gave me first prize; they clapped and clapped and wouldn't let me go."

47     Now suddenly she was Somebody, and as imprisoned in her difference as she had been in anonymity.

48     She began to be asked to perform at other high schools, even in colleges, then at city and statewide affairs. The first one she went to, I only recognized her that first moment when thin, shy, she almost drowned herself into the curtains. Then: Was this Emily? The control, the command, the convulsing and deadly clowning, the spell, then the roaring, stamping audience, unwilling to let this rare and precious laughter out of their lives.

49     Afterwards: You ought to do something about her with a gift like that — but without money or knowing how, what does one do? We have left it all to her, and the gift has as often eddied inside, clogged and clotted, as been used and growing.

---

2. Mail to U.S. troops overseas during World War II.

50   She is coming. She runs up the stairs two at a time with her light graceful step, and I know she is happy tonight. Whatever it was that occasioned your call did not happen today.

51   "Aren't you ever going to finish the ironing, Mother? Whistler painted his mother in a rocker. I'd have to paint mine standing over an ironing board." This is one of her communicative nights and she tells me everything and nothing as she fixes herself a plate of food out of the icebox.

52   She is lovely. Why did you want me to come in at all? Why were you concerned? She will find her way.

53   She starts up the stairs to bed. "Don't get me up with the rest in the morning." "But I thought you were having midterms." "Oh, those," she comes back in, kisses me, and says lightly, "in a couple of years when we'll all be atom-dead they won't matter a bit."

54   She has said it before. She *believes* it. But because I have been dredging the past, and all that compounds a human being is so heavy and meaningful in me, I cannot endure it tonight.

55   I will never total it all. I will never come in to say: She was a child seldom smiled at. Her father left me before she was a year old. I had to work her first six years when there was work, or I sent her home to his relatives. There were years she had care she hated. She was dark and thin and foreign-looking in a world where the prestige went to blondeness and curly hair and dimples, she was slow where glibness was prized. She was a child of anxious, not proud, love. We were poor and could not afford for her the soil of easy growth. I was a young mother, I was a distracted mother. There were the other children pushing up, demanding. Her younger sister seemed all that she was not. There were years she did not want me to touch her. She kept too much in herself, her life was such she had to keep too much in herself. My wisdom came too late. She has much to her and probably nothing will come of it. She is a child of her age, of depression, of war, of fear.

56   Let her be. So all that is in her will not bloom — but in how many does it? There is still enough left to live by. Only help her to know — help make it so there is cause for her to know — that she is more than this dress on the ironing board, helpless before the iron.

*(1956)*

# Nadine Gordimer (b. 1923)

A writer, critic, and editor, Nadine Gordimer is internationally known for her achievements in both the short story and the novel. Her work often focusses on the race relations and politics of her native South Africa. One critic has said that Gordimer "is one of the very few links between white and black in South Africa." Gordimer received a Nobel Prize for literature in 1991.

## Town and Country Lovers

1   Dr. Franz-Josef von Leinsdorf is a geologist absorbed in his work; wrapped up in it, as the saying goes — year after year the experience of his work enfolds him, swaddling him away from the landscapes, the cities and the people, wherever he lives: Peru, New Zealand, the United States. He's always been like that, his mother could confirm from their native Austria. There, even as a handsome small boy he presented only his profile to her: turned away to his bits of rock and stone. His few relaxations have not changed much since then. An occasional skiing trip, listening to music, reading poetry — Rainer Maria Rilke once stayed in his grandmother's hunting lodge in the forests of Styria and the boy was introduced to Rilke's poems while very young.

2   Layer upon layer, country after country, wherever his work takes him — and now he has been almost seven years in Africa. First the Côte d'Ivoire, and for the past five years, South Africa. The shortage of skilled manpower brought about his recruitment here. He has no interest in the politics of the countries he works in. His private preoccupation-within-the-preoccupation of his work has been research into underground water-courses, but the mining company that employs him in a senior though not executive capacity is interested only in mineral discovery. So he is much out in the field — which is the veld, here — seeking new gold, copper, platinum and uranium deposits. When he is at home — on this particular job, in this particular country, this city — he lives in a two-roomed flat in a suburban block with a landscaped garden, and does his shopping at a supermarket conveniently across the street. He is not married — yet. That is how his colleagues, and the typists and secretaries at the mining company's head office, would define his situation. Both men and women would describe him

as a good-looking man, in a foreign way, with the lower half of the face dark and middle-aged (his mouth is thin and curving, and no matter how close-shaven his beard shows like fine shot embedded in the skin round mouth and chin) and the upper half contradictorily young, with deep-set eyes (some would say grey, some black), thick eyelashes and brows. A tangled gaze: through which concentration and gleaming thoughtfulness perhaps appear as fire and langour. It is this that the women in the office mean when they remark he's not unattractive. Although the gaze seems to promise, he has never invited any of them to go out with him. There is the general assumption he probably has a girl who's been picked for him, he's bespoken by one of his own kind, back home in Europe where he comes from. Many of these well-educated Europeans have no intention of becoming permanent immigrants; neither the remnant of white colonial life nor idealistic involvement with Black Africa appeals to them.

3 One advantage, at least, of living in underdeveloped or half-developed countries is that flats are serviced. All Dr. von Leinsdorf has to do for himself is buy his own supplies and cook an evening meal if he doesn't want to go to a restaurant. It is simply a matter of dropping in to the supermarket on his way from his car to his flat after work in the afternoon. He wheels a trolley up and down the shelves, and his simple needs are presented to him in the form of tins, packages, plastic-wrapped meat, cheeses, fruit and vegetables, tubes, bottles ... At the cashiers' counters where customers must converge and queue there are racks of small items uncategorized, for last-minute purchase. Here, as the coloured girl cashier punches the adding machine, he picks up cigarettes and perhaps a packet of salted nuts or a bar of nougat. Or razor-blades, when he remembers he's running short. One evening in winter he saw that the cardboard display was empty of the brand of blades he preferred, and he drew the cashier's attention to this. These young coloured girls are usually pretty unhelpful, taking money and punching their machines in a manner that asserts with the time-serving obstinacy of the half-literate the limit of any responsibility towards customers, but this one ran an alert glance over the selection of razor-blades, apologized that she was not allowed to leave her post, and said she would see that the stock was replenished "next time." A day or two later she recognized him, gravely, as he took his turn before her counter — "I ahssed them, but it's out of stock. You can't get it. I did ahss about it." He said this didn't matter. "When it comes in, I can keep a few packets for you." He thanked her.

4 He was away with the prospectors the whole of the next week. He arrived back in town just before nightfall on Friday, and was on his way from car to flat with his arms full of briefcase, suitcase and canvas bags when someone stopped him by standing timidly in his path. He was about to dodge round unseeingly on the crowded pavement but she spoke. "We got the blades in now. I didn't see you in the shop this week, but I kept some for you when you come. So ..."

5    He recognized her. He had never seen her standing before, and she was wearing a coat. She was rather small and finely-made, for one of them. The coat was skimpy but no big backside jutted. The cold brought an apricot-graining of warm colour to her cheekbones, beneath which a very small face was quite delicately hollowed, and the skin was smooth, the subdued satiny colour of certain yellow wood. That crêpey hair, but worn drawn back flat and in a little knot pushed into one of the cheap wool chignons that (he recognized also) hung in the miscellany of small goods along with the razor-blades, at the supermarket. He said thanks, he was in a hurry, he'd only just got back from a trip — shifting the burdens he carried, to demonstrate. "Oh shame." She acknowledged his load. "But if you want I can run in and get it for you quickly. If you want."

6    He saw at once it was perfectly clear that all the girl meant was that she would go back to the supermarket, buy the blades and bring the packet to him there where he stood, on the pavement. And it seemed that it was this certainty that made him say, in the kindly tone of assumption used for an obliging underling, "I live just across there — *Atlantis* — that flat building. Could you drop them by, for me — number seven-hundred-and-eighteen, seventh floor — "

7    She had not before been inside one of these big flat buildings near where she worked. She lived a bus- and train-ride away to the West of the city, but this side of the black townships, in a township for people her tint. There was a pool with ferns, not plastic, and even a little waterfall pumped electrically over rocks, in the entrance of the building *Atlantis*; she didn't wait for the lift marked GOODS but took the one meant for whites and a white woman with one of those sausage-dogs on a lead got in with her but did not pay her any attention. The corridors leading to the flats were nicely glassed-in, not draughty.

8    He wondered if he should give her a twenty-cent piece for her trouble — ten cents would be right for a black; but she said, "Oh no — please, here — " standing outside his open door and awkwardly pushing back at his hand the change from the money he'd given her for the razor-blades. She was smiling, for the first time, in the dignity of refusing a tip. It was difficult to know how to treat these people, in this country; to know what they expected. In spite of her embarrassing refusal of the coin, she stood there, completely unassuming, fists thrust down the pockets of her cheap coat against the cold she'd come in from, rather pretty thin legs neatly aligned, knee to knee, ankle to ankle.

9    "Would you like a cup of coffee or something?"

10    He couldn't very well take her into his study-cum-living-room and offer her a drink. She followed him to his kitchen, but at the sight of her pulling out the single chair to drink her cup of coffee at the kitchen table, he said, "No — bring it in here — " and led the way into the big room where, among his books and his papers, his files of scientific correspondence (and the cigar boxes of stamps from

envelopes) his racks of records, his specimens of minerals and rocks, he lived alone.

11  It was no trouble to her; she saved him the trips to the supermarket and brought him his groceries two or three times a week. All he had to do was leave a list and the key under the doormat, and she would come up in her lunch-hour to collect them, returning to put his supplies in the flat after work. Sometimes he was home and sometimes not. He bought a box of chocolates and left it, with a note, for her to find; and that was acceptable, apparently, as a gratuity.

12  Her eyes went over everything in the flat although her body tried to conceal its sense of being out of place by remaining as still as possible, holding its contours in the chair offered her as a stranger's coat is set aside and remains exactly as left until the owner takes it up to go. "You collect?"

13  "Well, these are specimens — connected with my work."

14  "My brother used to collect. Miniatures. With brandy and whiskey and that, in them. From all over. Different countries."

15  The second time she watched him grinding coffee for the cup he had offered her she said, "You always do that? Always when you make coffee?"

16  "But of course. Is it no good, for you? Do I make it too strong?"

17  "Oh it's just I'm not used to it. We buy it ready — you know, it's in a bottle, you just add a bit to the milk or water."

18  He laughed, instructive: "That's not coffee, that's a synthetic flavouring. In my country we drink only real coffee, fresh, from the beans — you smell how good it is as it's being ground?"

19  She was stopped by the caretaker and asked what she wanted in the building? Heavy with the *bona fides* of groceries clutched to her body, she said she was working at number 718, on the seventh floor. The caretaker did not tell her not to use the whites' lift; after all, she was not black; her family was very light-skinned.

20  There was the item "grey button for trousers" on one of his shopping lists. She said as she unpacked the supermarket carrier "Give me the pants, so long, then," and sat on his sofa that was always gritty with fragments of pipe tobacco, sewing in and out through the four holds of the button with firm, fluent movements of the right hand, gestures supplying the articulacy missing from her talk. She had a little yokel's, peasant's (he thought of it) gap between her two front teeth when she smiled that he didn't much like, but, face ellipsed to three-quarter angle, eyes cast down in concentration with soft lips almost closed, this didn't much matter. He said, watching her sew, "You're a good girl"; and touched her.

21  She remade the bed every late afternoon when they left it and she dressed again before she went home. After a week there was a day when late afternoon became evening, and they were still in the bed.

22  "Can't you stay the night?"
23  "My mother," she said.
24  "Phone her. Make an excuse." He was a foreigner. He had been in the country five years, but he didn't understand that people don't usually have telephones in their houses, where she lived. She got up to dress. He didn't want that tender body to go out in the night cold and kept hindering her with the interruption of his hands; saying nothing. Before she put on her coat, when the body had already disappeared, he spoke. "But you must make some arrangement."
25  "Oh my mother!" Her face opened to fear and vacancy he could not read.
26  He was not entirely convinced the woman would think of her daughter as some pure and unsullied virgin ... "Why?"
27  The girl said, "S'e'll be scared. S'e'll be scared we get caught."
28  "Don't tell her anything. Say I'm employing you." In this country he was working in now there were generally rooms on the roofs of flat buildings for tenants' servants.
29  She said: "That's what I told the caretaker."

30  She ground fresh coffee beans every time he wanted a cup while he was working at night. She never attempted to cook anything until she had watched in silence while he did it the way he liked, and she learned to reproduce exactly the simple dishes he preferred. She handled his pieces of rock and stone, at first admiring the colours — "It'd make a beautiful ring or a necklace, ay." Then he showed her the striations, the formation of each piece, and explained what each was, and how, in the long life of the earth, it had been formed. He named the mineral it yielded, and what that was used for. He worked at his papers, writing, writing, every night, so it did not matter that they could not go out together to public places. On Sundays she got into his car in the basement garage and they drove to the country and picnicked away up in the Magaliesberg,[1] where there was no one. He read or poked about among the rocks; they climbed together, to the mountain pools. He taught her to swim. She had never seen the sea. She squealed and shrieked in the water, showing the gap between her teeth, as — it crossed his mind — she must do when among her own people. Occasionally he had to go out to dinner at the houses of colleagues from the mining company; she sewed and listened to the radio in the flat and he found her in bed, warm and already asleep, by the time he came in. He made his way into her body without speaking; she made him welcome without a word. Once he put on evening dress for a dinner at his country's consulate; watching him brush one or two fallen hairs from the shoulders of the dark jacket that sat so well on him, she saw a huge room all chandeliers and people dancing some

---

1. A mountain range north of Johannesburg.

dance from a costume film — stately, hand-to-hand. She supposed he was going to fetch, in her place in the car, a partner for the evening. They never kissed when either left the flat; he said, suddenly, kindly, pausing as he picked up cigarettes and keys, "Don't be lonely." And added, "Wouldn't you like to visit your family sometimes, when I have to go out?"

31   He had told her he was going home to his mother in the forests and mountains of his country near the Italian border (he showed her on the map) after Christmas. She had not told him how her mother, not knowing there was any other variety, assumed he was a medical doctor, so she had talked to her about the doctor's children and the doctor's wife who was a very kind lady, glad to have someone who could help out in the surgery as well as the flat.

32   She remarked wonderingly on his ability to work until midnight or later, after a day at work. She was so tired when she came home from her cash register at the supermarket that once dinner was eaten she could scarcely keep awake. He explained in a way she could understand that while the work she did was repetitive, undemanding of any real response from her intelligence, requiring little mental or physical effort and therefore unrewarding, his work was his greatest interest, it taxed his mental capacities to their limit, exercised all his concentration, and rewarded him constantly as much with the excitement of a problem presented as with the satisfaction of a problem solved. He said later, putting away his papers, speaking out of a silence: "Have you done other kinds of work?" She said, "I was in a clothing factory before. Sportbeau shirts; you know? But the pay's better in the shop."

33   Of course. Being a conscientious newspaper-reader in every country he lived in, he was aware that it was only recently that the retail consumer trade in this one had been allowed to employ coloureds as shop assistants; even punching a cash register represented advancement. With the continuing shortage of semi-skilled whites a girl like this might be able to edge a little farther into the white-collar category. He began to teach her to type. He was aware that her English was poor, even though, as a foreigner, in his ears her pronunciation did not offend, nor categorize her as it would in those of someone of his education whose mother tongue was English. He corrected her grammatical mistakes but missed the less obvious ones because of his own sometimes exotic English usage — she continued to use the singular pronoun "it" when what was required was the plural "they." Because he was a foreigner (although so clever, as she saw) she was less inhibited than she might have been by the words she knew she misspelled in her typing. While she sat at the typewriter she thought how one day she would type notes for him, as well as making coffee that way he liked it, and taking him inside her body without saying anything, and sitting (even if only through the empty streets of quiet Sundays) beside him in his car, like a wife.

34    On a summer night near Christmas — he had already bought and hidden a slightly showy but nevertheless good watch he thought she would like — there was a knocking at the door that brought her out of the bathroom and him to his feet, at his work-table. No one ever came to the flat at night; he had no friends intimate enough to drop in without warning. The summons was an imperious banging that did not pause and clearly would not stop until the door was opened.

35    She stood in the open bathroom doorway gazing at him across the passage into the living-room; her bare feet and shoulders were free of a big bath-towel. She said nothing, did not even whisper. The flat seemed to shake with the strong unhurried blows.

36    He made as if to go to the door, at last, but now she ran and clutched him by both arms. She shook her head wildly; her lips drew back but her teeth were clenched, she didn't speak. She pulled him into the bedroom, snatched some clothes from the clean laundry laid out on the bed and got into the wall-cupboard, thrusting the key at his hand. Although his arms and calves felt weakly cold he was horrified, distastefully embarrassed at the sight of her pressed back crouching there under his suits and coat; it was horrible and ridiculous. *Come out!* he whispered. *No! Come out!* She hissed: *Where? Where can I go?*

37    *Never mind! Get out of there!*

38    He put out his hand to grasp her. At bay, she said with all the force of her terrible whisper, baring the gap in her teeth: *I'll throw myself out the window.*

39    She forced the key into his hand like the handle of a knife. He closed the door on her face and drove the key home in the lock, then dropped it among the coins in his trouser pocket.

40    He unslotted the chain that was looped across the flat door. He turned the serrated knob of the Yale lock. The three policemen, two in plain clothes, stood there without impatience although they had been banging on the door for several minutes. The big dark one with an elaborate moustache held out in a hand wearing a plaited gilt ring some sort of identity card.

41    Dr. von Leinsdorf said quietly, the blood coming strangely back to legs and arms, "What is it?"

42    The sergeant told him they knew there was a coloured girl in the flat. They had had information; "I been watching this flat three months, I know."

43    "I am alone here." Dr. von Leinsdorf did not raise his voice.

44    "I know, I know who is here. Come — " And the sergeant and his two assistants went into the living-room, the kitchen, the bathroom (the sergeant picked up a bottle of after-shave cologne, seemed to study the French label) and the bedroom. The assistants removed the clean laundry that was laid upon the bed and then turned back the bedding, carrying the sheets over to be examined by the sergeant under the lamp. They talked to one another in Afrikaans, which the

Doctor did not understand. The sergeant himself looked under the bed, and lifted the long curtains at the window. The wall cupboard was of the kind that has no knobs; he saw that it was locked and began to ask in Afrikaans, then politely changed to English, "Give us the key."

45   Dr. von Leinsdorf said, "I'm sorry, I left it at my office — I always lock and take my keys with me in the mornings."

46   "It's no good, man, you better give me the key."

47   He smiled a little, reasonably. "It's on my office desk."

48   The assistants produced a screwdriver and he watched while they inserted it where the cupboard doors met, gave it quick, firm but not forceful leverage. He heard the lock give.

49   She had been naked, it was true, when they knocked. But now she was wearing a long-sleeved T-shirt with an appliquéd butterfly motif on one breast, and a pair of jeans. Her feet were still bare; she had managed, by feel, in the dark, to get into some of the clothing she had snatched from the bed, but she had no shoes. She had perhaps been weeping behind the cupboard door (her cheeks looked stained) but now her face was sullen and she was breathing heavily, her diaphragm contracting and expanding exaggeratedly and her breasts pushing against the cloth. It made her appear angry; it might simply have been that she was half-suffocated in the cupboard and needed oxygen. She did not look at Dr. von Leinsdorf. She would not reply to the sergeant's questions.

50   They were taken to the police station where they were at once separated and in turn led for examination by the district surgeon. The man's underwear was taken away and examined, as the sheets had been, for signs of his seed. When the girl was undressed, it was discovered that beneath her jeans she was wearing a pair of men's briefs with his name on the neatly-sewn laundry tag; in her haste, she had taken the wrong garment to her hiding-place.

51   Now she cried, standing there before the district surgeon in a man's underwear.

52   He courteously pretended not to notice. He handed briefs, jeans and T-shirt round the door, and motioned her to lie on a white-sheeted high table where he placed her legs apart, resting in stirrups, and put into her where the other had made his way so warmly a cold hard instrument that expanded wider and wider. Her thighs and knees trembled uncontrollably while the doctor looked into her and touched her deep inside with more hard instruments, carrying wafers of gauze.

53   When she came out of the examining room back to the charge office, Dr. von Leinsdorf was not there; they must have taken him somewhere else. She spent what was left of the night in a cell, as he must be doing; but early in the morning she was released and taken home to her mother's house in the coloured township by a white man who explained he was the clerk of the lawyer who had been engaged for her by Dr. von Leinsdorf. Dr. von Leinsdorf, the clerk said, had

also been bailed out that morning. He did not say when, or if she would see him again.

54 A statement made by the girl to the police was handed in to Court when she and the man appeared to meet charges of contravening the Immorality Act in a Johannesburg flat on the night of — December, 19——. *I lived with the white man in his flat. He had intercourse with me sometimes. He gave me tablets to take to prevent me becoming pregnant.*

55 Interviewed by the Sunday papers, the girl said, "I'm sorry for the sadness brought to my mother." She said she was one of nine children of a female laundry worker. She had left school in Standard Three because there was no money at home for gym clothes or a school blazer. She had worked as a machinist in a factory and a cashier in a supermarket. Dr. von Leinsdorf taught her to type his notes.

56 Dr. Franz-Josef von Leinsdorf, described as the grandson of a baroness, a cultured man engaged in international mineralogical research, said he accepted social distinctions between people but didn't think they should be legally imposed. "Even in my own country it's difficult for a person from a higher class to marry one from a lower class."

57 The two accused gave no evidence. They did not greet or speak to each other in Court. The Defence argued that the sergeant's evidence that they had been living together as man and wife was hearsay. (The woman with the dachshund, the caretaker?) The magistrate acquitted them because the State failed to prove carnal intercourse had taken place on the night of — December, 19——.

58 The girl's mother was quoted, with photograph, in the Sunday papers: "I won't let my daughter work as a servant for a white man again."

(1980)

# Margaret Laurence (1926–1987)

Born in Neepawa, Manitoba, and educated at United College, Winnipeg, Margaret Laurence travelled in Africa with her husband in the 1950s, and out of that experience came a novel, stories, a travel book, and translations of folk tales. Her later writings focus on her prairie background and a world she called Manawaka, in which she could explore generational, gender, and ethnic tensions and elaborate her anti-colonial feelings.

## The Loons

1 Just below the Manawaka, where the Wachakwa River ran brown and noisy over the pebbles, the scrub oak and grey-green willow and chokecherry bushes grew in a dense thicket. In a clearing at the centre of the thicket stood the Tonnerre family's shack. The basis of this dwelling was a small square cabin made of poplar poles and chinked with mud, which had been built by Jules Tonnerre some fifty years before, when he came back from Batoche with a bullet in his thigh, the year that Riel was hung and the voices of the Metis entered their long silence. Jules had only intended to stay the winter in the Wachakwa Valley, but the family was still there in the thirties, when I was a child. As the Tonnerres had increased, their settlement had been added to, until the clearing at the foot of the town hill was a chaos of lean-tos, wooden packing cases, warped lumber, discarded car tyres, ramshackle chicken coops, tangled strands of barbed wire and rusty tin cans.

2 The Tonnerres were French halfbreeds, and among themselves they spoke a *patois* that was neither Cree nor French. Their English was broken and full of obscenities. They did not belong among the Cree of the Galloping Mountain reservation, further north, and they did not belong among the Scots-Irish and Ukrainians of Manawaka, either. They were, as my Grandmother MacLeod would have put it, neither flesh, fowl, nor good salt herring. When their men were not working at odd jobs or as section hands on the C.P.R., they lived on relief. In the summers, one of the Tonnerre youngsters, with a face that seemed totally unfamiliar with laughter, would knock at the doors of the town's brick houses and offer for sale a lard-pail full of bruised wild strawberries, and if he got as much as a quarter he would

grab the coin and run before the customer had time to change her mind. Sometimes old Jules, or his son Lazarus, would get mixed up in a Saturday-night brawl, and would hit out at whoever was nearest, or howl drunkenly among the offended shoppers on Main Street, and then the Mountie would put them for the night in the barred cell underneath the Court House, and the next morning they would be quiet again.

3   Piquette Tonnerre, the daughter of Lazarus, was in my class at school. She was older than I, but she had failed several grades, perhaps because her attendance had always been sporadic and her interest in schoolwork negligible. Part of the reason she had missed a lot of school was that she had had tuberculosis of the bone, and had once spent many months in hospital. I knew this because my father was the doctor who had looked after her. Her sickness was almost the only thing I knew about her, however. Otherwise, she existed for me only as a vaguely embarrassing presence, with her hoarse voice and her clumsy limping walk and her grimy cotton dresses that were always miles too long. I was neither friendly nor unfriendly towards her. She dwelt and moved somewhere within my scope of vision, but I did not actually notice her very much until that peculiar summer when I was eleven.

4   "I don't know what to do about that kid," my father said at dinner one evening. "Piquette Tonnerre, I mean. The damn bone's flared up again. I've had her in hospital for quite a while now, and it's under control all right, but I hate like the dickens to send her home again."

5   "Couldn't you explain to her mother that she has to rest a lot?" my mother said.

6   "The mother's not there," my father replied. "She took off a few years back. Can't say I blame her. Piquette cooks for them, and she says Lazarus would never do anything for himself as long as she's there. Anyway, I don't think she'd take much care of herself, once she got back. She's only thirteen, after all. Beth, I was thinking — what about taking her up to Diamond Lake with us for the summer? A couple of months rest would give that bone a much better chance."

7   My mother looked stunned.

8   "But Ewen — what about Roddie and Vanessa?"

9   "She's not contagious," my father said. "And it would be company for Vanessa."

10  "Oh dear," my mother said in distress, "I'll bet anything she has nits in her hair."

11  "For Pete's sake," my father said crossly, "do you think Matron would let her stay in the hospital for all this time like that? Don't be silly, Beth."

12  Grandmother MacLeod, her delicately featured face as rigid as a cameo, now brought her mauve-veined hands together as though she were about to begin a prayer.

13  "Ewen, if that half-breed youngster comes along to Diamond Lake, I'm not going," she announced. "I'll go to Morag's for the summer."

14     I had trouble in stifling my urge to laugh, for my mother brightened visibly and quickly tried to hide it. If it came to a choice between Grandmother MacLeod and Piquette, Piquette would win hands down, nits or not.

15     "It might be quite nice for you, at that," she mused. "You haven't seen Morag for over a year, and you might enjoy being in the city for a while. Well, Ewen dear, you do what you think is best. If you think it would do Piquette some good, then we'll be glad to have her, as long as she behaves herself."

16     So it happened that several weeks later, when we all piled into my father's old Nash, surrounded by suitcases and boxes of provisions and toys for my ten-month-old brother, Piquette was with us and Grandmother MacLeod, miraculously, was not. My father would only be staying at the cottage for a couple of weeks, for he had to get back to his practice, but the rest of us would stay at Diamond Lake until the end of August.

17     Our cottage was not named, as many were, "Dew Drop Inn" or "Bide-a-Wee," or "Bonnie Doon." The sign on the roadway bore in austere letters only our name, MacLeod. It was not a large cottage, but it was on the lakefront. You could look out the windows and see, through the filigree of the spruce trees, the water glistening greenly as the sun caught it. All around the cottage were ferns, and sharp-branched raspberry bushes, and moss that had grown over fallen tree trunks. If you looked carefully among the weeds and grass, you could find wild strawberry plants which were in white flower now and in another month would bear fruit, the fragrant globes hanging like miniature scarlet lanterns on the thin hairy stems. The two grey squirrels were still there, gossiping at us from the tall spruce beside the cottage, and by the end of the summer they would again be tame enough to take pieces of crust from my hands. The broad moose antlers that hung above the back door were a little more bleached and fissured after the winter, but otherwise everything was the same. I raced joyfully around my kingdom, greeting all the places I had not seen for a year. My brother, Roderick, who had not been born when we were here last summer, sat on the car rug in the sunshine and examined a brown spruce cone, meticulously turning it round and round in his small and curious hands. My mother and father toted the luggage from car to cottage, exclaiming over how well the place had wintered, no broken windows, thank goodness, no apparent damage from storm-felled branches or snow.

18     Only after I had finished looking around did I notice Piquette. She was sitting on the swing, her lame leg held stiffly out, and her other foot scuffling the ground as she swung slowly back and forth. Her long hair hung black and straight around her shoulders, and her broad coarse-featured face bore no expression — it was blank, as though she no longer dwelt within her own skull, as though she had gone elsewhere. I approached her very hesitantly.

19   "Want to come and play?"

20   Piquette looked at me with a sudden flash of scorn.

21   "I ain't a kid," she said.

22   Wounded, I stamped angrily away, swearing I would not speak to her for the rest of the summer. In the days that followed, however, Piquette began to interest me, and I began to interest her. My reasons did not appear bizarre to me. Unlikely as it may seem I had only just realised that the Tonnerre family, whom I had always heard called half-breeds, were actually Indians, or as near as made no difference. My acquaintance with Indians was not extensive. I did not remember ever having seen a real Indian, and my new awareness that Piquette sprang from the people of Big Bear and Poundmaker, of Tecumseh, of the Iroquois who had eaten Father Brebeuf's heart — all this gave her an instant attraction in my eyes. I was a devoted reader of Pauline Johnson[1] at this age, and sometimes would orate aloud in an exalted voice, *West Wind, blow from your prairie nest; Blow from the mountains, blow from the west* — and so on. It seemed to me that Piquette must be in some way a daughter of the forest, a kind of junior prophetess of the wilds, who might impart to me, if I took the right approach, some of the secrets which she undoubtedly knew — where the whip-poorwill made her nest, how the coyote reared her young, or whatever it was that it said in Hiawatha.[2]

23   I set about gaining Piquette's trust. She was not allowed to go swimming, with her bad leg, but I managed to lure her down to the beach — or rather, she came because there was nothing else to do. The water was always icy, for the lake was fed by springs, but I swam like a dog, thrashing my arms and legs around at such a speed and with such an output of energy that I never grew cold. Finally, when I had had enough, I came out and sat beside Piquette on the sand. When she saw me approaching, her hand squashed flat the sand castle she had been building, and she looked at me sullenly, without speaking.

24   "Do you like this place?" I asked, after a while, intending to lead on from there into the question of forest lore.

25   Piquette shrugged. "It's okay. Good as anywhere."

26   "I love it," I said. "We come here every summer."

27   "So what?" Her voice was distant, and I glanced at her uncertainly, wondering what I could have said wrong.

28   "Do you want to come for a walk?" I asked her. "We wouldn't need to go far. If you just walk around the point there, you come to a bay where great big reeds grow in the water, and all kinds of fish hang around there. Want to? Come on."

29   She shook her head.

---

1. (1861–1913), poet; daughter of a Mohawk chief and an English woman.
2. *The Song of Hiawatha* (1855), a long narrative poem by Henry Wadsworth Longfellow.

30    "Your dad said I ain't supposed to do no more walking than I got to."

31    I tried another line.

32    "I bet you know a lot about the woods and all that, eh?" I began respectfully.

33    Piquette looked at me from her large dark unsmiling eyes.

34    "I don't know what in hell you're talkin' about," she replied. "You nuts or somethin'? If you mean where my old man, and me, and all them live, you better shut up, by Jesus, you hear?"

35    I was startled and my feelings were hurt, but I had a kind of dogged perseverance. I ignored her rebuff.

36    "You know something, Piquette? There's loons here, on this lake. You can see their nests just up the shore there, behind those logs. At night, you can hear them even from the cottage, but it's better to listen from the beach. My dad says we should listen and try to remember how they sound because in a few years when more cottages are built at Diamond Lake and more people come in, the loons will go away."

37    Piquette was picking up stones and snail shells and then dropping them again.

38    "Who gives a good goddamn?" she said.

39    It became increasingly obvious that, as an Indian, Piquette was a dead loss. That evening I went out by myself, scrambling through the bushes that overhung the steep path, my feet slipping on the fallen spruce needles that covered the ground. When I reached the shore, I walked along the firm damp sand to the small pier that my father had built, and sat down there. I heard someone else crashing through the undergrowth and the bracken, and for a moment I thought Piquette had changed her mind, but it turned out to be my father. He sat beside me on the pier and we waited, without speaking.

40    At night the lake was like black glass with a streak of amber which was the path of the moon. All around, the spruce trees grew tall and close-set, branches blackly sharp against the sky, which was lightened by a cold flickering of stars. Then the loons began their calling. They rose like phantom birds from the nests on the shore, and flew out onto the dark still surface of the water.

41    No one can ever describe that ululating sound, the crying of the loons, and no one who has heard it can ever forget it. Plaintive, and yet with a quality of chilling mockery, those voices belonged to a world separated by aeons from our neat world of summer cottages and the lighted lamps of home.

42    "They must have sounded just like that," my father remarked, "before any person ever set foot here."

43    Then he laughed. "You could say the same, of course, about sparrows, or chipmunks, but somehow it only strikes you that way with the loons."

44    "I know," I said.

45 Neither of us suspected that this would be the last time we would ever sit here together on the shore, listening. We stayed for perhaps half an hour, and then we went back to the cottage. My mother was reading beside the fireplace. Piquette was looking at the burning birch log, and not doing anything.

46 "You should have come along," I said, although in fact I was glad she had not.

47 "Not me," Piquette said. "You wouldn' catch me walkin' way down there jus' for a bunch of squawkin' birds."

48 Piquette and I remained ill at ease with one another. I felt I had somehow failed my father, but I did not know what was the matter, nor why she would not or could not respond when I suggested exploring the woods or playing house. I thought it was probably her slow and difficult walking that held her back. She stayed most of the time in the cottage with my mother, helping her with the dishes or with Roddie, but hardly ever talking. Then the Duncans arrived at their cottage, and I spend my days with Mavis, who was my best friend. I could not reach Piquette at all, and I soon lost interest in trying. But all that summer she remained as both a reproach and a mystery to me.

49 That winter, my father died of pneumonia, after less than a week's illness. For some time I saw nothing around me, being completely immersed in my own pain and my mother's. When I looked outward once more, I scarcely noticed that Piquette Tonnerre was no longer at school. I do not remember seeing her at all until four years later, one Saturday night when Mavis and I were having Cokes in the Regal Café. The jukebox was booming like tuneful thunder, and beside it, leaning lightly on its chrome and its rainbow glass, was a girl.

50 Piquette must have been seventeen then, although she looked about twenty. I stared at her, astounded that anyone could have changed so much. Her face, so stolid and expressionless before, was animated now with a gaiety that was almost violent. She laughed and talked very loudly with the boys around her. Her lipstick was bright carmine, and her hair was cut short and frizzily permed. She had not been pretty as a child, and she was not pretty now, for her features were still heavy and blunt. But her dark and slightly slanted eyes were beautiful, and her skin-tight skirt and orange sweater displayed to enviable advantage a soft and slender body.

51 She saw me, and walked over. She teetered a little, but it was not due to her once-tubercular leg, for her limp was almost gone.

52 "Hi, Vanessa." Her voice still had the same hoarseness. "Long time no see, eh?"

53 "Hi," I said. "Where've you been keeping yourself, Piquette?"

54 "Oh, I been around," she said. "I been away almost two years now. Been all over the place — Winnipeg, Regina, Saskatoon. Jesus, what I could tell you! I come back this summer, but I ain't stayin'. You kids goin' to the dance?"

55 "No," I said abruptly, for this was a sore point with me. I was fifteen, and thought I was old enough to go to the Saturday-night dances at the Flamingo. My mother, however, thought otherwise.

56 "Y'oughta come," Piquette said. "I never miss one. It's just about the on'y thing in this jerkwater town that's any fun. Boy, you couldn' catch me stayin' here. I don' give a shit about this place. It stinks."

57 She sat down beside me, and I caught the harsh over-sweetness of her perfume.

58 "Listen, you wanna know something, Vanessa?" she confided, her voice only slightly blurred. "Your dad was the only person in Manawaka that ever done anything good to me."

59 I nodded speechlessly. I was certain she was speaking the truth. I knew a little more than I had that summer at Diamond Lake, but I could not reach her now any more than I had then. I was ashamed, ashamed of my own timidity, the frightened tendency to look the other way. Yet I felt no real warmth towards her — I only felt that I ought to, because of that distant summer and because my father had hoped she would be company for me, or perhaps that I would be for her, but it had not happened that way. At this moment, meeting her again, I had to admit that she repelled and embarrassed me, and I could not help despising the self-pity in her voice. I wished she would go away. I did not want to see her. I did not know what to say to her. It seemed that we had nothing to say to one another.

60 "I'll tell you something else," Piquette went on. "All the old bitches an' biddies in this town will sure be surprised. I'm gettin' married this fall — my boyfriend, he's an English fella, works in the stockyards in the city there, a very tall guy, got blond wavy hair. Gee, is he ever handsome. Got this real classy name. Alvin Gerald Cummings — some handle, eh? They call him Al."

61 For the merest instant, then, I saw her. I really did see her, for the first and only time in all the years we had both lived in the same town. Her defiant face, momentarily, became unguarded and unmasked, and in her eyes there was a terrifying hope.

62 "Gee, Piquette — " I burst out awkwardly, "that's swell. That's really wonderful. Congratulations — good luck — I hope you'll be happy — "

63 As I mouthed the conventional phrases, I could only guess how great her need must have been, that she had been forced to seek the very things she so bitterly rejected.

64 When I was eighteen, I left Manawaka and went away to college. At the end of my first year, I came back home for the summer. I spent the first few days in talking non-stop with my mother, as we exchanged all the news that somehow had not found its way into letters — what had happened in my life and what had happened here in Manawaka while I was away. My mother searched her memory for events that concerned people I knew.

65     "Did I ever write to you about Piquette Tonnerre, Vanessa?" she asked one morning.

66     "No, I don't think so," I replied. "Last I heard of her, she was going to marry some guy in the city. Is she still there?"

67     My mother looked perturbed, and it was a moment before she spoke, as though she did not know how to express what she had to tell and wished she did not need to try.

68     "She's dead," she said at last. Then, as I stared at her, "Oh, Vanessa, when it happened, I couldn't help thinking of her as she was that summer — so sullen and gauche and badly dressed. I couldn't help wondering if we could have done something more at that time — but what could we do? She used to be around in the cottage there with me all day, and honestly, it was all I could do to get a word out of her. She didn't even talk to your father very much, although I think she liked him, in her way."

69     "What happened?" I asked.

70     "Either her husband left her, or she left him," my mother said. "I don't know which. Anyway, she came back here with two youngsters, both only babies — they must have been born very close together. She kept house, I guess, for Lazarus and her brothers, down the valley there, in the old Tonnerre place. I used to see her on the street sometimes, but she never spoke to me. She'd put on an awful lot of weight, and she looked a mess, to tell you the truth, a real slattern, dressed any old how. She was up in court a couple of times — drunk and disorderly, of course. One Saturday night last winter, during the coldest weather, Piquette was alone in the shack with the children. The Tonnerres made home brew all the time, so I've heard, and Lazarus said later she'd been drinking most of the day when he and the boys went out that evening. They had an old woodstove there — you know the kind, with exposed pipes. The shack caught fire. Piquette didn't get out, and neither did the children."

71     I did not say anything. As so often with Piquette, there did not seem to be anything to say. There was a kind of silence around the image in my mind of the fire and the snow, and I wished I could put from my memory the look that I had seen once in Piquette's eyes.

72     I went up to Diamond Lake for a few days that summer, with Mavis and her family. The MacLeod cottage had been sold after my father's death, and I did not even go to look at it, not wanting to witness my long-ago kingdom possessed now by strangers. But one evening I went down to the shore by myself.

73     The small pier which my father had built was gone, and in its place there was a large and solid pier built by the government, for Galloping Mountain was now a national park, and Diamond Lake had been renamed Lake Wapakata, for it was felt that an Indian name would have a greater appeal to tourists. The one store had become several dozen, and the settlement had all the attributes of a flourishing resort —

hotels, a dance-hall, cafés with neon signs, the penetrating odours of potato chips and hot dogs.

74  I sat on the government pier and looked out across the water. At night the lake at least was the same as it had always been, darkly shining and bearing within its black glass the streak of amber that was the path of the moon. There was no wind that evening, and everything was quiet all around me. It seemed too quiet, and then I realized that the loons were no longer here. I listened for some time, to make sure, but never once did I hear that long-drawn call, half mocking and half plaintive, spearing through the stillness across the lake.

75  I did not know what had happened to the birds. Perhaps they had gone away to some far place of belonging. Perhaps they had been unable to find such a place, and had simply died out, having ceased to care any longer whether they lived or not.

76  I remembered how Piquette had scorned to come along, when my father and I sat there and listened to the lake birds. It seemed to me now that in some unconscious and totally unrecognised way, Piquette might have been the only one, after all, who had heard the crying of the loons.

*(1966)*

# Timothy Findley (b. 1930)

Once an actor, Timothy Findley now writes short stories, novels, plays, and screenplays. He is one of Canada's most versatile and ambitious literary figures. His novel The Wars won the Governor General's Award in 1977. In "Dreams," as in much of his other work, Findley's characters move between the realms of the rational and the irrational.

## Dreams

*For R.E. Turner*

1. Doctor Menlo was having a problem: he could not sleep and his wife — the other Doctor Menlo — was secretly staying awake in order to keep an eye on him. The trouble was, in spite of her concern and in spite of all her efforts, Doctor Menlo — whose name was Mimi — was always nodding off because of her exhaustion.

2. She had tried drinking coffee, but this had no effect. She detested coffee and her system had a built-in rejection mechanism. She also prescribed herself a week's worth of Dexedrine to see if that would do the trick. *Five mg at bedtime* — all to no avail. And even though she put the plastic bottle of small orange hearts beneath her pillow and kept augmenting her intake, she would wake half an hour later with a dreadful start to discover the night was moving on to morning.

3. Everett Menlo had not yet declared the source of his problem. His restless condition had begun about ten days ago and had barely raised his interest. Soon, however, the time spent lying awake had increased from one to several hours and then, on Monday last, to all-night sessions. Now he lay in a state of rigid apprehension — eyes wide open, arms above his head, his hands in fists — like a man in pain unable to shut it out. His neck, his back and his shoulders constantly harried him with cramps and spasms. Everett Menlo had become a full-blown insomniac.

4. Clearly, Mimi Menlo concluded, her husband was refusing sleep because he believed something dreadful was going to happen the moment he closed his eyes. She had encountered this sort of fear in one or two of her patients. Everett, on the other hand, would not dis-

cuss the subject. If the problem had been hers, he would have said *such things cannot occur if you have gained control of yourself.*

5   Mimi began to watch for the dawn. She would calculate its approach by listening for the increase of traffic below the bedroom window. The Menlos' home was across the road from the Manulife Centre — corner of Bloor and Bay streets. Mimi's first sight of daylight always revealed the high, white shape of its terraced storeys. Their own apartment building was of a modest height and colour — twenty floors of smoky glass and polished brick. The shadow of the Manulife would crawl across the bedroom floor and climb the wall behind her, grey with fatigue and cold.

6   The Menlo beds were an arm's length apart, and lying like a rug between them was the shape of a large, black dog of unknown breed. All night long, in the dark of his well, the dog would dream and he would tell the content of his dreams the way that victims in a trance will tell of being pursued by posses of their nameless fears. He whimpered, he cried and sometimes he howled. His legs and his paws would jerk and flail and his claws would scrabble desperately against the parquet floor. Mimi — who loved this dog — would lay her hand against his side and let her fingers dabble in his coat in vain attempts to soothe him. Sometimes, she had to call his name in order to rouse him from his dreams because his heart would be racing. Other times, she smiled and thought: *at least there's one of us getting some sleep.* The dog's name was Thurber and he dreamed in beige and white.

7   Everett and Mimi Menlo were both psychiatrists. His field was schizophrenia; hers was autistic children. Mimi's venue was the Parkin Institute at the University of Toronto; Everett's was the Queen Street Mental Health Centre. Early in their marriage they had decided never to work as a team and not — unless it was a matter of financial life and death — to accept employment in the same institution. Both had always worked with the kind of physical intensity that kills, and yet they gave the impression this was the only tolerable way in which to function. It meant there was always a sense of peril in what they did, but the peril — according to Everett — made their lives worth living. This, at least, had been his theory twenty years ago when they were young.

8   Now, for whatever unnamed reason, peril had become his enemy and Everett Menlo had begun to look and behave and lose his sleep like a haunted man. But he refused to comment when Mimi asked him what was wrong. Instead, he gave the worst of all possible answers a psychiatrist can hear who seeks an explanation of a patient's silence: he said there was *absolutely nothing wrong.*

9   "You're sure you're not coming down with something?"
10  "Yes."
11  "And you wouldn't like a massage?"
12  "I've already told you: no."

13 "Can I get you anything?"
14 "No."
15 "And you don't want to talk?"
16 "That's right."
17 "Okay, Everett ..."
18 "Okay, what?"
19 "Okay, nothing. I only hope you get some sleep tonight."
20 Everett stood up. "Have you been spying on me, Mimi?"
21 "What do you mean by *spying*?"
22 "Watching me all night long."
23 "Well, Everett, I don't see how I can fail to be aware you aren't asleep when we share this bedroom. I mean — I can hear you grinding your teeth. I can see you lying there wide awake."
24 "When?"
25 "All the time. You're staring at the ceiling."
26 "I've never stared at the ceiling in my whole life. I sleep on my stomach."
27 "You sleep on your stomach *if* you sleep. But you have not been sleeping. Period. No argument."
28 Everett Menlo went to his dresser and got out a pair of clean pyjamas. Turning his back on Mimi, he put them on.
29 Somewhat amused at the coyness of this gesture, Mimi asked what he was hiding.
30 "Nothing!" he shouted at her.
31 Mimi's mouth fell open. Everett never yelled. His anger wasn't like that; it manifested itself in other ways, in silence and withdrawal, never shouts.
32 Everett was staring at her defiantly. He had slammed the bottom drawer of his dresser. Now he was fumbling with the wrapper of a pack of cigarettes.
33 Mimi's stomach tied a knot.
34 Everett hadn't touched a cigarette for weeks.
35 "Please don't smoke those," she said. "You'll only be sorry if you do."
36 "And you," he said, "will be sorry if I don't."
37 "But, dear ... ," said Mimi.
38 "Leave me for Christ's sake alone!" Everett yelled.
39 Mimi gave up and sighed and then she said: "all right. Thurber and I will go and sleep in the living-room. Goodnight."
40 Everett sat on the edge of his bed. His hands were shaking.
41 "Please," he said — apparently addressing the floor. "Don't leave me here alone. I couldn't bear that."
42 This was perhaps the most chilling thing he could have said to her. Mimi was alarmed; her husband was genuinely terrified of something and he would not say what it was. If she had not been who she was — if she had not known what she knew — if her years of training had not prepared her to watch for signs like this, she might have been better off. As it was, she had to face the possibility the strongest, most

sensible man on earth was having a nervous breakdown of major proportions. Lots of people have breakdowns, of course, but not, she had thought, the gods of reason.

43 "All right," she said — her voice maintaining the kind of calm she knew a child afraid of the dark would appreciate. "In a minute I'll get us something to drink. But first I'll go and change. ..."

44 Mimi went into the sanctum of the bathroom, where her nightgown waited for her — a portable hiding-place hanging on the back of the door. "You stay here," she said to Thurber, who had padded after her. "Mama will be out in just a moment."

45 Even in the dark, she could gauge Everett's tension. His shadow — all she could see of him — twitched from time to time and the twitching took on a kind of lurching rhythm, something like the broken clock in their living-room.

46 Mimi lay on her side and tried to close her eyes. But her eyes were tied to a will of their own and would not obey her. Now she, too, was caught in the same irreversible tide of sleeplessness that bore her husband backward through the night. Four or five times she watched him lighting cigarettes — blowing out the matches, courting disaster in the bedclothes — conjuring the worst of deaths for the three of them: a flaming pyre on the twentieth floor.

47 All this behaviour was utterly unlike him; foreign to his code of disciplines and ethics; alien to everything he said and believed. *Openness, directness, sharing of ideas, encouraging imaginative response to every problem. Never hide troubles. Never allow despair ...* These were his directives in everything he did. Now, he had thrown them over.

48 One thing was certain. She was not the cause of his sleeplessness. She didn't have affairs and neither did he. He might be ill — but whenever he'd been ill before, there had been no trauma; never a trauma like this one, at any rate. Perhaps it was something about a patient — one of his tougher cases; a wall in the patient's condition they could not break through; some circumstance of someone's lack of progress — a sudden veering towards a catatonic state, for instance — something that Everett had not foreseen that had stymied him and was slowly ... what? Destroying his sense of professional control? His self-esteem? His scientific certainty? If only he would speak.

49 Mimi thought about her own worst case: a child whose obstinant refusal to communicate was currently breaking her heart and, thus, her ability to help. If ever she had needed Everett to talk to, it was now. All her fellow doctors were locked in a battle over this child; they wanted to take him away from her. Mimi refused to give him up; he might as well have been her own flesh and blood. Everything had been done — from gentle holding sessions to violent bouts of manufactured anger — in her attempt to make the child react. She was staying with him every day from the moment he was roused to the moment he was induced to sleep with drugs.

50  His name was Brian Bassett and he was eight years old. He sat on the floor in the furthest corner he could achieve in one of the observation-isolation rooms where all the autistic children were placed when nothing else in their treatment — nothing of love or expertise — had managed to break their silence. Mostly, this was a signal they were coming to the end of life.

51  There in his four-square, glass-box room, surrounded by all that can tempt a child if a child can be tempted — toys and food and storybook companions — Brian Bassett was in the process, now, of fading away. His eyes were never closed and his arms were restrained. He was attached to three machines that nurtured him with all that science can offer. But of course, the spirit and the will to live cannot be fed by force to those who do not want to feed.

52  Now, in the light of Brian Bassett's utter lack of willing contact with the world around him — his utter refusal to communicate — Mimi watched her husband through the night. Everett stared at the ceiling, lit by the Manulife building's distant lamps, borne on his back further and further out to sea. She had lost him, she was certain.

53  When, at last, he saw that Mimi had drifted into her own and welcome sleep, Everett rose from the bed and went out into the hall, past the simulated jungle of the solarium, until he reached the dining-room. There, all the way till dawn, he amused himself with two decks of cards and endless games of Dead Man's Solitaire.

54  Thurber rose and shuffled after him. The dining-room was one of Thurber's favourite places in all his confined but privileged world, for it was here — as in the kitchen — that from time to time a hand descended filled with the miracle of food. But whatever it was that his master was doing up there above him on the table-top, it wasn't anything to do with feeding or with being fed. The playing cards had an old and dusty dryness to their scent and they held no appeal for the dog. So he once again lay down and he took up his dreams, which at least gave his paws some exercise. This way, he failed to hear the advent of a new dimension to his master's problems. This occurred precisely at 5:45 A.M. when the telephone rang and Everett Menlo, having rushed to answer it, waited breathless for a minute while he listened and then said: "yes" in a curious, strangulated fashion. Thurber — had he been awake — would have recognized in his master's voice the signal for disaster.

55  For weeks now, Everett had been working with a patient who was severely and uniquely schizophrenic. This patient's name was Kenneth Albright, and while he was deeply suspicious, he was also oddly caring. Kenneth Albright loved the detritus of life, such as bits of woolly dust and wads of discarded paper. He loved all dried-up leaves that had drifted from their parent trees and he loved the dead bees that had curled up to die along the window-sill of his ward. He also loved the

spiderwebs seen high up in the corners of the rooms where he sat on plastic chairs and ate with plastic spoons.

56   Kenneth Albright talked a lot about his dreams. But his dreams had become, of late, a major stumbling block in the process of his recovery. Back in the days when Kenneth had first become Doctor Menlo's patient, the dreams had been overburdened with detail: "overcast," as he would say, "with characters" and over-produced, again in Kenneth's phrase, "as if I were dreaming the dreams of Cecil B. de Mille."

57   Then he had said: "but a person can't really dream someone else's dreams. Or can they, Doctor Menlo?"

58   "No" had been Everett's answer — definite and certain.

59   Everett Menlo had been delighted, at first, with Kenneth Albright's dreams. They had been immensely entertaining — complex and filled with intriguing detail. Kenneth himself was at a loss to explain the meaning of these dreams, but as Everett had said, it wasn't Kenneth's job to explain. That was Everett's job. His job and his pleasure. For quite a long while, during these early sessions, Everett had written out the dreams, taken them home and recounted them to Mimi.

60   Kenneth Albright was a paranoid schizophrenic. Four times now, he had attempted suicide. He was a fiercely angry man at times — and at other times as gentle and as pleasant as a docile child. He had suffered so greatly, in the very worst moments of his disease, that he could no longer work. His job — it was almost an incidental detail in his life and had no importance for him, so it seemed — was returning reference books, in the Metro Library, to their places in the stacks. Sometimes — mostly late of an afternoon — he might begin a psychotic episode of such profound dimensions that he would attempt his suicide right behind the counter and even once, in the full view of everyone, while riding in the glass-walled elevator. It was after this last occasion that he was brought, in restraints, to be a resident patient at the Queen Street Mental Health Centre. He had slashed his wrists with a razor — but not before he had also slashed and destroyed an antique copy of *Don Quixote*, the pages of which he pasted to the walls with blood.

61   For a week thereafter, Kenneth Albright — just like Brian Bassett — had refused to speak or to move. Everett had him kept in an isolation cell, force-fed and drugged. Slowly, by dint of patience, encouragement and caring even Kenneth could recognize as genuine, Everett Menlo had broken through the barrier. Kenneth was removed from isolation, pampered with food and cigarettes, and he began relating his dreams.

62   At first there seemed to be only the dreams and nothing else in Kenneth's memory. Broken pencils, discarded toys and the telephone directory all had roles to play in these dreams but there were never any people. All the weather was bleak and all the landscapes were

empty. Houses, motor cars and office buildings never made an appearance. Sounds and smells had some importance, the wind would blow, the scent of unseen fires was often described. Stairwells were plentiful, leading nowhere, all of them rising from a subterranean world that Kenneth either did not dare to visit or would not describe.

63   The dreams had little variation, one from another. The themes had mostly to do with loss and with being lost. The broken pencils were all given names and the discarded toys were given to one another as companions. The telephone books were the sources of recitations — hours and hours of repeated names and numbers, some of which — Everett had noted with surprise — were absolutely accurate.

64   All of this held fast until an incident occurred one morning that changed the face of Kenneth Albright's schizophrenia forever; an incident that stemmed — so it seemed — from something he had dreamed the night before.

65   Bearing in mind his previous attempts at suicide, it will be obvious that Kenneth Albright was never far from sight at the Queen Street Mental Health Centre. He was, in fact, under constant observation; constant, that is, as human beings and modern technology can manage. In the ward to which he was ultimately consigned, for instance, the toilet cabinets had no doors and the shower-rooms had no locks. Therefore, a person could not ever be alone with water, glass or shaving utensils. (All the razors were cordless automatics.) Scissors and knives were banned, as were pieces of string and rubber bands. A person could not even kill his feet and hands by binding up his wrists and ankles. Nothing poisonous was anywhere available. All the windows were barred. All the double doors between this ward and the corridors beyond were doors with triple locks and a guard was always near at hand.

66   Still, if people want to die, they will find a way. Mimi Menlo would discover this to her everlasting sorrow with Brian Bassett. Everett Menlo would discover this to his everlasting horror with Kenneth Albright.

67   On the morning of April 19th, a Tuesday, Everett Menlo, in the best of health, had welcomed a brand-new patient into his office. This was Anne Marie Wilson, a young and brilliant pianist whose promising career had been halted mid-flight by a schizophrenic incident involving her ambition. She was, it seemed, no longer able to play and all her dreams were shattered. The cause was simple, to all appearances: Anne Marie had a sense of how, precisely, the music should be and she had not been able to master it accordingly. "Everything I attempt is terrible," she had said — in spite of all her critical accolades and all her professional success. Other doctors had tried and failed to break the barriers in Anne Marie, whose hands had taken on a life of their own, refusing altogether to work for her. Now it was Menlo's turn and hope was high.

68    Everett had been looking forward to his session with this prodigy. He loved all music and he thought to find some means within its discipline to reach her. She seemed so fragile, sitting there in the sunlight, and he had just begun to take his first notes when the door flew open and Louise, his secretary, had said: "I'm sorry, Doctor Menlo. There's a problem. Can you come with me at once?"

69    Everett excused himself.

70    Anne Marie was left in the sunlight to bide her time. Her fingers were moving around in her lap and she put them in her mouth to make them quiet.

71    Even as he'd heard his secretary speak, Everett had known the problem would be Kenneth Albright. Something in Kenneth's eyes had warned him there was trouble on the way: a certain wariness that indicated all was not as placid as it should have been, given his regimen of drugs. He had stayed long hours in one position, moving his fingers over his thighs as if to dry them on his trousers; watching his fellow patients come and go with abnormal interest — never, however, rising from his chair. An incident was on the horizon and Everett had been waiting for it, hoping it would come.

72    Louise had said that Doctor Menlo was to go at once to Kenneth Albright's ward. Everett had run the whole way. Only after the attendant had let him past the double doors, did he slow his pace to a hurried walk and wipe his brow. He didn't want Kenneth to know how alarmed he had been.

73    Coming to the appointed place, he paused before he entered, closing his eyes, preparing himself for whatever he might have to see. *Other people have killed themselves: I've seen it often enough*, he was thinking. *I simply won't let it affect me.* Then he went in.

74    The room was small and white — a dining-room — and Kenneth was sitting down in a corner, his back pressed out against the walls on either side of him. His head was bowed and his legs drawn up and he was obviously trying to hide without much success. An intern was standing above him and a nurse was kneeling down beside him. Several pieces of bandaging with blood on them were scattered near Kenneth's feet and there was a white enamel basin filled with pinkish water on the floor beside the nurse.

75    "Morowetz," Everett said to the intern. "Tell me what happened here." He said this just the way he posed such questions when he took the interns through the wards at examination time, quizzing them on symptoms and prognoses.

76    But Morowetz the intern had no answer. He was puzzled. What had happened had no sane explanation.

77    Everett turned to Charterhouse, the nurse.

78    "On the morning of April 19th, at roughly ten-fifteen, I found Kenneth Albright covered with blood," Ms Charterhouse was to write in her report. "His hands, his arms, his face and his neck were stained.

I would say the blood was fresh and the patient's clothing — mostly his shirt — was wet with it. Some — a very small amount of it — had dried on his forehead. The rest was uniformly the kind of blood you expect to find free-flowing from a wound. I called for assistance and meanwhile attempted to ascertain where Mister Albright might have been injured. I performed this examination without success. I could find no source of bleeding anywhere on Mister Albright's body."

79   Morowetz concurred.
80   The blood was someone else's.
81   "Was there a weapon of any kind?" Doctor Menlo had wanted to know.
82   "No, sir. Nothing," said Charterhouse.
83   "And was he alone when you found him?"
84   "Yes, sir. Just like this in the corner."
85   "And the others?"
86   "All the patients in the ward were examined," Morowetz told him.
87   "And?"
88   "Not one of them was bleeding."
89   Everett said: "I see."
90   He looked down at Kenneth.
91   "This is Doctor Menlo, Kenneth. Have you anything to tell me?"
92   Kenneth did not reply.
93   Everett said: "When you've got him back in his room and tranquillized, will you call me, please?"
94   Morowetz nodded.
95   The call never came. Kenneth had fallen asleep. Either the drugs he was given had knocked him out cold, or he had opted for silence. Either way, he was incommunicado.
96   No one was discovered bleeding. Nothing was found to indicate an accident, a violent attack, an epileptic seizure. A weapon was not located. Kenneth Albright had not a single scratch on his flesh from stem, as Everett put it, to gudgeon. The blood, it seemed, had fallen like the rain from heaven: unexplained and inexplicable.
97   Later, as the day was ending, Everett Menlo left the Queen Street Mental Health Centre. He made his way home on the Queen streetcar and the Bay bus. When he reached the apartment, Thurber was waiting for him. Mimi was at a goddamned meeting.
98   That was the night Everett Menlo suffered the first of his failures to sleep. It was occasioned by the fact that, when he awakened sometime after three, he had just been dreaming. This, of course, was not unusual — but the dream itself was perturbing. There was someone lying there, in the bright white landscape of a hospital dining-room. Whether it was a man or a woman could not be told, it was just a human body, lying down in a pool of blood.
99   Kenneth Albright was kneeling beside this body; pulling it open the way a child will pull a Christmas present open — yanking at its strings and ribbons, wanting only to see the contents. Everett saw this scene

from several angles, never speaking, never being spoken to. In all the time he watched — the usual dream eternity — the silence was broken only by the sound of water dripping from an unseen tap. Then, Kenneth Albright rose and was covered with blood, the way he had been that morning. He stared at Doctor Menlo, looked right through him and departed. Nothing remained in the dining-room but plastic tables and plastic chairs and the bright red thing on the floor that once had been a person. Everett Menlo did not know and could not guess who this person might have been. He only knew that Kenneth Albright had left this person's body in Everett Menlo's dream.

100   Three nights running, the corpse remained in its place and every time that Everett entered the dining-room in the nightmare he was certain he would find out who it was. On the fourth night, fully expecting to discover he himself was the victim, he beheld the face and saw it was a stranger.

101   *But there are no strangers in dreams*; he knew that now after twenty years of practice. *There are no strangers; there are only people in disguise.*

102   Mimi made one final attempt in Brian Bassett's behalf to turn away the fate to which his other doctors — both medical and psychiatric — had consigned him. Not that, as a group, they had failed to expend the full weight of all they knew and all they could do to save him. One of his medical doctors — a woman whose name was Juliet Bateman — had moved a cot into his isolation room and stayed with him twenty-four hours a day for over a week. But her health had been undermined by this and when she succumbed to the Shanghai flu she removed herself for fear of infecting Brian Bassett.

103   The parents had come and gone on a daily basis for months in a killing routine of visits. But parents, their presence and their loving, are not the answer when a child has fallen into an autistic state. They might as well have been strangers. And so they had been advised to stay away.

104   Brian Bassett was eight years old — *unlucky eight*, as one of his therapists had said — and in every other way, in terms of physical development and mental capability, he had always been a perfectly normal child. Now, in the final moments of his life, he weighed a scant thirty pounds, when he should have weighed twice that much.

105   Brian had not been heard to speak a single word in over a year of constant observation. Earlier — long ago as seven months — a few expressions would visit his face from time to time. Never a smile — but often a kind of sneer, a passing of judgement, terrifying in its intensity. Other times, a pinched expression would appear — a signal of the shyness peculiar to autistic children, who think of light as being unfriendly.

106   Mimi's militant efforts in behalf of Brian had been exemplary. Her fellow doctors thought of her as *Bassett's crazy guardian angel*. They

begged her to remove herself in order to preserve her health. Being wise, being practical, they saw that all her efforts would not save him. But Mimi's version of being a guardian angel was more like being a surrogate warrior: a hired gun or a samurai. Her cool determination to thwart the enemies of silence, stillness and starvation gave her strengths that even she had been unaware were hers to command.

107   Brian Bassett, seated in his corner on the floor, maintained a solemn composure that lent his features a kind of unearthly beauty. His back was straight, his hands were poised, his hair was so fine he looked the very picture of a spirit waiting to enter a newborn creature. Sometimes Mimi wondered if this creature Brian Bassett waited to inhabit could be human. She thought of all the animals she had ever seen in all her travels and she fell upon the image of a newborn fawn as being the most tranquil and the most in need of stillness in order to survive. If only all the natural energy and curiosity of a newborn beast could have entered into Brian Bassett, surely, they would have transformed the boy in the corner into a vibrant, joyous human being. But it was not to be.

108   On the 29th of April — one week and three days after Everett had entered into his crisis of insomnia — Mimi sat on the floor in Brian Bassett's isolation room, gently massaging his arms and legs as she held him in her lap.

109   His weight, by now, was shocking — and his skin had become translucent. His eyes had not been closed for days — for weeks — and their expression might have been carved in stone.

110   "Speak to me. Speak," she whispered to him as she cradled his head beneath her chin. "Please at least speak before you die."

111   Nothing happened. Only silence.

112   Juliet Bateman — wrapped in a blanket — was watching through the observation glass as Mimi lifted up Brian Bassett and placed him in his cot. The cot had metal sides — and the sides were raised. Juliet Bateman could see Brian Bassett's eyes and his hands as Mimi stepped away.

113   Mimi looked at Juliet and shook her head. Juliet closed her eyes and pulled her blanket tighter like a skin that might protect her from the next five minutes.

114   Mimi went around the cot to the other side and dragged the IV stand in closer to the head. She fumbled for a moment with the long plastic lifelines — anti-dehydrants, nutrients — and she adjusted the needles and brought them down inside the nest of the cot where Brian Bassett lay and she lifted up his arm in order to insert the tubes and bind them into place with tape.

115   This was when it happened — just as Mimi Menlo was preparing to insert the second tube.

116   Brian Bassett looked at her and spoke.

117   "No," he said. "Don't."

118   *Don't* meant death.

119 Mimi paused — considered — and set the tube aside. Then she withdrew the tube already in place and she hung them both on the IV stand.

120 *All right*, she said to Brian Bassett in her mind, *you win*.

121 She looked down then with her arm along the side of the cot — and one hand trailing down so Brian Bassett could touch it if he wanted to. She smiled at him and said to him: "not to worry. None of us is ever going to trouble you again." He watched her carefully. "Goodbye, Brian," she said. "I love you."

122 Juliet Bateman saw Mimi Menlo say all this and was fairly sure she had read the words on Mimi's lips just as they had been spoken.

123 Mimi started out of the room. She was determined now there was no turning back and that Brian Bassett was free to go his way. But just as she was turning the handle and pressing her weight against the door — she heard Brian Bassett speak again.

124 "Goodbye," he said.

125 And died.

126 Mimi went back and Juliet Bateman, too, and they stayed with him another hour before they turned out his lights. "Someone else can cover his face," said Mimi. "I'm not going to do it." Juliet agreed and they came back out to tell the nurse on duty that their ward had died and their work with him was over.

127 On the 30th of April — a Saturday — Mimi stayed home and made her notes and she wondered if and when she would weep for Brian Bassett. Her hand, as she wrote, was steady and her throat was not constricted and her eyes had no sensation beyond the burning itch of fatigue. She wondered what she looked like in the mirror, but resisted that discovery. Some things could wait. Outside it rained. Thurber dreamed in the corner. Bay Street rumbled in the basement.

128 Everett, in the meantime, had reached his own crisis and because of his desperate straits a part of Mimi Menlo's mind was on her husband. Now he had not slept for almost ten days. *We really ought to consign ourselves to hospital beds*, she thought. Somehow, the idea held no persuasion. It occurred to her that laughter might do a better job, if only they could find it. The brain, when over-extended, gives us the most surprisingly simple propositions, she concluded. *Stop*, it says to us. *Lie down and sleep*.

129 Five minutes later, Mimi found herself still sitting at the desk, with her fountain pen capped and her fingers raised to her lips in an attitude of gentle prayer. It required some effort to re-adjust her gaze and re-establish her focus on the surface of the window glass beyond which her mind had wandered. Sitting up, she had been asleep.

130 Thurber muttered something and stretched his legs and yawned, still asleep. Mimi glanced in his direction. *We've both been dreaming,* she thought, *but his dream continues.*

131 Somewhere behind her, the broken clock was attempting to strike the hour of three. Its voice was dull and rusty, needing oil.

132   Looking down, she saw the words BRIAN BASSETT written on the page before her and it occurred to her that, without this person, the words were nothing more than extrapolations from the alphabet — something fanciful we call a "name" in the hope that, one day, it will take on meaning.

133   She thought of Brian Bassett with his building blocks — pushing the letters around on the floor and coming up with more acceptable arrangements: *TINA STERABBS ... IAN BRETT BASS ... BEST STAB the RAIN*: a sentence. He had known all along, of course, that *BRIAN BASSETT* wasn't what he wanted because it wasn't what he was. He had come here against his will, was held here against his better judgement, fought against his captors and finally escaped.

134   But where was here to Brett Bass? Where was here to Tina Sterabbs? Like Brian Bassett, they had all been here in someone else's dreams, and had to wait for someone else to wake before they could make their getaway.

135   Slowly, Mimi uncapped her fountain pen and drew a firm black line through Brian Bassett's name. *We dreamed him*, she wrote, *that's all. And then we let him go.*

136   Seeing Everett standing in the doorway, knowing he had just returned from another Kenneth Albright crisis, she had no sense of apprehension. All this was only as it should be. Given the way that everything was going, it stood to reason Kenneth Albright's crisis had to come in this moment. If he managed, at last, to kill himself then at least her husband might begin to sleep again.

137   Far in the back of her mind a carping, critical voice remarked that any such thoughts were *deeply unfeeling and verging on the barbaric*. But Mimi dismissed this voice and another part of her brain stepped forward in her defence. *I will weep for Kenneth Albright*, she thought, *when I can weep for Brian Bassett. Now, all that matters is that Everett and I survive.*

138   Then she strode forward and put out her hand for Everett's briefcase, set the briefcase down and helped him out of his topcoat. She was playing wife. It seemed to be the thing to do.

139   For the next twenty minutes Everett had nothing to say, and after he had poured himself a drink and after Mimi had done the same, they sat in their chairs and waited for Everett to catch his breath.

140   The first thing he said when he finally spoke was: "finish your notes?"

141   "Just about," Mimi told him. "I've written everything I can for now." She did not elaborate. "You're home early," she said, hoping to goad him into saying something new about Kenneth Albright.

142   "Yes," he said. "I am." But that was all.

143   Then he stood up — threw back the last of his drink and poured another. He lighted a cigarette and Mimi didn't even wince. He had been smoking now three days. The atmosphere between them had

been, since then, enlivened with a magnetic kind of tension. But it was a moribund tension, slowly beginning to dissipate.

Mimi watched her husband's silent torment now with a kind of clinical detachment. This was the result, she liked to tell herself, of her training and her discipline. The lover in her could regard Everett warmly and with concern, but the psychiatrist in her could also watch him as someone suffering a nervous breakdown, someone who could not be helped until the symptoms had multiplied and declared themselves more openly.

Everett went into the darkest corner of the room and sat down hard in one of Mimi's straight-backed chairs: the ones inherited from her mother. He sat, prim, like a patient in a doctor's office, totally unrelaxed and nervy; expressionless. Either he had come to receive a deadly diagnosis, or he would get a clean bill of health.

Mimi glided over to the sofa in the window, plush and red and deeply comfortable; a place to recuperate. The view — if she chose to turn only slightly sideways — was one of the gentle rain that was falling onto Bay Street. Sopping-wet pigeons huddled on the windowsill; people across the street in the Manulife building were turning on their lights.

A renegade robin, nesting in their eaves, began to sing.

Everett Menlo began to talk.

"Please don't interrupt," he said at first.

"You know I won't," said Mimi. It was a rule that neither one should interrupt the telling of a case until they had been invited to do so.

Mimi put her fingers into her glass so the ice-cubes wouldn't click. She waited.

Everett spoke — but he spoke as if in someone else's voice, perhaps the voice of Kenneth Albright. This was not entirely unusual. Often, both Mimi and Everett Menlo spoke in the voices of their patients. What was unusual, this time, was that, speaking in Kenneth's voice, Everett began to sweat profusely — so profusely that Mimi was able to watch his shirt front darkening with perspiration.

"As you know," he said, "I have not been sleeping."

This was the understatement of the year. Mimi was silent. "I have not been sleeping because — to put it in a nutshell — I have been afraid to dream."

Mimi was somewhat startled by this. Not by the fact that Everett was afraid to dream, but only because she had just been thinking of dreams herself.

"I have been afraid to dream, because in all my dreams there have been bodies. Corpses. Murder victims."

Mimi — not really listening — idly wondered if she had been one of them.

"In all my dreams, there have been corpses," Everett repeated. "But I am not the murderer. Kenneth Albright is the murderer, and up to this moment, he has left behind him fifteen bodies: none of them people I recognize."

Mimi nodded. The ice-cubes in her drink were beginning to freeze her fingers. Any minute now, she prayed, they would surely melt.

"I gave up dreaming almost a week ago," said Everett, "thinking that if I did, the killing pattern might be altered; broken." Then he said tersely; "it was not. The killings have continued. ..."

"How do you know the killings have continued, Everett, if you've given up dreaming? Wouldn't this mean he had no place to hide the bodies?"

In spite of the fact she had disobeyed their rule about not speaking, Everett answered her.

"I know they are being continued because I have seen the blood."

"Ah, yes. I see."

"No, Mimi. No. You don't see. The blood is not a figment of my imagination. The blood, in fact, is the only thing not dreamed." He explained the stains on Kenneth Albright's hands and arms and clothes and he said: "It happens every day. We have searched his person for signs of cuts and gashes — even for internal and rectal bleeding. Nothing. We have searched his quarters and all the other quarters in his ward. His ward is locked. His ward is isolated in the extreme. None of his fellow patients was ever found bleeding — never had cause to bleed. There were no injuries — no self-inflicted wounds. We thought of animals. Perhaps a mouse — a rat. But nothing. Nothing. Nothing ... We also went so far as to strip-search all the members of the staff who entered that ward and I, too, offered myself for this experiment. Still nothing. Nothing. No one had bled."

Everett was now beginning to perspire so heavily he removed his jacket and threw it on the floor. Thurber woke and stared at it, startled. At first, it appeared to be the beast that had just pursued him through the woods and down the road. But, then, it sighed and settled and was just a coat; a rumpled jacket lying down on the rug.

Everett said: "we had taken samples of the blood on the patient's hands — on Kenneth Albright's hands and on his clothing and we had these samples analyzed. No. It was not his own blood. No, it was not the blood of an animal. No, it was not the blood of a fellow patient. No, it was not the blood of any members of the staff. ...."

Everett's voice had risen.

"Whose blood was it?" he almost cried. "Whose the hell was it?"

Mimi waited.

Everett Menlo lighted another cigarette. He took a great gulp of his drink.

"Well ..." He was calmer now; calmer of necessity. He had to marshall the evidence. He had to put it all in order — bring it into line with reason. "Did this mean that — somehow — the patient had managed to leave the premises — do some bloody deed and return without our knowledge of it? That is, after all, the only possible explanation. Isn't it?"

173 Mimi waited.
174 "Isn't it?" he repeated.
175 "Yes," she said. "It's the only possible explanation."
176 "Except there is no way out of that place. There is absolutely no way out."
177 Now, there was a pause.
178 "But one," he added — his voice, again, a whisper.
179 Mimi was silent. Fearful — watching his twisted face.
180 "Tell me," Everett Menlo said — the perfect innocent, almost the perfect child in quest of forbidden knowledge.
181 "Answer me this — be honest: is there blood in dreams?"
182 Mimi could not respond. She felt herself go pale. Her husband — after all, the sanest man alive — had just suggested something so completely mad he might as well have handed over his reason in a paper bag and said to her, *burn this.*
183 "The only place that Kenneth Albright goes, I tell you, is into dreams," Everett said. "That is the only place beyond the ward into which the patient can or does escape."
184 Another — briefer — pause.
185 "It is real blood, Mimi. And he gets it all from dreams. *My dreams.*"
186 They waited for this to settle.
187 Everett said: "I'm tired. I'm tired. I cannot bear this any more. I'm tired. ..."
188 Mimi thought, *good. No matter what else happens, he will sleep tonight.*
189 He did. And so, at last, did she.

190 Mimi's dreams were rarely of the kind that engender fear. She dreamt more gentle scenes with open spaces that did not intimidate. She would dream quite often of water and of animals. Always, she was nothing more than an observer; roles were not assigned her; often, this was sad. Somehow, she seemed at times locked out, unable to participate. These were the dreams she endured when Brian Bassett died: field trips to see him in some desert setting; underwater excursions to watch him floating amongst the seaweed. He never spoke, and, indeed, he never appeared to be aware of her presence.
191 That night, when Everett fell into his bed exhausted and she did likewise, Mimi's dream of Brian Bassett was the last she would ever have of him and somehow, in the dream, she knew this. What she saw was what, in magical terms, would be called a disappearing act. Brian Bassett vanished. Gone.

192 Sometime after midnight on May Day morning, Mimi Menlo awoke from her dream of Brian to the sound of Thurber thumping the floor in a dream of his own.

193     Everett was not in his bed and Mimi cursed. She put on her wrapper and her slippers and went beyond the bedroom into the hall.

194     No lights were shining but the street lamps far below and the windows gave no sign of stars.

195     Mimi made her way past the jungle, searching for Everett in the living-room. He was not there. She would dream of this one day; it was a certainty.

196     "Everett?"

197     He did not reply.

198     Mimi turned and went back through the bedroom.

199     "Everett?"

200     She heard him. He was in the bathroom and she went in through the door.

201     "Oh," she said, when she saw him. "Oh, my God."

202     Everett Menlo was standing in the bathtub, removing his pyjamas. They were soaking wet, but not with perspiration. They were soaking wet with blood.

203     For a moment, holding his jacket, letting its arms hang down across his belly and his groin, Everett stared at Mimi, blank-eyed from his nightmare.

204     Mimi raised her hand to her mouth. She felt as one must feel, if helpless, watching someone burn alive.

205     Everett threw the jacket down and started to remove his trousers. His pyjamas, made of cotton, had been green. His eyes were blinded now with blood and his hands reached out to find the shower taps.

206     "Please don't look at me," he said. "I ... Please go away."

207     Mimi said: "no." She sat on the toilet seat. "I'm waiting here," she told him, "until we both wake up."

*(1988)*

# Alice Munro (b. 1931)

Munro spent her youth in southwestern Ontario, the setting for many of her short stories. Her unaffected but finely subtle style and her focus on the lives of adolescent and adult women have twice won her the Governor General's Award.

## Boys and Girls

1  My father was a fox farmer. That is, he raised silver foxes, in pens; and in the fall and early winter, when their fur was prime, he killed them and skinned them and sold their pelts to the Hudson's Bay Company or the Montreal Fur Traders. These companies supplied us with heroic calendars to hang, one on each side of the kitchen door. Against a background of cold blue sky and black pine forests and treacherous northern rivers, plumed adventurers planted the flags of England and France; magnificent savages bent their backs to the portage.

2  For several weeks before Christmas, my father worked after supper in the cellar of our house. The cellar was whitewashed, and lit by a hundred-watt bulb over the worktable. My brother Laird and I sat on the top step and watched. My father removed the pelt inside-out from the body of the fox, which looked surprisingly small, mean and rat-like, deprived of its arrogant weight of fur. The naked, slippery bodies were collected in a sack and buried at the dump. One time the hired man, Henry Bailey, had taken a swipe at me with the sack, saying, "Christmas present!" My mother thought that was not funny. In fact she disliked the whole pelting operation — that was what the killing, skinning, and preparation of the furs was called — and wished it did not have to take place in the house. There was the smell. After the pelt had been stretched inside-out on a long board my father scraped away delicately, removing the little clotted webs of blood vessels, the bubbles of fat; the smell of blood and animal fat, with the strong primitive odor of the fox itself, penetrated all parts of the house. I found it reassuringly seasonal, like the smell of oranges and pine needles.

3  Henry Bailey suffered from bronchial troubles. He would cough and cough until his narrow face turned scarlet, and his light blue, derisive eyes filled up with tears; then he took the lid off the stove, and, standing well back, shot out a great clot of phlegm — hsss — straight into

the heart of the flames. We admired him for this performance and for his ability to make his stomach growl at will, and for his laughter, which was full of high whistlings and gurglings and involved the whole faulty machinery of his chest. It was sometimes hard to tell what he was laughing at, and always possible that it might be us.

4   After we had been sent to bed we could smell fox and still hear Henry's laugh, but these things, reminders of the warm, safe, brightly lit downstairs world, seemed lost and diminished, floating on the stale cold air upstairs. We were afraid at night in the winter. We were not afraid of *outside* though this was the time of year when snowdrifts curled around our house like sleeping whales and the wind harassed us all night, coming up from the buried fields, the frozen swamp, with its old bugbear chorus of threats and misery. We were afraid of *inside*, the room where we slept. At this time the upstairs of our house was not finished. A brick chimney went up one wall. In the middle of the floor was a square hole, with a wooden railing around it; that was where the stairs came up. On the other side of the stairwell were the things that nobody had any use for any more — a soldiery roll of linoleum, standing on end, a wicker baby carriage, a fern basket, china jugs and basins with cracks in them, a picture of the Battle of Balaclava,[1] very sad to look at. I had told Laird, as soon as he was old enough to understand such things, that bats and skeletons lived over there; whenever a man escaped from the county jail, twenty miles away, I imagined that he had somehow let himself in the window and was hiding behind the linoleum. But we had rules to keep us safe. When the light was on, we were safe as long as we did not step off the square of worn carpet which defined our bedroom-space; when the light was off no place was safe but the beds themselves. I had to turn out the light kneeling on the end of my bed, and stretching as far as I could to reach the cord.

5   In the dark we lay on our beds, our narrow life rafts, and fixed our eyes on the faint light coming up the stairwell, and sang songs. Laird sang "Jingle Bells," which he would sing any time, whether it was Christmas or not, and I sang "Danny Boy." I loved the sound of my own voice, frail and supplicating, rising in the dark. We could make out the tall frosted shapes of the windows now, gloomy and white. When I came to the part *When I am dead, as dead I well may be* — a fit of shivering caused not by the cold sheets but by pleasurable emotion almost silenced me. *You'll kneel and say an Ave there above me* — What is an Ave? Every day I forgot to find out.

6   Laird went straight from singing to sleep. I could hear his long, satisfied, bubbly breaths. Now for the time that remained to me, the most perfectly private and perhaps the best time of the whole day, I

---

1. One of the battles in the Crimean War of 1853–1856, in which Britain and France allied with Turkey against Tsarist Russia.

arranged myself tightly under the covers and went on with one of the stories I was telling myself from night to night. These stories were about myself, when I had grown a little older; they took place in a world that was recognizably mine, yet one that presented opportunities for courage, boldness and self-sacrifice, as mine never did. I rescued people from a bombarded building (it had discouraged me that the real war had gone on so far away from Jubilee). I shot two rabid wolves who were menacing the schoolyard (the teachers cowered terrified at my back). I rode a fine horse spiritedly down the main street of Jubilee, acknowledging the townspeople's gratitude for some yet-to-be-worked-out piece of heroism (nobody ever rode a horse there, except King Billy in the Orangemen's Day[2] parade). There was always riding and shooting in these stories, though I had only been on a horse twice — bareback because we did not own a saddle — and the second time I had slid right around and dropped under the horse's feet; it had stepped placidly over me. I really was learning to shoot, but I could not hit anything yet, not even tin cans on fence posts.

7  Alive, the foxes inhabited a world my father made for them. It was surrounded by a high guard fence, like a medieval town, with a gate that was padlocked at night. Along the streets of this town were ranged large, sturdy pens. Each of them had a real door that a man could go through, a wooden ramp along the wire, for the foxes to run up and down on, and a kennel — something like a clothes chest with airholes — where they slept in winter and had their young. There were feeding and watering dishes attached to the wire in such a way that they could be emptied and cleaned from the outside. The dishes were made of old tin cans, and the ramps and kennels of odds and ends of old lumber. Everything was tidy and ingenious; my father was tirelessly inventive and his favorite book in the world was Robinson Crusoe.[3] He had fitted a tin drum on a wheelbarrow, for bringing water down to the pens. This was my job in summer, when the foxes had to have water twice a day. Between nine and ten o'clock in the morning, and again after supper, I filled the drum at the pump and trundled it down through the barnyard to the pens, where I parked it, and filled my watering can and went along the streets. Laird came too, with his little cream and green gardening can, filled too full and knocking against his legs and slopping water on his canvas shoes. I

---

2. Irish Protestant association named after William of Orange, who later became William III ("King Billy") of England, defeating the Catholic James II. The society holds annual parades on July 12 to commemorate the Battle of the Boyne in 1690, in which James II's army was defeated.
3. Daniel Defoe's novel (1719) about a shipwrecked sailor who survives on a desert island through his ability to improvise and devise ingenious contraptions.

had the real watering can, my father's, though I could only carry it three-quarters full.

8   The foxes all had names, which were printed on a tin plate and hung beside their doors. They were not named when they were born, but when they survived the first year's pelting and were added to the breeding stock. Those my father had named were called names like Prince, Bob, Wally and Betty. Those I had named were called Star or Turk, or Maureen or Diana. Laird named one Maud after a hired girl we had when he was little, one Harold after a boy at school, and one Mexico, he did not say why.

9   Naming them did not make pets out of them, or anything like it. Nobody but my father ever went into the pens, and he had twice had blood-poisoning bites. When I was bringing them their water they prowled up and down on the paths they had made inside their pens, barking seldom — they saved that for nighttime, when they might get up a chorus of community frenzy — but always watching me, their eyes burning, clear gold, in their pointed, malevolent faces. They were beautiful for their delicate legs and heavy, aristocratic tails and the bright fur sprinkled on dark down their backs — which gave them their name — but especially for their faces, drawn exquisitely sharp in pure hostility, and their golden eyes.

10  Besides carrying water I helped my father when he cut the long grass, and the lamb's quarter and flowering money-musk that grew between the pens. He cut with the scythe and I raked into piles. Then he took a pitchfork and threw fresh-cut grass all over the top of the pens, to keep the foxes cooler and shade their coats, which were browned by too much sun. My father did not talk to me unless it was about the job we were doing. In this he was quite different from my mother, who, if she was feeling cheerful, would tell me all sorts of things — the name of a dog she had had when she was a little girl, the names of boys she had gone out with later on when she was grown up, and what certain dresses of hers had looked like — she could not imagine now what had become of them. Whatever thoughts and stories my father had were private, and I was shy of him and would never ask him questions. Nevertheless I worked willingly under his eyes, and with a feeling of pride. One time a feed salesman came down into the pens to talk to him and my father said, "Like to have you meet my new hired man." I turned away and raked furiously, red in the face with pleasure.

11  "Could of fooled me," said the salesman. "I thought it was only a girl."

12  After the grass was cut, it seemed suddenly much later in the year. I walked on stubble in the earlier evening, aware of the reddening skies, the entering silences, of fall. When I wheeled the tank out of the gate and put the padlock on, it was almost dark. One night at this time I saw my mother and father standing talking on the little rise of ground we called the gangway, in front of the barn. My father had just

come from the meathouse; he had his stiff bloody apron on, and a pail of cut-up meat in his hand.

13   It was an odd thing to see my mother down at the barn. She did not often come out of the house unless it was to do something — hang out the wash or dig potatoes in the garden. She looked out of place, with her bare lumpy legs, not touched by the sun, her apron still on and damp across the stomach from the supper dishes. Her hair was tied up in a kerchief, wisps of it falling out. She would tie her hair up like this in the morning, saying she did not have time to do it properly, and it would stay tied up all day. It was true, too; she really did not have time. These days our back porch was piled with baskets of peaches and grapes and pears, bought in town, and onions and tomatoes and cucumbers grown at home, all waiting to be made into jelly and jam preserves, pickles and chili sauce. In the kitchen there was a fire in the stove all day, jars clinked in boiling water, sometimes a cheesecloth bag was strung on a pole between two chairs straining blue-black grape pulp for jelly. I was given jobs to do and I would sit at the table peeling peaches that had been soaked in the hot water, or cutting up onions, my eyes smarting and streaming. As soon as I was done I ran out of the house, trying to get out of earshot before my mother thought of what she wanted me to do next. I hated the hot dark kitchen in the summer, the green blinds and the flypapers, the same old oilcloth table and wavy mirror and bumpy linoleum. My mother was too tired and preoccupied to talk to me, she had no heart to tell about the Normal School Graduation Dance; sweat trickled over her face and she was always counting under her breath, pointing at jars, dumping cups of sugar. It seemed to me that work in the house was endless, dreary and peculiarly depressing; work done out of doors, and in my father's service, was ritualistically important.

14   I wheeled the tank up to the barn, where it was kept, and I heard my mother saying, "Wait till Laird gets a little bigger, then you'll have a real help."

15   What my father said I did not hear. I was pleased by the way he stood listening, politely as he would to a salesman or a stranger, but with an air of wanting to get on with his real work. I felt my mother had no business down here and I wanted him to feel the same way. What did she mean about Laird? He was no help to anybody. Where was he now? Swinging himself sick on the swing, going around in circles, or trying to catch caterpillars. He never once stayed with me till I was finished.

16   "And then I can use her more in the house," I heard my mother say. She had a dead-quiet, regretful way of talking about me that always made me uneasy. "I just get my back turned and she runs off. It's not like I had a girl in the family at all."

17   I went and sat on a feed bag in the corner of the barn, not wanting to appear when this conversation was going on. My mother, I felt, was not to be trusted. She was kinder than my father and more easily

fooled, but you could not depend on her, and the real reasons for the things she said and did were not to be known. She loved me, and she sat up late at night making a dress of the difficult style I wanted, for me to wear when school started, but she was also my enemy. She was always plotting. She was plotting now to get me to stay in the house more, although she knew I hated it (*because* she knew I hated it) and keep me from working for my father. It seemed to me she would do this simply out of perversity, and to try her power. It did not occur to me that she could be lonely, or jealous. No grown-up could be; they were too fortunate. I sat and kicked my heels monotonously against a feed bag, raising dust, and did not come out till she was gone.

18   At any rate, I did not expect my father to pay any attention to what she said. Who could imagine Laird doing my work — Laird remembering the padlock and cleaning out the watering dishes with a leaf on the end of a stick, or even wheeling the tank without tumbling over? It showed how little my mother knew about the way things really were.

19   I have forgotten to say what the foxes were fed. My father's bloody apron reminded me. They were fed horsemeat. At this time most farmers still kept horses, and when a horse got too old to work, or broke a leg or got down and would not get up, as they sometimes did, the owner would call my father, and he and Henry went out to the farm in the truck. Usually they shot and butchered the horse there, paying the farmer from five to twelve dollars. If they had already too much meat on hand, they would bring the horse back alive, and keep it for a few days or weeks in our stable, until the meat was needed. After the war the farmers were buying tractors and gradually getting rid of horses altogether, so it sometimes happened that we got a good healthy horse, that there was just no use for any more. If this happened in the winter we might keep the horse in our stable till spring, for we had plenty of hay and if there was a lot of snow — and the plow did not always get our road cleared — it was convenient to be able to go to town with a horse and cutter.[4]

20   The winter I was eleven years old we had two horses in the stable. We did not know what names they had had before, so we called them Mack and Flora. Mack was an old black workhorse, sooty and indifferent. Flora was a sorrel mare, a driver. We took them both out in the cutter. Mack was slow and easy to handle. Flora was given to fits of violent alarm, veering at cars and even at other horses, but we loved her speed and high-stepping, her general air of gallantry and abandon. On Saturdays we went down to the stable and as soon as we opened the door on its cosy, animal-smelling darkness Flora threw up her head, rolled her eyes, whinnied despairingly and pulled herself

---

4. Light, horse-drawn sleigh.

through a crisis of nerves on the spot. It was not safe to go into her stall; she would kick.

21 This winter also I began to hear a great deal more on the theme my mother had sounded when she had been talking in front of the barn. I no longer felt safe. It seemed that in the minds of the people around me there was a steady undercurrent of thought, not to be deflected, on this one subject. The word *girl* had formerly seemed to me innocent and unburdened, like the word *child*; now it appeared that it was no such thing. A girl was not, as I had supposed, simply what I was; it was what I had to become. It was a definition, always touched with emphasis, with reproach and disappointment. Also it was a joke on me. Once Laird and I were fighting, and for the first time ever I had to use all my strength against him: even so, he caught and pinned my arm for a moment, really hurting me. Henry saw this, and laughed, saying, "Oh, that there Laird's gonna show you, one of these days!" Laird was getting a lot bigger. But I was getting bigger too.

22 My grandmother came to stay with us for a few weeks and I heard other things. "Girls don't slam doors like that." "Girls keep their knees together when they sit down." And worse still, when I asked some questions, "That's none of girls' business." I continued to slam the doors and sit as awkwardly as possible, thinking that by such measures I kept myself free.

23 When spring came, the horses were let out in the barnyard. Mack stood against the barn wall trying to scratch his neck and haunches, but Flora trotted up and down and reared at fences, clattering her hooves against the rails. Snow drifts dwindled quickly, revealing the hard gray and brown earth, the familiar rise and fall of the ground, plain and bare after the fantastic landscape of winter. There was a great feeling of opening-out, of release. We just wore rubbers now, over our shoes; our feet felt ridiculously light. One Saturday we went out to the stable and found all the doors open, letting in the unaccustomed sunlight and fresh air. Henry was there, just idling around looking at his collection of calendars which were tacked up behind the stalls in a part of the stable my mother had probably never seen.

24 "Come to say goodbye to your old friend Mack?" Henry said. "Here, you give him a taste of oats." He poured some oats into Laird's cupped hands and Laird went to feed Mack. Mack's teeth were in bad shape. He ate very slowly, patiently shifting the oats around in his mouth, trying to find a stump of a molar to grind it on. "Poor old Mack," said Henry mournfully. "When a horse's teeth's gone, he's gone. That's about the way."

25 "Are you going to shoot him today?" I said. Mack and Flora had been in the stable so long I had almost forgotten they were going to be shot.

26 Henry didn't answer me. Instead he started to sing in a high, trembly, mocking-sorrowful voice. *Oh, there's no more work, for poor Uncle*

*Ned, he's gone where the good darkies go.*[5] Mack's thick, blackish tongue worked diligently at Laird's hand. I went out before the song was ended and sat down on the gangway.

27   I had never seen them shoot a horse, but I knew where it was done. Last summer Laird and I had come upon a horse's entrails before they were buried. We had thought it was a big black snake, coiled up in the sun. That was around the field that ran up beside the barn. I thought that if we went inside the barn, and found a side crack or a knothole to look through, we would be able to see them do it. It was not something I wanted to see: just the same, if a thing really happened, it was better to see it, and know.

28   My father came down from the house, carrying the gun.
29   "What are you doing here?" he said.
30   "Nothing."
31   "Go on up and play around the house."
32   He sent Laird out of the stable. I said to Laird, "Do you want to see them shoot Mack?" and without waiting for an answer led him around to the front door of the barn, opened it carefully, and went in. "Be quiet or they'll hear us," I said. We could hear Henry and my father talking in the stable, then the heavy, shuffling steps of Mack being backed out of his stall.

33   In the loft it was cold and dark. Thin, crisscrossed beams of sunlight fell through the cracks. The hay was low. It was a rolling country, hills and hollows, slipping under our feet. About four feet up was a beam going around the walls. We piled hay up in one corner and I boosted Laird up and hoisted myself. The beam was not very wide; we crept along it with our hands flat on the barn walls. There were plenty of knotholes, and I found one that gave me the view I wanted — a corner of the barnyard, the gate, part of the field. Laird did not have a knothole and began to complain.

34   I showed him a widened crack between two boards. "Be quiet and wait. If they hear you you'll get us into trouble."

35   My father came in sight carrying the gun. Henry was leading Mack by the halter. He dropped it and took out his cigarette paper and tobacco; he rolled cigarettes for my father and himself. While this was going on Mack nosed around in the old, dead grass along the fence. Then my father opened the gate and they took Mack through. Henry led Mack away from the path to a patch of ground and they talked together, not loud enough for us to hear. Mack again began searching for a mouthful of fresh grass, which was not to be found. My father walked away in a straight line, and stopped short at a distance which seemed to suit him. Henry was walking away from Mack too, but sideways, still negligently holding on to the halter. My father raised

---

5. Lines from "Old Uncle Ned" by American popular songwriter Stephen Foster (1826–1864).

the gun and Mack looked up as if he had noticed something and my father shot him.

36  Mack did not collapse at once but swayed, lurched sideways and fell, first on his side: then he rolled over on his back and, amazingly, kicked his legs for a few seconds in the air. At this Henry laughed, as if Mack had done a trick for him. Laird, who had drawn a long, groaning breath of surprise when the shot was fired, said out loud, "He's not dead." And it seemed to me it might be true. But his legs stopped, he rolled on his side again, his muscles quivered and sank. The two men walked over and looked at him in a businesslike away; they bent down and examined his forehead where the bullet had gone in, and now I saw his blood on the brown grass.

37  "Now they just skin him and cut him up," I said. "Let's go." My [scared?] legs were a little shaky and I jumped gratefully down into the hay. "Now you've seen how they shoot a horse," I said in a congratulatory way, as if I had seen it many times before. "Let's see if any barn cat's had kittens in the hay." Laird jumped. He seemed young and obedient again. Suddenly I remembered how, when he was little, I had brought him into the barn and told him to climb the ladder to the top beam. That was in the spring, too, when the hay was low. I had done it out of a need for excitement, a desire for something to happen so that I could tell about it. He was wearing a little bulky brown and white checked coat, made down from one of mine. He went all the way up just as I told him, and sat down on the top beam with all the hay far below him on one side, and the barn floor and some old machinery on the other. Then I ran screaming to my father. "Laird's up on the top beam!" My father came, my mother came, my father went up the ladder talking very quietly and brought Laird down under his arm, at which my mother leaned against the ladder and began to cry. They said to me, "Why weren't you watching him?" but nobody ever knew the truth. Laird did not know enough to tell. But whenever I saw the brown and white checked coat hanging in the closet, or at the bottom of the rag bag, which was where it ended up, I felt a weight in my stomach, the sadness of unexorcised guilt.

38  I looked at Laird, who did not even remember this, and I did not like the look on his thin, winter-pale face. His expression was not frightened or upset, but remote, concentrating. "Listen," I said, in an unusually bright and friendly voice, "you aren't going to tell, are you?"

39  "No," he said absently.

40  "Promise."

41  "Promise," he said. I grabbed the hand behind his back to make sure he was not crossing his fingers. Even so, he might have a nightmare; it might come out that way. I decided I had better work hard to get all thoughts of what he had seen out of his mind — which, it seemed to me, could not hold very many things at a time. I got some money I had saved and that afternoon we went into Jubilee and saw

a show, with Judy Canova,⁶ at which we both laughed a great deal. After that I thought it would be all right.

42   Two weeks later I knew they were going to shoot Flora. I knew from the night before, when I heard my mother ask if the hay was holding out all right, and my father said, "Well, after tomorrow there'll just be the cow, and we should be able to put her out to grass in another week." So I knew it was Flora's turn in the morning.

43   This time I didn't think of watching it. That was something to see just one time. I had not thought about it very often since, but sometimes when I was busy, working at school, or standing in front of the mirror combing my hair and wondering if I would be pretty when I grew up, the whole scene would flash into my mind: I would see the easy, practised way my father raised the gun, and hear Henry laughing when Mack kicked his legs in the air. I did not have any great feeling of horror and opposition, such as a city child might have had; I was too used to seeing the death of animals as a necessity by which we lived. Yet I felt a little ashamed, and there was a new wariness, a sense of holding-off, in my attitude to my father and his work.

44   It was a fine day, and we were going around the yard picking up tree branches that had been torn off in winter storms. This was something we had been told to do, and also we wanted to use them as a teepee. We heard Flora whinny, and then my father's voice and Henry's shouting and we ran down to the barnyard to see what was going on.

45   The stable door was open. Henry had just brought Flora out, and she had broken away from him. She was running free in the barnyard, from one end to the other. We climbed up on the fence. It was exciting to see her running, whinnying, going up on her hind legs, prancing and threatening like a horse in a Western movie, an unbroken ranch horse, though she was just an old driver, an old sorrel mare. My father and Henry ran after her and tried to grab the dangling halter. They tried to work her into a corner, and they had almost succeeded when she made a run between them, wild-eyed, and disappeared around the corner of the barn. We heard the rails clatter down as she got over the fence, and Henry yelled, "She's into the field now!"

46   That meant she was in the long L-shaped field that ran up by the house. If she got around the center, heading towards the lane, the gate was open; the truck had been driven into the field this morning. My father shouted to me, because I was on the other side of the fence, nearest to the lane, "Go shut the gate!"

47   I could run very fast. I ran across the garden, past the tree where our swing was hung, and jumped across a ditch into the lane. There was the open gate. She had not got out, I could not see her up on the road; she must have run to the other end of the field. The gate was heavy. I lifted it out of the gravel and carried it across the roadway. I

---

6. American comedian known for her yodelling in "hillbilly" movies of the 1940s.

had it halfway across when she came in sight, galloping straight towards me. There was just time to get the chain on. Laird came scrambling through the ditch to help me.

48  Instead of shutting the gate, I opened it as wide as I could. I did not make any decision to do this, it was just what I did. Flora never slowed down: she galloped straight past me, and Laird jumped up and down, yelling, "Shut it, shut it!" even after it was too late. My father and Henry appeared in the field a moment too late to see what I had done. They only saw Flora heading for the township road. They would think I had not got there in time.

49  They did not waste any time asking about it. They went back to the barn and got the gun and the knives they used, and put these in the truck; then they turned the truck around and came bouncing up the field toward us. Laird called to them, "Let me go too, let me go too!" and Henry stopped the truck and they took him in. I shut the gate after they were all gone.

50  I supposed Laird would tell. I wondered what would happen to me. I had never disobeyed my father before, and I could not understand why I had done it. Flora would not really get away. They would catch up with her in the truck. Or if they did not catch her this morning somebody would see her and telephone us this afternoon or tomorrow. There was no wild country here for her to run to, only farms. What was more, my father had paid for her, we needed the meat to feed the foxes, we needed the foxes to make our living. All I had done was make more work for my father who worked hard enough already. And when my father found out about it he was not going to trust me any more; he would know that I was not entirely on his side. I was on Flora's side, and that made me no use to anybody, not even to her. Just the same, I did not regret it; when she came running at me and I held the gate open, that was the only thing I could do.

51  I went back to the house, and my mother said, "What's all the commotion?" I told her that Flora kicked down the fence and got away. "Your poor father," she said, "now he'll have to go chasing over the countryside. Well, there isn't any use planning dinner before one." She put up the ironing board. I wanted to tell her, but thought better of it and went upstairs and sat on my bed.

52  Lately I had been trying to make my part of the room fancy, spreading the bed with old lace curtains, and fixing myself a dressing table with some leftovers of cretonne for a skirt. I planned to put up some kind of barricade between my bed and Laird's, to keep my section separate from his. In the sunlight, the lace curtains were just dusty rags. We did not sing at night any more. One night when I was singing Laird said, "You sound silly," and I went right on but the next night I did not start. There was not so much need to anyway, we were no longer afraid. We knew it was just old furniture over there, old jumble and confusion. We did not keep to the rules. I still stayed awake after Laird was asleep and told myself stories, but even in these stories

something different was happening, mysterious alterations took place. A story might start off in the old way, with a spectacular danger, a fire or wild animals, and for a while I might rescue people; then things would change around, and instead, somebody would be rescuing me. It might be a boy from our class at school, or even Mr. Campbell, our teacher, who tickled girls under the arms. And at this point the story concerned itself at great length with what I looked like — how long my hair was, and what kind of dress I had on; by the time I had these details worked out the real excitement of the story was lost.

53  It was later than one o'clock when the truck came back. The tarpaulin was over the back, which meant there was meat in it. My mother had to heat dinner all over again. Henry and my father had changed from their bloody overalls into ordinary working overalls in the barn, and they washed their arms and necks and faces at the sink, and splashed water on their hair and combed it. Laird lifted his arm to show off a streak of blood. "We shot Flora," he said, "and cut her up in fifty pieces."

54  "Well I don't want to hear about it," my mother said. "And don't come to my table like that."

55  My father made him go and wash the blood off.

56  We sat down and my father said grace and Henry pasted his chewing gum on the end of his fork, the way he always did; when he took it off he would have us admire the pattern. We began to pass the bowls of steaming, overcooked vegetables. Laird looked across the table at me and said proudly, distinctly, "Anyway it was her fault Flora got away."

57  "What?" my father said.

58  "She could of shut the gate and she didn't. She just open' it up and Flora run out."

59  "Is that right?" my father said.

60  Everybody at the table was looking at me. I nodded, swallowing food with great difficulty. To my shame, tears flooded my eyes.

61  My father made a curt sound of disgust. "What did you do that for?"

62  I did not answer. I put down my fork and waited to be sent from the table, still not looking up.

63  But this did not happen. For some time nobody said anything, then Laird said matter-of-factly, "She's crying."

64  "Never mind," my father said. He spoke with resignation, even good humour, the words which absolved and dismissed me for good. "She's only a girl," he said.

65  I didn't protest that, even in my heart. Maybe it was true.

(1968)

# Alistair MacLeod (b. 1936)

Raised on the Prairies and in Nova Scotia, MacLeod teaches English and creative writing at the University of Windsor. He has published two volumes of short stories, The Lost Salt Gift of Blood (1976) and As Birds Bring Forth the Sun (1986), and a novel, No Great Mischief (1999).

## The Boat

1. There are times even now, when I awake at four o'clock in the morning with the terrible fear that I have overslept; when I imagine that my father is waiting for me in the room below the darkened stairs or that the shorebound men are tossing pebbles against my window while blowing their hands and stomping their feet impatiently on the frozen steadfast earth. There are times when I am half out of bed and fumbling for socks and mumbling for words before I realize that I am foolishly alone, that no one waits at the base of the stairs and no boat rides restlessly in the waters by the pier.

2. At such times only the grey corpses on the overflowing ashtray beside my bed bear witness to the extinction of the latest spark and silently await the crushing out of the most recent of their fellows. And then because I am afraid to be alone with death, I dress rapidly, make a great to-do about clearing my throat, turn on both faucets in the sink and proceed to make loud splashing ineffectual noises. Later I go out and walk the mile to the all-night restaurant.

3. In the winter it is a very cold walk and there are often tears in my eyes when I arrive. The waitress usually gives a sympathetic little shiver and says, "Boy, it must be really cold out there; you got tears in your eyes."

4. "Yes," I say, "it sure is; it really is."

5. And then the three or four of us who are always in such places at such times make uninteresting little protective chit-chat until the dawn reluctantly arrives. Then I swallow the coffee which is always bitter and leave with a great busy rush because by that time I have to worry about being late and whether I have a clean shirt and whether my car will start and about all the other countless things one must worry about when he teaches at a great Midwestern university. And I know then that that day will go by as have all the days of the past ten

years, for the call and the voices and the shapes and the boat were not really there in the early morning's darkness and I have all kinds of comforting reality to prove it. They are only shadows and echoes, the animals a child's hands make on the wall by lamplight, and the voices from the rain barrel; the cuttings from an old movie made in the black and white of long ago.

6   I first became conscious of the boat in the same way and at almost the same time that I became aware of the people it supported. My earliest recollection of my father is a view from the floor of gigantic rubber boots and then of being suddenly elevated and having my face pressed against the stubble of his cheek, and of how it tasted of salt and of how he smelled of salt from his red-soled rubber boots to the shaggy whiteness of his hair.

7   When I was very small, he took me for my first ride in the boat. I rode the half-mile from our house to the wharf on his shoulders and I remember the sound of his rubber boots galumphing along the gravel beach, the tune of the indecent little song he used to sing, and the odour of the salt.

8   The floor of the boat was permeated with the same odour and in its constancy I was not aware of change. In the harbour we made our little circle and returned. He tied the boat by its painter, fastened the stern to its permanent anchor and lifted me high over his head to the solidity of the wharf. Then he climbed up the little iron ladder that led to the wharf's cap, placed me once more upon his shoulders and galumphed off again.

9   When we returned to the house everyone made a great fuss over my precocious excursion and asked, "How did you like the boat?" "Were you afraid in the boat?" "Did you cry in the boat?" They repeated "the boat" at the end of all their questions and I knew it must be very important to everyone.

10   My earliest recollection of my mother is of being alone with her in the mornings while my father was away in the boat. She seemed to be always repairing clothes that were "torn in the boat," preparing food "to be eaten in the boat" or looking for "the boat" through our kitchen window which faced upon the sea. When my father returned about noon, she would ask, "Well, how did things go in the boat today?" It was the first question I remember asking: "Well, how did things go in the boat today?" "Well, how did things go in the boat today?"

11   The boat in our lives was registered at Pork Hawkesbury. She was what Nova Scotians called a Cape Island boat and was designed for the small inshore fishermen who sought the lobsters of the spring and mackerel of summer and later the cod and haddock and hake. She was thirty-two feet long and nine wide, and was powered by an engine from a Chevrolet truck. She had a marine clutch and a high speed reverse gear and was painted light green with the name *Jenny Lynn* stencilled in black letters on her bow and painted on an oblong plate across her stern. Jenny Lynn had been my mother's maiden name and

the boat was called after her as another link in the chain of tradition. Most of the boats that berthed at the wharf bore the names of some female member of their owner's household.

12  I say this now as if I knew it all then. All at once, all about the boat dimensions and engines, and as if on the day of my first childish voyage I noticed the difference between a stencilled name and a painted name. But of course it was not that way at all, for I learned it all very slowly and there was not time enough.

13  I learned first about our house which was one of about fifty which marched around the horseshoe of our harbour and the wharf which was its heart. Some of them were so close to the water that during a storm the sea spray splashed against their windows while others were built farther along the beach as was the case with ours. The houses and their people, like those of the neighbouring towns and villages, were the result of Ireland's discontent and Scotland's Highland Clearances[1] and America's War of Independence. Impulsive emotional Catholic Celts who could not bear to live with England and shrewd determined Protestant Puritans who, in the years after 1776, could not bear to live without.

14  The most important room in our house was one of those oblong old-fashioned kitchens heated by a wood- and coal-burning stove. Behind the stove was a box of kindlings and beside it a coal scuttle. A heavy wooden table with leaves that expanded or reduced its dimensions stood in the middle of the floor. There were five wooden home-made chairs which had been chipped and hacked by a variety of knives. Against the east wall, opposite the stove, there was a couch which sagged in the middle and had a cushion for a pillow, and above it a shelf which contained matches, tobacco, pencils, odd fish-hooks, bits of twine, and a tin can filled with bills and receipts. The south wall was dominated by a window which faced the sea and on the north there was a five-foot board which bore a variety of clothes hooks and the burdens of each. Beneath the board there was a jumble of odd footwear, mostly of rubber. There was also, on this wall, a barometer, a map of the marine area and a shelf which held a tiny radio. The kitchen was shared by all of us and was a buffer zone between the immaculate order of ten other rooms and the disruptive chaos of the single room that was my father's.

15  My mother ran her house as her brothers ran their boats. Everything was clean and spotless and in order. She was tall and dark and powerfully energetic. In later years she reminded me of the women of Thomas Hardy, particularly Eustacia Vye,[2] in a physical way. She fed and clothed a family of seven children, making all of the meals and

---

1. In the early nineteenth century, Scottish landlords evicted tenant farmers to make way for sheep.
2. A character in Thomas Hardy's *The Return of the Native* (1878).

*[margin note: admiration?]*

most of the clothes. She grew miraculous gardens and magnificent flowers and raised broods of hens and ducks. She would walk miles on berry-picking expeditions and hoist her skirts to dig for clams when the tide was low. She was fourteen years younger than my father, whom she had married when she was twenty-six and had been a local beauty for a period of ten years. My mother was of the sea as were all of her people, and her horizons were the very literal ones she scanned with her dark and fearless eyes.

16   Between the kitchen clothes rack and barometer, a door opened into my father's bedroom. It was a room of disorder and disarray. It was as if the wind which so often clamoured about the house succeeded in entering this single room and after whipping it into turmoil stole quietly away to renew its knowing laughter from without.

17   My father's bed was against the south wall. It always looked rumpled and unmade because he lay on top of it more than he slept within any folds it might have had. Beside it, there was a little brown table. An archaic goose-necked reading light, a battered table radio, a mound of wooden matches, one or two packages of tobacco, a deck of cigarette papers and an overflowing ashtray cluttered its surface. The brown larvae of tobacco shreds and the grey flecks of ash covered both the table and the floor beneath it. The once-varnished surface of the table was disfigured by numerous black scars and gashes inflicted by the neglected burning cigarettes of many years. They had tumbled from the ashtray unnoticed and branded their statements permanently and quietly into the wood until the odour of their burning caused the snuffing out of their lives. At the bed's foot there was a single window which looked upon the sea.

18   Against the adjacent wall there was a battered bureau and beside it there was a closet which held his single ill-fitting serge suit, the two or three white shirts that strangled him and the square black shoes that pinched. When he took off his more friendly clothes, the heavy woollen sweaters, mitts and socks which my mother knitted for him and the woollen and doeskin shirts, he dumped them unceremoniously on a single chair. If a visitor entered the room while he was lying on the bed, he would be told to throw the clothes on the floor and take their place upon the chair.

19   Magazines and books covered the battered bureau and competed with the clothes for domination of the chair. They further overburdened the heroic little table and lay on top of the radio. They filled a baffling and unknowable cave beneath the bed, and in the corner by the bureau they spilled from the walls and grew up from the floor.

20   The magazines were the most conventional: *Time, Newsweek, Life, Maclean's, Family Herald, Reader's Digest*. They were the result of various cut-rate subscriptions or the gift subscriptions associated with Christmas, "the two whole years for only $3.50."

21   The books were more varied. There were a few hard-cover magnificents and bygone Book-of-the-Month wonders and some were

Christmas or birthday gifts. The majority of them, however, were used paperbacks which came from those second-hand bookstores which advertise in the backs of magazines: "Miscellaneous Used Paperbacks 10¢ Each." At first he sent for them himself, although my mother resented the expense, but in later years they came more and more often from my sisters who had moved to the cities. Especially at first they were very weird and varied. Mickey Spillane and Ernest Haycox[3] vied with Dostoyevsky and Faulkner, and the Penguin Poets edition of Gerard Manley Hopkins[4] arrived in the same box as a little book on sex technique called *Getting the Most Out of Love*. The former had been assiduously annotated by a very fine hand using a very blue-inked fountain pen while the latter had been studied by someone with very large thumbs, the prints of which were still visible in the margins. At the slightest provocation it would open almost automatically to particularly graphic and well-smudged pages.

22   When he was not in the boat, my father spent most of his time lying on the bed in his socks, the top two buttons of his trousers undone, his discarded shirt on the ever-ready chair and the sleeves of the woollen Stanfield underwear, which he wore both summer and winter, drawn half way up to his elbows. The pillows propped up the whiteness of his head and the goose-necked lamp illuminated the pages in his hands. The cigarettes smoked and smouldered on the ashtray and on the table and the radio played constantly, sometimes low and sometimes loud. At midnight and at one, two, three and four, one could sometimes hear the radio, his occasional cough, the rustling thud of a completed book being tossed to the corner heap, or the movement necessitated by his sitting on the edge of the bed to roll the thousandth cigarette. He seemed never to sleep, only to doze, and the light shone constantly from his window to the sea.

23   My mother despised the room and all it stood for and she had stopped sleeping in it after I was born. She despised disorder in rooms and in houses and in hours and in lives, and she had not read a book since high school. There she had read *Ivanhoe*[5] and considered it a colossal waste of time. Still the room remained, like a solid rock of opposition in the sparkling waters of a clear deep harbour, opening off the kitchen where we really lived our lives, with its door always open and its contents visible to all.

24   The daughters of the room and of the house were very beautiful. They were tall and willowy like my mother and had her fine facial features set off by the reddish copper-coloured hair that had apparently once been my father's before it turned to white. All of them were very

---

3. Popular pulp fiction authors. Mickey Spillane wrote lurid and violent crime novels; Ernest Haycox wrote Western adventure stories.
4. (1844–1889), a poet and Jesuit priest.
5. 1820 novel by Sir Walter Scott (1772–1832).

clever in school and helped my mother a great deal about the house. When they were young they sang and were very happy and very nice to me because I was the youngest and the family's only boy.

25  My father never approved of their playing about the wharf like the other children, and they went there only when my mother sent them on an errand. At such times they almost always overstayed, playing screaming games of tag or hide-and-seek in and about the fishing shanties, the piled traps and tubs of trawl, shouting down to the perch that swam languidly about the wharf's algae-covered piles, or jumping in and out of the boats that tugged gently at their lines. My mother was never uneasy about them at such times, and when her husband criticized her she would say, "Nothing will happen to them there," or "They could be doing worse things in worse places."

26  By about the ninth or tenth grade my sisters one by one discovered my father's bedroom and then the change would begin. Each would go into the room one morning when he was out. She would go with the ideal hope of imposing order or with the more practical objective of emptying the ashtray, and later she would be found spellbound by the volume in her hand. My mother's reaction was always abrupt, bordering on the angry. "Take your nose out of that trash and come and do your work," she would say, and once I saw her slap my youngest sister so hard that the print of her hand was scarletly emblazoned upon her daughter's cheek while the broken-spined paperback fluttered uselessly to the floor.

27  Thereafter my mother would launch a campaign against what she had discovered but could not understand. At times although she was not overly religious she would bring in God to bolster her arguments, saying, "In the next world God will see to those who waste their lives reading useless books when they should be about their work." Or without theological aid, "I would like to know how books help anyone to live a life." If my father were in, she would repeat the remarks louder than necessary, and her voice would carry into his room where he lay upon his bed. His usual reaction was to turn up the volume of the radio, although that action in itself betrayed the success of the initial thrust.

28  Shortly after my sisters began to read the books, they grew restless and lost interest in darning socks and baking bread, and all of them eventually went to work as summer waitresses in the Sea Food Restaurant. The restaurant was run by a big American concern from Boston and catered to the tourists that flooded the area during July and August. My mother despised the whole operation. She said the restaurant was not run by "our people," and "our people" did not eat there, and that it was run by outsiders for outsiders.

29  "Who are these people anyway?" she would ask, tossing back her dark hair, "and what do they, though they go about with their cameras for a hundred years, know about the way it is here, and what do they care about me and mine, and why should I care about them?"

30  She was angry that my sisters should even conceive of working in such a place and more angry when my father made no move to prevent it, and she was worried about herself and about her family and about her life. Sometimes she would say softly to her sisters, "I don't know what's the matter with my girls. It seems none of them are interested in any of the right things." And sometimes there would be bitter savage arguments. One afternoon I was coming in with three mackerel I'd been given at the wharf when I heard her say, "Well I hope you'll be satisfied when they come home knocked up and you'll have had your way."

31  It was the most savage thing I'd ever heard my mother say. Not just the words but the way she said them, and I stood there in the porch afraid to breathe for what seemed like the years from ten to fifteen, feeling the damp moist mackerel with their silver glassy eyes growing clammy against my leg.

32  Through the angle in the screen door I saw my father who had been walking into his room wheel around on one of his rubber-booted heels and look at her with his blue eyes flashing like clearest ice beneath the snow that was his hair. His usually ruddy face was drawn and grey, reflecting the exhaustion of a man of sixty-five who had been working in those rubber boots for eleven hours on an August day, and for a fleeting moment I wondered what I would do if he killed my mother while I stood there in the porch with those three foolish mackerel in my hand. Then he turned and went into his room and the radio blared forth the next day's weather forecast and I retreated under the noise and returned again, stamping my feet and slamming the door too loudly to signal my approach. My mother was busy at the stove when I came in, and did not raise her head when I threw the mackerel in a pan. As I looked into my father's room, I said, "Well, how did things go in the boat today?" and he replied, "Oh not too badly, all things considered." He was lying on his back and lighting the first cigarette and the radio was talking about the Virginia coast.

33  All of my sisters made good money on tips. They bought my father an electric razor which he tried to use for a while and they took out even more magazine subscriptions. They bought my mother a great many clothes of the type she was very fond of, the wide-brimmed hats and the brocaded dresses, but she locked them all in trunks and refused to wear any of them.

34  On one August day my sisters prevailed upon my father to take some of their restaurant customers for an afternoon ride in the boat. The tourists with their expensive clothes and cameras and sun glasses awkwardly backed down the iron ladder at the wharf's side to where my father waited below, holding the rocking *Jenny Lynn* in snug against the wharf with one hand on the iron ladder and steadying his descending passengers with the other. They tried to look both prim and wind-blown like the girls in the Pepsi-Cola ads and did the best they could, sitting on the thwarts where the newspapers were spread

to cover the splattered blood and fish entrails, crowding to one side so that they were in danger of capsizing the boat, taking the inevitable pictures or merely trailing their fingers through the water of their dreams.

35   All of them liked my father very much and, after he'd brought them back from their circles in the harbour, they invited him to their rented cabins which were located high on a hill overlooking the village to which they were so alien. He proceeded to get very drunk up there with the beautiful view and the strange company and the abundant liquor, and late in the afternoon he began to sing.

36   I was just approaching the wharf to deliver my mother's summons when he began, and the familiar yet unfamiliar voice that rolled down from the cabins made me feel as I had never felt before in my young life or perhaps as I had always felt without really knowing it, and I was ashamed yet proud, young yet old and saved yet forever lost, and there was nothing I could do to control my legs which trembled nor my eyes which wept for what they could not tell.

37   The tourists were equipped with tape recorders and my father sang for more than three hours. His voice boomed down the hill and bounced off the surface of the harbour, which was an unearthly blue on that hot August day, and was then reflected to the wharf and the fishing shanties where it was absorbed amidst the men who were baiting their lines for the next day's haul.

38   He sang all the old sea chanties which had come across from the old world and by which men like him had pulled ropes for generations, and he sang the East Coast sea songs which celebrated the sealing vessels of Northumberland Strait and the long liners of the Grand Banks, and of Anticosti, Sable Island, Grand Manan, Boston Harbor, Nantucket and Block Island. Gradually he shifted to the seemingly unending Gaelic drinking songs with their twenty or more verses and inevitable refrains, and the men in the shanties smiled at the coarseness of some of the verses and at the thought that the singer's immediate audience did not know what they were applauding nor recording to take back to staid old Boston. Later as the sun was setting he switched to the laments and the wild and haunting Gaelic war songs of those spattered Highland ancestors he had never seen, and when his voice ceased, the savage melancholy of three hundred years seemed to hang over the peaceful harbour and the quiet boats and the men leaning in the doorways of their shanties with their cigarettes glowing in the dusk and the women looking to the sea from their open windows with their children in their arms.

39   When he came home he threw the money he had earned on the kitchen table as he did with all his earnings but my mother refused to touch it and the next day he went with the rest of the men to bait his trawl in the shanties. The tourists came to the door that evening and my mother met them there and told them that her husband was not in although he was lying on the bed only a few feet away with the

radio playing and the cigarette upon his lips. She stood in the doorway until they reluctantly went away.

40   In the winter they sent him a picture which had been taken on the day of the singing. On the back it said, "To Our Ernest Hemingway" and the "Our" was underlined. There was also an accompanying letter telling how much they had enjoyed themselves, how popular the tape was proving and explaining who Ernest Hemingway was. In a way it almost did look like one of those unshaven, taken-in-Cuba pictures of Hemingway. He looked both massive and incongruous in the setting. His bulky fisherman's clothes were too big for the green and white lawn chair in which he sat, and his rubber boots seemed to take up all of the well-clipped grass square. The beach umbrella jarred with his sunburned face and because he had already been singing for some time, his lips which chapped in the winds of spring and burned in the water glare of summer had already cracked in several places, producing tiny flecks of blood at their corners and on the whiteness of his teeth. The bracelets of brass chain which he wore to protect his wrists from chafing seemed abnormally large and his broad leather belt had been slackened and his heavy shirt and underwear were open at the throat revealing an uncultivated wilderness of white chest hair bordering on the semicontrolled stubble of his neck and chin. His blue eyes had looked directly into the camera and his hair was whiter than the two tiny clouds which hung over his left shoulder. The sea was behind him and its immense blue flatness stretched out to touch the arching blueness of the sky. It seemed very far away from him or else he was so much in the foreground that he seemed too big for it.

41   Each year another of my sisters would read the books and work in the restaurant. Sometimes they would stay out quite late on the hot summer nights and when they came up the stairs my mother would ask them many long and involved questions which they resented and tried to avoid. Before ascending the stairs they would go into my father's room and those of us who waited above could hear them throwing his clothes off the chair before sitting on it or the squeak of the bed as they sat on its edge. Sometimes they would talk to him a long time, the murmur of their voices blending with the music of the radio into a mysterious vapour-like sound which floated softly up the stairs.

42   I say this again as if it all happened at once and as if all my sisters were of identical ages and like so many lemmings going into another sea and, again, it was of course not that way at all. Yet go they did, to Boston, to Montreal, to New York with the young men they met during the summers and later married in those far-away cities. The young men were very articulate and handsome and wore fine clothes and drove expensive cars and my sisters, as I said, were very tall and beautiful with their copper-coloured hair and were tired of darning socks and baking bread.

43   One by one they went. My mother had each of her daughters for fifteen years, then lost them for two and finally forever. None married

a fisherman. My mother never accepted any of the young men, for in her eyes they seemed always a combination of the lazy, the effeminate, the dishonest and the unknown. They never seemed to do any physical work and she could not comprehend their luxurious vacations and she did not know whence they came nor who they were. And in the end she did not really care, for they were not of her people and they were not of her sea.

I say this now with a sense of wonder at my own stupidity in thinking I was somehow free and would go on doing well in school and playing and helping in the boat and passing into my early teens while streaks of grey began to appear in my mother's dark hair and my father's rubber boots dragged sometimes on the pebbles of the beach as he trudged home from the wharf. And there were but three of us in the house that had at one time been so loud.

Then during the winter that I was fifteen he seemed to grow old and ill at once. Most of January he lay upon the bed, smoking and reading and listening to the radio while the wind howled about the house and the needle-like snow blistered off the ice-covered harbour and the doors flew out of people's hands if they did not cling to them like death.

In February when the men began overhauling their lobster traps he still did not move, and my mother and I began to knit lobster trap headings in the evenings. The twine was as always very sharp and harsh, and blisters formed upon our thumbs and little paths of blood snaked quietly down between our fingers while the seals that had drifted down from distant Labrador wept and moaned like human children on the ice-floes of the Gulf.

In the daytime my mother's brother who had been my father's partner as long as I could remember also came to work upon the gear. He was a year older than my mother and was tall and dark and the father of twelve children.

By March we were very far behind and although I began to work very hard in the evenings I knew it was not hard enough and that there were but eight weeks left before the opening of the season on May first. And I knew that my mother worried and that my uncle was uneasy and that all of our very lives depended on the boat being ready with her gear and two men, by the date of May the first. And I knew then that *David Copperfield* and *The Tempest* and all those friends I had dearly come to love must really go forever. So I bade them all good-bye.

The night after my first full day at home and after my mother had gone upstairs he called me into his room where I sat upon the chair beside his bed. "You will go back tomorrow," he said simply.

I refused then, saying I had made my decision and was satisfied.

"That is no way to make a decision," he said, "and if you are satisfied I am not. It is best that you go back." I was almost angry then and told him as all children do that I wished he would leave me alone and stop telling me what to do.

52     He looked at me a long time then, lying there on the same bed on which he had fathered me those sixteen years before, fathered me his only son, out of who knew what emotions when he was already fifty-six and his hair had turned to snow. Then he swung his legs over the edge of the squeaking bed and sat facing me and looked into my own dark eyes with his crystal blue and placed his hand upon my knee. "I am not telling you to do anything," he said softly, "only asking you."

53     The next morning I returned to school. As I left, my mother followed me to the porch and said, "I never thought a son of mine would choose useless books over the parents that gave him life."

54     In the weeks that followed he got up rather miraculously and the gear was ready and the *Jenny Lynn* was freshly painted by the last two weeks of April when the ice began to break up and the lonely screaming gulls returned to haunt the silver herring as they flashed within the sea.

55     On the first day of May the boats raced out as they had always done, laden down almost to the gunwales with their heavy cargoes of traps. They were almost like living things as they plunged through the waters of the spring and manoeuvred between the still floating icebergs of crystal white and emerald green on their way to the traditional grounds that they sought out every May. And those of us who sat that day in the high school on the hill, discussing the water imagery of Tennyson, watched them as they passed back and forth beneath us until by afternoon the piles of traps which had been stacked upon the wharf were no longer visible but were spread about the bottom of the sea. And the *Jenny Lynn* went too, all day, with my uncle tall and dark, like a latter-day Tashtego[6] standing at the tiller with his legs wide apart and guiding her deftly between the floating pans of ice and my father in the stern standing in the same way with his hands upon the ropes that lashed the cargo to the deck. And at night my mother asked, "Well, how did things go in the boat today?"

56     And the spring wore on and the summer came and school ended in the third week of June and the lobster season on July first and I wished that the two things I loved so dearly did not exclude each other in a manner that was so blunt and too clear.

57     At the conclusion of the lobster season my uncle said he had been offered a berth on a deep sea dragger and had decided to accept. We all knew that he was leaving the *Jenny Lynn* forever and that before the next lobster season he would buy a boat of his own. He was expecting another child and would be supporting fifteen people by the next spring and could not chance my father against the family that he loved.

58     I joined my father then for the trawling season, and he made no protest and my mother was quite happy. Through the summer we

---

6. A character in Herman Melville's *Moby Dick* (1851).

baited the tubs of trawl in the afternoon and set them at sunset and revisited them in the darkness of the early morning. The men would come tramping by our house at four A.M. and we would join them and walk with them to the wharf and be on our way before the sun rose out of the ocean where it seemed to spend the night. If I was not up they would toss pebbles to my window and I would be very embarrassed and tumble downstairs to where my father lay fully clothed atop his bed, reading his book and listening to his radio and smoking his cigarette. When I appeared he would swing off his bed and put on his boots and be instantly ready and then we would take the lunches my mother had prepared the night before and walk off toward the sea. He would make no attempt to wake me himself.

59   It was in many ways a good summer. There were few storms and we were out almost every day and we lost a minimum of gear and seemed to land a maximum of fish and I tanned dark and brown after the manner of my uncles.

60   My father did not tan — he never tanned — because of his reddish complexion, and the salt water irritated his skin as it had for sixty years. He burned and reburned over and over again and his lips still cracked so that they bled when he smiled, and his arms, especially the left, still broke out into the oozing saltwater boils as they had ever since as a child I had first watched him soaking and bathing them in a variety of ineffectual solutions. The chafe-preventing bracelets of brass linked chain that all the men wore about their wrists in early spring were his the full season and he shaved but painfully and only once a week.

61   And I saw then, that summer, many things that I had seen all my life as if for the first time and I thought that perhaps my father had never been intended for a fisherman either physically or mentally. At least not in the manner of my uncles; he had never really loved it. And I remembered that, one evening in his room when we were talking about *David Copperfield*, he had said that he had always wanted to go to the university and I had dismissed it then in the way one dismisses his father's saying he would like to be a tight-rope walker, and we had gone on to talk about the Peggottys and how they loved the sea.

62   And I thought then to myself that there were many things wrong with all of us and all our lives and I wondered why my father, who was himself an only son, had not married before he was forty and then I wondered why he had. I even thought that perhaps he had had to marry my mother and checked the dates on the flyleaf of the Bible where I learned that my oldest sister had been born a prosaic eleven months after the marriage, and I felt myself then very dirty and debased for my lack of faith and for what I had thought and done.

63   And then there came into my heart a very great love for my father and I thought it was very much braver to spend a life doing what you really do not want rather than selfishly following forever your own

dreams and inclinations. And I knew then that I could never leave him alone to suffer the iron-tipped harpoons which my mother would forever hurl into his soul because he was a failure as a husband and a father who had retained none of his own. And I felt that I had been very small in a little secret place within me and that even the completion of high school was for me a silly shallow selfish dream.

So I told him one night very resolutely and very powerfully that I would remain with him as long as he lived and we would fish the sea together. And he made no protest but only smiled through the cigarette smoke that wreathed his bed and replied, "I hope you will remember what you've said."

The room was now so filled with books as to be almost Dickensian, but he would not allow my mother to move or change them and he continued to read them, sometimes two or three a night. They came with great regularity now, and there were more hard covers, sent by my sisters who had gone so long ago and now seemed so distant and so prosperous, and sent also pictures of small red-haired grandchildren with baseball bats and dolls which he placed upon his bureau and which my mother gazed at wistfully when she thought no one would see. Red-haired grandchildren with baseball bats and dolls who would never know the sea in hatred or in love.

And so we fished through the heat of August and into the cooler days of September when the water was so clear we could almost see the bottom and the white mists rose like delicate ghosts in the early morning dawn. And one day my mother said to me, "You have given added years to his life."

And we fished on into October when it began to roughen and we could no longer risk night sets but took our gear out each morning and returned at the first sign of the squalls; and on into November when we lost three tubs of trawl and the clear blue water turned to a sullen grey and the trochoidal waves rolled rough and high and washed across our bows and decks as we ran within their troughs. We wore heavy sweaters now and the awkward rubber slickers and the heavy woollen mitts which soaked and froze into masses of ice that hung from our wrists like the limbs of gigantic monsters until we thawed them against the exhaust pipe's heat. And almost every day we would leave for home before noon, driven by the blasts of the northwest wind, coating our eyebrows with ice and freezing our eyelids closed as we leaned into a visibility that was hardly there, charting our course from the compass and the sea, running with the waves and between them but never confronting their towering might.

And I stood at the tiller now, on these homeward lunges, stood in the place and in the manner of my uncle, turning to look at my father and to shout over the roar of the engine and the slop of the sea to where he stood in the stern, drenched and dripping with the snow and the salt and the spray and his bushy eyebrows caked in ice. But on

November twenty-first, when it seemed we might be making the final run of the season, I turned and he was not there and I knew even in that instant that he would never be again.

69   On November twenty-first the waves of the grey Atlantic are very very high and the waters are very cold and there are no signposts on the surface of the sea. You cannot tell where you have been five minutes before and in the squalls of snow you cannot see. And it takes longer than you would believe to check a boat that has been running before a gale and turn her ever so carefully in a wide and stupid circle, with timbers creaking and straining, back into the face of the storm. And you know it is useless and that your voice does not carry the length of the boat and that even if you knew the original spot, the relentless waves would carry such a burden perhaps a mile or so by the time you could return. And you know also, the final irony, that your father like your uncles and all the men that form your past, cannot swim a stroke.

70   The lobster beds off the Cape Breton coast are still very rich and now, from May to July, their offerings are packed in crates of ice, and thundered by the gigantic transport trucks, day and night, through New Glasgow, Amherst, Saint John and Bangor and Portland and into Boston where they are tossed still living into boiling pots of water, their final home.

71   And though the prices are higher and the competition tighter, the grounds to which the *Jenny Lynn* once went remain untouched and unfished as they have for the last ten years. For if there are no signposts on the sea in storm there are certain ones in calm and the lobster bottoms were distributed in calm before any of us can remember and the grounds my father fished were those his father fished before him and there were others before and before and before. Twice the big boats have come from forty and fifty miles, lured by the promise of the grounds, and strewn the bottom with their traps and twice they have returned to find their buoys cut adrift and their gear lost and destroyed. Twice the Fisheries Officer and the Mounted Police have come and asked many long and involved questions and twice they have received no answers from the men leaning in the doors of their shanties and the women standing at their windows with their children in their arms. Twice they have gone away saying: "There are no legal boundaries in the Marine area"; "No one can own the sea"; "Those grounds don't wait for anyone."

72   But the men and the women, with my mother dark among them, do not care for what they say, for to them the grounds are sacred and they think they wait for me.

73   It is not an easy thing to know that your mother lives alone on an inadequate insurance policy and that she is too proud to accept any other aid. And that she looks through her lonely window onto the ice of winter and the hot flat calm of summer and the rolling waves of fall. And that she lies awake in the early morning's darkness when the rub-

ber boots of the men scrunch upon the gravel as they pass beside her house on their way down to the wharf. And she knows that the footsteps never stop, because no man goes from her house, and she alone of all the Lynns has neither son nor son-in-law that walks toward the boat that will take him to the sea. And it is not an easy thing to know that your mother looks upon the sea with love and on you with bitterness because the one has been so constant and the other so untrue.

But neither is it easy to know that your father was found on November twenty-eighth, ten miles to the north and wedged between two boulders at the base of the rock-strewn cliffs where he had been hurled and slammed so many many times. His hands were shredded ribbons as were his feet which had lost their boots to the suction of the sea, and his shoulders came apart in our hands when we tried to move him from the rocks. And the fish had eaten his testicles and the gulls had pecked out his eyes and the white-green stubble of his whiskers had continued to grow in death, like the grass on graves, upon the purple, bloated mass that was his face. There was not much left of my father, physically, as he lay there with the brass chains on his wrists and the seaweed in his hair.

- Conflict between mother & father.
  Traditional (1974)
- Father kind of "did what he had to do" for the family survive. Like mother in Boys and Girls.
  – Father gets rashes every year and doesn't want to be there.
- Father is also traditional – his father before him fished the grounds and he wants his only son to do so aswell. This sacrificing of his life is keeping his only son there to continue the tradition.
- Sadness in ending – with death of father the son may continue to fish for his father. Sacrificial death.

# Margaret Atwood (b. 1939)

*Equally at home with essays, fiction, and poetry, Atwood has also achieved some of her considerable stature from her work as a literary critic. Her interest in fictional form is demonstrated in "Happy Endings," an amusing survey of the bare-bones possibilities of fiction.*

## Happy Endings

1 John and Mary meet.
2 What happens next?
3 If you want a happy ending, try A.

4 A. John and Mary fall in love and get married. They both have worthwhile and remunerative jobs which they find stimulating and challenging. They buy a charming house. Real estate values go up. Eventually, when they can afford live-in help, they have two children, to whom they are devoted. The children turn out well. John and Mary have a stimulating and challenging sex life and worthwhile friends. They go on fun vacations together. They retire. They both have hobbies which they find stimulating and challenging. Eventually they die. This is the end of the story.

5 B. Mary falls in love with John but John doesn't fall in love with Mary. He merely uses her body for selfish pleasure and ego gratification of a tepid kind. He comes to her apartment twice a week and she cooks him dinner, you'll notice that he doesn't even consider her worth the price of a dinner out, and after he's eaten he fucks her and after that he falls asleep, while she does the dishes so he won't think she's untidy, having all those dirty dishes lying around, and puts on fresh lipstick so she'll look good when he wakes up, but when he wakes up he doesn't even notice, he puts on his socks and his shorts and his pants and his shirt and his tie and his shoes, the reverse order from the one in which he took them off. He doesn't take off Mary's clothes, she takes them off herself, she acts as if she's dying for it every time, not because she likes sex exactly, she doesn't, but she wants John to think she does because if they do it often enough surely he'll get used to her, he'll come to depend on her and they will get married, but John goes out the door with

hardly so much as a good-night and three days later he turns up at six o'clock and they do the whole thing over again.

6  Mary gets run-down. Crying is bad for your face, everyone knows that and so does Mary but she can't stop. People at work notice. Her friends tell her John is a rat, a pig, a dog, he isn't good enough for her, but she can't believe it. Inside John, she thinks, is another John, who is much nicer. This other John will emerge like a butterfly from a cocoon, a jack from a box, a pit from a prune, if the first John is only squeezed enough.

7  One evening John complains about the food. He has never complained about the food before. Mary is hurt.

8  Her friends tell her they've seen him in a restaurant with another woman, whose name is Madge. It's not even Madge that finally gets to Mary: it's the restaurant. John has never taken Mary to a restaurant. Mary collects all the sleeping pills and aspirins she can find, and takes them and a half a bottle of sherry. You can see what kind of a woman she is by the fact that it's not even whiskey. She leaves a note for John. She hopes he'll discover her and get her to the hospital in time and repent and then they can get married, but this fails to happen and so she dies.

9  John marries Madge and everything continues as in A.

10 C. John, who is an older man, falls in love with Mary, and Mary, who is only twenty-two, feels sorry for him because he's worried about his hair falling out. She sleeps with him even though she's not in love with him. She met him at work. She's in love with someone called James, who is twenty-two and not yet ready to settle down.

11  John on the contrary settled down long ago: this is what is bothering him. John has a steady, respectable job and is getting ahead in his field, but Mary isn't impressed by him, she's impressed by James, who has a motorcycle and a fabulous record collection. But James is often away on his motorcycle, being free. Freedom isn't the same for girls, so in the meantime Mary spends Thursday evenings with John. Thursdays are the only days John can get away.

12  John is married to a woman called Madge and they have two children, a charming house which they bought just before the real estate values went up, and hobbies which they find stimulating and challenging, when they have the time. John tells Mary how important she is to him, but of course he can't leave his wife because a commitment is a commitment. He goes on about this more than is necessary and Mary finds it boring, but older men can keep it up longer so on the whole she has a fairly good time.

13  One day James breezes in on his motorcycle with some top-grade California hybrid and James and Mary get higher than you'd believe possible and they climb into bed. Everything becomes very underwater, but along comes John, who has a key to Mary's apartment. He finds them stoned and entwined. He's hardly in any position to

be jealous, considering Madge, but nevertheless he's overcome with despair. Finally he's middle-aged, in two years he'll be bald as an egg and he can't stand it. He purchases a handgun, saying he needs it for target practice — this is the thin part of the plot, but it can be dealt with later — and shoots the two of them and himself.

Madge, after a suitable period of mourning, marries an understanding man called Fred and everything continues as in A, but under different names.

15 D. Fred and Madge have no problems. They get along exceptionally well and are good at working out any little difficulties that may arise. But their charming house is by the seashore and one day a giant tidal wave approaches. Real estate values go down. The rest of the story is about what caused the tidal wave and how they escape from it. They do, though thousands drown, but Fred and Madge are virtuous and lucky. Finally on high ground they clasp each other, wet and dripping and grateful, and continue as in A.

16 E. Yes, but Fred has a bad heart. The rest of the story is about how kind and understanding they both are until Fred dies. Then Madge devotes herself to charity work until the end of A. If you like, it can be "Madge," "cancer," "guilty and confused," and "bird watching."

17 F. If you think this is all too bourgeois, make John a revolutionary and Mary a counterespionage agent and see how far that gets you. Remember, this is Canada. You'll still end up with A, though in between you may get a lustful brawling saga of passionate involvement, a chronicle of our times, sort of.

18 You'll have to face it, the endings are the same however you slice it. Don't be deluded by any other endings, they're all fake, either deliberately fake, with malicious intent to deceive, or just motivated by excessive optimism if not downright sentimentality.

19 The only authentic ending is the one provided here:
20 *John and Mary die. John and Mary die. John and Mary die.*

21 So much for endings. Beginnings are always more fun. True connoisseurs, however, are known to favor the stretch in between, since it's the hardest to do anything with.

22 That's about all that can be said for plots, which anyway are just one thing after another, a what and a what and a what.

23 Now try How and Why.

(1983)

# Toni Cade Bambara (b. 1939)

Born in New York, Bambara has written short stories, novels, and screenplays in which she presents portraits of black urban life in America. In "The Lesson," she offers an unsentimental, lively, and humorous explanation of the neighbourhood and wider world of her adolescent protagonists.

## The Lesson

1   Back in the days when everyone was old and stupid or young and foolish and me and Sugar were the only ones just right, this lady moved on our block with nappy hair and proper speech and no makeup. And quite naturally we laughed at her, laughed the way we did at the junk man who went about his business like he was some big-time president and his sorry-ass horse his secretary. And we kinda hated her too, hated the way we did the winos who cluttered up our parks and pissed on our handball walls and stank up our hallways so you couldn't halfway play hide-and-seek without a goddamn gas mask. Miss Moore was her name. The only woman on the block with no first name. And she was black as hell, cept for her feet, which were fish-white and spooky. And she was always planning these boring-ass things for us to do, us being my cousin, mostly, who lived on the block cause we all moved North the same time and to the same apartment then spread out gradual to breathe. And our parents would yank our heads into some kinda shape and crisp up our clothes so we'd be presentable for travel with Miss Moore, who always looked like she was going to church, though she never did. Which is just one of the things grownups talked about when they talked behind her back like a dog. But when she came calling with some sachet she'd sewed up or some gingerbread she'd made or some book, why then they'd all be too embarrassed to turn her down and we'd get handed over all spruced up. She'd been to college and said it was only right that she should take responsibility for the young ones' education, and she not even related by marriage or blood. So they'd go for it. Specially, Aunt Gretchen. She been screwed into the go-along for so long, it's a blood-deep natural thing with her. Which is how she got saddled with me and Sugar and Junior in the first place while our mothers were in a la-de-da apartment up the block having a good ole time.

2   So this one day Miss Moore rounds us all up at the mailbox and it's puredee hot and she's knockin herself out about arithmetic. And school suppose to let up in summer I heard, but she don't never let up. And the starch in my pinafore scratching the shit outta me and I'm really hating this nappy-head bitch and her goddamn college degree. I'd much rather go to the pool or to the show where it's cool. So me and Sugar leaning on the mailbox being surly, which is a Miss Moore word. And Flyboy checking out what everybody brought for lunch. And Fat Butt already wasting his peanut-butter-and-jelly sandwich like the pig he is. And Junebug punchin on Q.T.'s arm for potato chips. And Rosie Giraffe shifting from one hip to the other waiting for somebody to step on her foot or ask her if she from Georgia so she can kick ass, preferably Mercedes'. And Miss Moore asking us do we know what money is, like we a bunch of retards. I mean real money, she say, like it's only poker chips or monopoly papers we lay on the grocer. So right away I'm tired of this and say so. And would much rather snatch Sugar and go to the Sunset and terrorize the West Indian kids and take their hair ribbons and their money too. And Miss Moore files that remark away for next week's lesson on brotherhood, I can tell. And finally I say we oughta get to the subway cause it's cooler and besides we might meet some cute boys. Sugar done swiped her mama's lipstick, so we ready.

3   So we heading down the street and she's boring us silly about what things cost and what our parents make and how much goes for rent and how money ain't divided up right in this country. And then she gets to the part about we all poor and live in the slums, which I don't feature. And I'm ready to speak on that, but she steps out in the street and hails two cabs just like that. Then she hustles half the crew in with her and hands me a five-dollar bill and tells me to calculate 10 percent tip for the driver. And we're off. Me and Sugar and Junebug and Flyboy hangin out the window and hollering to everybody, putting lipstick on each other cause Flyboy a faggot anyway, and making farts with our sweaty armpits. But I'm mostly trying to figure how to spend this money. But they all fascinated with the meter ticking and Junebug starts laying bets as to how much it'll read when Flyboy can't hold his breath no more. The Sugar lays bets as to how much it'll be when we get there. So I'm stuck. Don't nobody want to go for my plan, which is to jump out at the next light and run off to the first bar-b-que we can find. Then the driver tells us to get the hell out cause we there already. And the meter reads eighty-five cents. And I'm stalling to figure out the tip and Sugar say give him a dime. And I decide he don't need it so bad as I do, so later for him. But then he tries to take off with Junebug foot still in the door as we talk about his mama something ferocious. Then we check out that we on Fifth Avenue and everybody dressed up in stockings. One lady in a fur coat, hot as it is. White folks crazy.

4   "This is the place," Miss Moore say, presenting it to us in the voice she uses at the museum. "Let's look in the windows before we go in."

5   "Can we steal?" Sugar asks very serious like she's getting the ground rules squared away before she plays. "I beg your pardon," say Miss Moore, and we fall out. So she leads us around the windows of the toy store and me and Sugar screaming, "This is mine, that's mine, I gotta have that, that was made for me, I was born for that," till Big Butt drowns us out.

6   "Hey, I'm going to buy that there."
7   "That there? You don't even know what it is, stupid."
8   "I do so," he say punching on Rosie Giraffe. "It's a microscope."
9   "Whatcha gonna do with a microscope, fool?"
10  "Look at things."
11  "Like what, Ronald?" ask Miss Moore. And Big Butt ain't got the first notion. So here go Miss Moore gabbing about the thousands of bacteria in a drop of water and the somethinorother in a speck of blood and the million and one living things in the air around us is invisible to the naked eye. And what she say that for? Junebug go to town on that "naked" and we rolling. Then Miss Moore ask what it cost. So we all jam into the window smudgin it up and the price tag say $300. So then she ask how long'd take for Big Butt and Junebug to save up their allowances. "Too long," I say. "Yeh," adds Sugar, "outgrown it by that time." And Miss Moore say no, you never outgrow learning instruments. "Why, even medical students and interns and," blah, blah, blah. And we ready to choke Big Butt for bringing it up in the first damn place.

12  "This here costs four hundred eighty dollars," says Rosie Giraffe. So we pile up all over her to see what she pointin out. My eyes tell me it's a chunk of glass cracked with something heavy, and different-color inks dipped into the splits, then the whole thing put into a oven or something. But for $480 it don't make sense.

13  "That's a paperweight made of semi-precious stones fused together under tremendous pressure," she explains slowly, with her hands doing the mining and all the factory work.

14  "So what's a paperweight?" asks Rosie Giraffe.
15  "To weigh paper with, dumbbell," say Flyboy, the wise man from the East.
16  "Not exactly," say Miss Moore, which is what she say when you warm or way off too. "It's to weight paper down so it won't scatter and make your desk untidy." So right away me and Sugar curtsy to each other and then to Mercedes who is more the tidy type.
17  "We don't keep paper on top of the desk in my class," say Junebug, figuring Miss Moore crazy or lyin one.
18  "At home, then," she say. "Don't you have a calendar and a pencil case and a blotter and a letter-opener on your desk at home where you do your homework?" And she know damn well what our homes look like cause she nosys around in them every chance she gets.
19  "I don't even have a desk," say Junebug. "Do we?"
20  "No. And I don't get no more homework neither," say Big Butt.

21  "And I don't even have a home," say Flyboy like he do at school to keep white folks off his back and sorry for him. Send this poor kid to camp posters, is his specialty.

22  "I do," says Mercedes. "I have a box of stationery on my desk and a picture of my cat. My godmother bought the stationery and the desk. There's big rose on each sheet and the envelopes smell like roses."

23  "Who wants to know about your smelly-ass stationery," says Rosie Giraffe fore I can get my two cents in.

24  "It's important to have a work area all your own so that ..."

25  "Will you look at this sailboat, please," say Flyboy, cuttin her off and pointin to the thing like it was his. So once again we tumble all over each other to gaze at this magnificent thing in the toy store which is just big enough to maybe sail two kittens across the pond if you strap them to the posts tight. We all start reciting the price tag like we in assembly. "Handcrafted sailboat of fiberglass at one thousand one hundred ninety-five dollars."

26  "Unbelievable," I hear myself say and am really stunned. I read it again for myself just in case the group recitation put me in a trance. Same thing. For some reason this pisses me off. We look at Miss Moore and she lookin at us, waiting for I dunno what.

27  "Who'd pay all that when you can buy a sailboat for a quarter at Pop's, a tube of glue for a dime, and a ball of string for eight cents? It must have a motor and a whole lot else besides," I say. "My sailboat cost me about fifty cents."

28  "But will it take water?" say Mercedes with her smart ass.

29  "Took mine to Alley Pond Park once," say Flyboy. "String broke. Lost it. Pity."

30  "Sailed mine in Central Park and it keeled over and sank. Had to ask my father for another dollar."

31  "And you got the strap," laugh Big Butt. "The jerk didn't even have a string on it. My old man wailed on his behind."

32  Little Q.T. was staring hard at the sailboat and you could see he wanted it bad. But he too little and somebody'd just take it from him. So what the hell. "This boat for kids, Miss Moore?"

33  "Parents silly to buy something like that just to get all broke up," say Rosie Giraffe.

34  "That much money it should last forever," I figure.

35  "My father'd buy it for me if I wanted it."

36  "Your father, my ass," say Rosie Giraffe getting a chance to finally push Mercedes.

37  "Must be rich people shop here," say Q.T.

38  "You are a very bright boy," say Flyboy. "What was your first clue?" And he rap him on the head with the back of his knuckles, since Q.T. the only one he could get away with. Though Q.T. liable to come up behind you years later and get his licks in when you half expect it.

39    "What I want to know is," I says to Miss Moore though I never talk to her, I wouldn't give the bitch that satisfaction, "is how much a real boat costs? I figure a thousand'd get you a yacht any day."

40    "Why don't you check that out," she says, "and report back to the group?" Which really pains my ass. If you gonna mess up a perfectly good swim day least you could do is have some answers. "Let's go in," she say like she got something up her sleeve. Only she don't lead the way. So me and Sugar turn the corner to where the entrance is, but when we get there I kinda hang back. Not that I'm scared, what's there to be afraid of, just a toy store. But I feel funny, shame. But what I got to be ashamed about? Got as much right to go in as anybody. But somehow I can't seem to get hold of the door, so I step away for Sugar to lead. But she hangs back too. And I look at her and she looks at me and this is ridiculous. I mean, damn, I have never ever been shy about doing nothing or going nowhere. But then Mercedes steps up and then Rosie Giraffe and Big Butt crowd in behind and shove, and next thing we all stuffed into the doorway with only Mercedes squeezing past us, smoothing out her jumper and walking right down the aisle. Then the rest of us tumble in like a glued-together jigsaw done all wrong. And people lookin at us. And it's like the time me and Sugar crashed into the Catholic church on a dare. But once we got in there and everything so hushed and holy and the candles and the bowin and the handkerchiefs on all the drooping heads, I just couldn't go through with the plan. Which was for me to run up to the altar and do a tap dance while Sugar played the nose flute and messed around in the holy water. And Sugar kept giving me the elbow. Then later teased me so bad I tied her up in the shower and turned it on and locked her in. And she'd be there till this day if Aunt Gretchen hadn't finally figured I was lyin about the boarder takin a shower.

41    Same thing in the store. We all walkin on tiptoe and hardly touchin the games and puzzles and things. And I watched Miss Moore who is steady watchin us like she waiting for a sign. Like Mama Drewery watches the sky and sniffs the air and takes note of just how much slant is in the bird formation. Then me and Sugar bump smack into each other, so busy gazing at the toys, 'specially the sailboat. But we don't laugh and go into our fat-day bump-stomach routine. We just stare at that price tag. Then Sugar runs a finger over the whole boat. And I'm jealous and want to hit her. Maybe not her, but I sure want to punch somebody in the mouth.

42    "Watcha bring us here for, Miss Moore?"

43    "You sound angry, Sylvia. Are you mad about something?" Givin me one of them grins like she tellin a grown-up joke that never turns out to be funny. And she's lookin very closely at me like maybe she plannin to do my portrait from memory. I'm mad, but I won't give her that satisfaction. So I slouch around the store bein very bored and say, "Let's go."

44   Me and Sugar at the back of the train watchin the tracks whizzin by large then small then gettin gobbled up in the dark. I'm thinking about this tricky toy I saw in the store. A clown that somersaults on a bar then does chin-ups just cause you yank lightly at his leg. Cost $35. I could see me askin my mother for a $35 birthday clown. "You wanna who that costs what?" she'd say, cocking her head to the side to get a better view of the hole in my head. Thirty-five dollars could buy new bunk beds for Junior and Gretchen's boy. Thirty-five dollars and the whole household could go visit Granddaddy Nelson in the country. Thirty-five dollars would pay for the rent and the piano bill too. Who are these people that spend that much for performing clowns and $1,000 for toy sailboats? What kinda work they do and how they live and how come we ain't in on it? Where we are is who we are, Miss Moore always pointin out. But it don't necessarily have to be that way, she always adds then waits for somebody to say that poor people have to wake up and demand their share of the pie and don't none of us know what kind of pie she talkin about in the first damn place. But she ain't so smart cause I still got her four dollars from the taxi and she sure ain't gettin it. Messin up my day with this shit. Sugar nudges me in my pocket and winks.

45   Miss Moore lines us up in front of the mailbox where we started from, seem like years ago, and I got a headache for thinkin so hard. And we lean all over each other so we can hold up under the draggy-ass lecture she always finishes us off with at the end before we thank her for borin us to tears. But she just looks at us like she readin tea leaves. Finally she say, "Well, what did you think of F.A.O. Schwartz?"

46   Rosie Giraffe mumbles, "White folks crazy."

47   "I'd like to go there again when I get my birthday money," says Mercedes, and we shove her out the pack so she has to lean on the mailbox by herself.

48   "I'd like a shower. Tiring day," say Flyboy.

49   Then Sugar surprises me by sayin, "You know, Miss Moore, I don't think all of us here put together eat in a year what that sailboat costs." And Miss Moore lights up like somebody goosed her. "And?" she say, urging Sugar on. Only I'm standin on her foot so she don't continue.

50   "Imagine for a minute what kind of society it is in which some people can spend on a toy what it would cost to feed a family of six or seven. What do you think?"

51   "I think," say Sugar pushing me off her feet like she never done before, cause I whip her ass in a minute, "that this is not much of a democracy if you ask me. Equal chance to pursue happiness means an equal crack at the dough, don't it?" Miss Moore is beside herself and I am disgusted with Sugar's treachery. So I stand on her foot one more time to see if she'll shove me. She shuts up and Miss Moore looks at me, sorrowfully I'm thinkin. And somethin weird is going on, I can feel it in my chest.

52 "Anybody else learn anything today?" lookin dead at me. I walk away and Sugar has to run to catch up and don't even seem to notice when I shrug her arm off my shoulder.
53 "Well, we got four dollars anyway," she says.
54 "Uh hunh."
55 "We could go to Hascombs and get half a chocolate layer and then go to the Sunset and still have plenty money for potato chips and ice-cream sodas."
56 "Uh hunh."
57 "Race you to Hascombs," she say.
58 We start down the block and she gets ahead which is O.K. by me cause I'm going to the West End and then over the Drive to think this day through. She can run if she want to and even run faster. But ain't nobody gonna beat me at nuthin.

(1972)

# Thomas King (b. 1943)

Born in Oklahoma of Greek-German and Cherokee parents, King is a Canadian as well as an American citizen. While teaching Native Studies at the University of Lethbridge, he began his creative writing career. He has published poems and short stories in many Canadian periodicals and edited a special issue of Canadian Fiction Magazine (1987) and All My Relations: An Anthology of Contemporary Canadian Native Writing (1990). He is currently a member of the English Department at the University of Guelph.

## The One About Coyote Going West

1. This one is about Coyote. She was going west. Visiting her relations. That's what she said. You got to watch that one. Tricky one. Full of bad business. No, no, no, no, that one says. I'm just visiting.
2. Going to see Raven.
3. Boy, I says. That's another tricky one.
4. Coyote comes by my place. She wag her tail. Make them happy noises. Sit on my porch. Look around. With them teeth. With that smile. Coyote put her nose in my tea. My good tea. Get that nose out of my tea, I says.
5. I'm going to see my friends, she says. Tell those stories. Fix this world. Straighten it up.
6. Oh boy, pretty scary that, Coyote fix the world, again.
7. Sit down, I says. Eat some food. Hard work that fix up the world. Maybe you have a song. Maybe you have a good joke.
8. Sure, says Coyote. That one wink her ears. Lick her whiskers.
9. I tuck my feet under that chair. Got to hide my toes. Sometimes that tricky one leave her skin sit in that chair. Coyote skin. No Coyote. Sneak around. Bite them toes. Make you jump.
10. I been reading those books, she says.
11. You must be one smart Coyote, I says.
12. You bet, she says.
13. Maybe you got a good story for me, I says.
14. I been reading about that history, says Coyote. She tricks that nose back in my tea. All about who found us Indians.

15   Ho, I says. I like those old ones. Them ones are the best. You tell me your story, I says. Maybe some biscuits will visit us. Maybe some moose-meat stew come along, listen to your story.
16   Okay, she says and she sings her story song.

>   Snow's on the ground the snakes are asleep.
>   Snow's on the ground my voice is strong.
>   Snow's on the ground the snakes are asleep.
>   Snow's on the ground my voice is strong.

17   She sings like that. With that tail, wagging. With that smile. Sitting there.
18   Maybe I tell you the one about Eric the Lucky and the Vikings play hockey for the Old-timers, find us Indians in Newfoundland, she says.
19   Maybe I tell you the one about Christopher Cartier looking for something good to eat. Find us Indians in a restaurant in Montreal.
20   Maybe I tell you the one about Jacques Columbus come along that river, Indians waiting for him. We all wave and say, here we are, here we are.
21   Everyone knows those stories, I says. White man stories. Baby stories you got in your mouth.
22   No, no, no, no, says the Coyote. I read these ones in that old book.
23   Ho, I says. You are trying to bite my toes. Everyone knows who found us Indians. Eric the Lucky and that Christopher Cartier and that Jacques Columbus come along later. Those ones get lost. Float about. Walk around. Get mixed up. Ho, ho, ho, ho, those ones cry, we are lost. So we got to find them. Help them out. Feed them. Show them around.
24   Boy, I says. Bad mistake that one.
25   You are very wise, grandmother, says Coyote, bring her eyes down. Like she is sleepy. Maybe you know who discovered Indians.
26   Sure, I says. Everyone knows that. It was Coyote. She was the one.
27   Oh, grandfather, that Coyote says. Tell me that story. I love those stories about that sneaky one. I don't think I know that story, she says.
28   All right, I says. Pay attention.
29   Coyote was heading west. That's how I always start this story. There was nothing else in this world. Just Coyote. She could see all the way, too. No mountains then. No rivers then. No forests then. Pretty flat then. So she starts to make things. So she starts to fix this world.
30   This is exciting, says Coyote, and she takes her nose out of my tea.
31   Yes, I says. Just the beginning, too. Coyote got a lot of things to make.
32   Tell me, grandmother, says Coyote. What does the clever one make first?

33   Well, I says. Maybe she makes that tree grows by the river. Maybe she makes that buffalo. Maybe she makes that mountain. Maybe she makes them clouds.

34   Maybe she makes that beautiful rainbow, says Coyote.

35   No, I says. She don't make that thing. Mink makes that.

36   Maybe she makes that beautiful moon, says Coyote.

37   No, I says. She don't do that either. Otter finds that moon in a pond later on.

38   Maybe she makes the oceans with that blue water, says Coyote.

39   No, I says. Oceans are already here. She don't do any of that. The first thing Coyote makes, I tell Coyote, is a mistake.

40   Boy, Coyote sit up straight. Them eyes pop open. That tail stop wagging. That one swallow that smile.

41   Big one, too, I says. Coyote is going west thinking of things to make. That one is trying to think of everything to make at once. So she don't see that hole. So she falls in that hole. Then those thoughts bump around. They run into each other. Those ones fall out of Coyote's ears. In that hole. Ho, that Coyote cries. I have fallen into a hole. I must have made a mistake. And she did.

42   So, there is that hole. And there is that Coyote in that hole. And there is that big mistake in that hole with Coyote. Ho, says that mistake. You must be Coyote.

43   That mistake is real big and that hole is small. Not much room. I don't want to tell you what that mistake looks like. First mistake in the world. Pretty scary. Boy, I can't look. I got to close my eyes. You better close your eyes, too, I tell Coyote.

44   Okay, I'll do that, she says, and she puts her hands over her eyes. But she don't fool me. I can see she's peeking.

45   Don't peek, I says.

46   Okay, she says. I won't do that.

47   Well, you know, that Coyote thinks about the hole. And she thinks about how she's going to get out of that hole. She thinks how she's going to get that big mistake back in her head.

48   Say, says that mistake. What is that you're thinking about?

49   I'm thinking of a song, says Coyote. I'm thinking of a song to make this hole bigger.

50   That's a good idea, says that mistake. Let me hear your hole song.

51   But that's not what Coyote sings. She sings a song to make the mistake smaller. But that mistake hears her. And that mistake grabs Coyote's nose. And that one pulls off her mouth so she can't sing. And that one jumps up and down on Coyote until she is flat. Then that one leaps out of that hole, wanders around looking for things to do.

52   Well, Coyote is feeling pretty bad, all flat her nice fur coat full of stomp holes. So she thinks hard, and she thinks about a healing song. And she tries to sing a healing song, but her mouth is in other places. So she thinks harder and tries to sing that song through her nose. But

that nose don't make any sound, just drip a lot. She tries to sing that song out her ears, but those ears don't hear anything.

53 So, that silly one thinks real hard and tries to sing out her butt-hole. Pssst! Pssst! That is what that butt-hole says, and right away things don't smell so good in that hole. Pssst.

54 Boy, Coyote thinks. Something smells.

55 That Coyote lies there flat and practise and practise. Pretty soon, maybe two days, maybe one year, she teach that butt-hole to sing. That song. That healing song. So that butt-hole sings that song. And Coyote begins to feel better. And Coyote don't feel so flat anymore. Pssst! Pssst! Things still smell pretty bad, but Coyote is okay.

56 That one look around in that hole. Find her mouth. Put that mouth back. So, she says to that butt-hole. Okay, you can stop singing now. You can stop making them smells now. But, you know, that butt-hole is liking all that singing, and so that butt-hole keeps on singing.

57 Stop that, says Coyote. You going to stink up the whole world. But it don't. So Coyote jumps out of that hole and runs across the prairies real fast. But that butt-hole follows her. Pssst. Pssst. Coyote jumps into a lake, but that butt-hole don't drown. It just keeps on singing.

58 Hey, who is doing all that singing, someone says.

59 Yes, and who is making that bad smell, says another voice.

60 It must be Coyote, says a third voice.

61 Yes, says a fourth voice. I believe it is Coyote.

62 That Coyote sit in my chair, put her nose in my tea, say, I know who that voice is. It is that big mistake playing a trick. Nothing else is made yet.

63 No, I says. That mistake is doing other things.

64 Then those voices are spirits, says Coyote.

65 No, I say. Them voices belong to them ducks.

66 Coyote stand up on my chair. Hey, she says, where did them ducks come from?

67 Calm down, I says. This story is going to be okay. This story is doing just fine. This story knows where it is going. Sit down. Keep your skin on.

68 So.

69 Coyote look around, and she see them four ducks. In that lake. Ho, she says. Where did you ducks come from? I didn't make you yet.

70 Yes, says them ducks. We were waiting around, but you didn't come. So we got tired of waiting. So we did it ourselves.

71 I was in a hole, says Coyote.

72 Psst. Psst.

73 What's that noise, says them ducks. What's that bad smell?

74 Never mind, says Coyote. Maybe you've seen something go by. Maybe you can help me find something I lost. Maybe you can help me get it back.

75 Those ducks swim around and talk to themselves. Was it something awful to look at? Yes, says Coyote, it certainly was. Was it

something with ugly fur? Yes, says Coyote, I think it had that, too. Was it something that made a lot of noise? ask them ducks. Yes, it was pretty noisy, says Coyote. Did it smell bad, them ducks want to know. Yes, says Coyote. I guess you ducks have seen my something.

76   Yes, says them ducks. It is right there behind you.
77   So that Coyote turn around, and there is nothing there.
78   It's still behind you, says those ducks.
79   So Coyote turn around again but she don't see anything.
80   Psst! Psst!
81   Boy, says those ducks. What a noise! What a smell! They say that, too. What an ugly thing with all that fur!
82   Never mind, says that Coyote, again. That is not what I'm looking for. I'm looking for something else.
83   Maybe you're looking for Indians, says those ducks.
84   Well, that Coyote is real surprised because she hasn't created Indians, either. Boy, says that one, mischief is everywhere. This world is getting bent.
85   All right.
86   So Coyote and those ducks are talking, and pretty soon they hear a noise. And pretty soon there is something coming. And those ducks says, oh, oh, oh, oh. They say that like they see trouble, but it is not trouble. What comes along is a river.
87   Hello, says that river. Nice day. Maybe you want to take a swim. But Coyote don't want to swim, and she looks at the river and she looks at that river again. Something's not right here, she says. Where are those rocks? Where are those rapids? What did you do with them waterfalls? How come you're so straight?
88   And Coyote is right. That river is nice and straight and smooth without any bumps or twists. It runs both ways, too, not like a modern river.
89   We got to fix this, says Coyote, and she does. She puts some rocks in that river, and she fixes it so it only runs one way. She puts a couple of waterfalls in and makes a bunch of rapids where things get shallow fast.
90   Coyote is tired with all this work, and those ducks are tired just watching. So that Coyote sits down. So she closes her eyes. So she puts her nose in her tail. So those ducks shout, wake up, wake up! Something big is heading this way! And they are right.
91   Mountain comes sliding along, whistling. Real happy mountain. Nice and round. This mountain is full of grapes and other good things to eat. Apples, peaches, cherries. Howdy-do, says that polite mountain, nice day for whistling.
92   Coyote looks at that mountain, and that one shakes her head. Oh, no, she says, this mountain is all wrong. How come you're so nice and round. Where are those craggy peaks? Where are all them cliffs? What happened to all that snow? Boy, we got to fix this thing, too. So she does.

93    Grandfather, grandfather, says that Coyote, sit in my chair, put her nose in my tea. Why is that Coyote changing all those good things?

94    That is a real sly one, ask me that question. I look at those eyes. Grab them ears. Squeeze that nose. Hey, let go my nose, that Coyote says.

95    Okay, I says. Coyote still in Coyote skin. I bet you know why Coyote change that happy river. Why she change that mountain sliding along whistling.

96    No, says that Coyote, look around my house, lick her lips, make them baby noises.

97    Maybe it's because she is mean, I says.

98    Oh, no, says Coyote. That one is sweet and kind.

99    Maybe it's because that one is not too smart.

100   Oh, no, says Coyote. That Coyote is very wise.

101   Maybe it's because she made a mistake.

102   Oh, no, says Coyote. She made one of those already.

103   All right, I says. Then Coyote must be doing the right thing. She must be fixing up the world so it is perfect.

104   Yes, says Coyote. That must be it. What does that brilliant one do next?

105   Everyone knows what Coyote does next, I says. Little babies know what Coyote does next.

106   Oh no, says Coyote. I have never heard this story. You are a wonderful storyteller. You tell me your good Coyote story.

107   Boy, you got to watch that one all the time. Hide them toes.

108   Well, I says. Coyote thinks about that river. And she thinks about that mountain. And she thinks somebody is fooling around. So she goes looking around. She goes looking for that one who is messing up the world.

109   She goes to the north, and there is nothing. She goes to the south, and there is nothing there, either. She goes to the east, and there is still nothing there. She goes to the west, and there is a pile of snow tires.

110   And there is some televisions. And there is some vacuum cleaners. And there is a bunch of pastel sheets. And there is an air humidifier. And there is a big mistake sitting on a portable gas barbecue reading a book. Big book. Department store catalogue.

111   Hello, says that mistake. Maybe you want a hydraulic jack.

112   No, says that Coyote. I don't want one of them. But she don't tell that mistake what she wants because she don't want to miss her mouth again. But when she thinks about being flat and full of stomp holes, that butt-hole wakes up and begins to sing. Pssst. Pssst.

113   What's that noise? says that big mistake.

114   I'm looking for Indians, says that Coyote, real quick. Have you seen any?

115   What's that bad smell?

116    Never mind, says Coyote. Maybe you have some Indians around here.
117    I got some toaster ovens, says that mistake.
118    We don't need that stuff, says Coyote. You got to stop making all those things. You're going to fill up this world.
119    Maybe you want a computer with a colour monitor. That mistake keeps looking through that book and those things keep landing in piles all around Coyote.
120    Stop, stop, cries Coyote. Golf cart lands on her foot. Golf balls bounce off her head. You got to give me that book before the world gets lopsided.
121    These are good things, says that mistake. We need these things to make up the world. Indians are going to need this stuff.
122    We don't have any Indians, says Coyote.
123    And that mistake can see that that's right. Maybe we better make some Indians, says that mistake. So that one looks in that catalogue, but it don't have any Indians. And Coyote don't know how to do that, either. She has already made four things.
124    I've made four things already, she says. I got to have help.
125    We can help, says some voices and it is those ducks come swimming along. We can help you make Indians, says the white duck. Yes, we can do that, says the green duck. We have been thinking about this, says that blue duck. We have a plan, says the red duck.
126    Well, that Coyote don't know what to do. So she tells them ducks to go ahead because this story is pretty long and it's getting late and everyone wants to go home.
127    You still awake, I says to Coyote. You still here?
128    Oh yes, grandmother, says Coyote. What do those clever ducks do?
129    So I tell Coyote that those ducks lay some eggs. Ducks do that, you know. That white duck lay an egg, and it is blue. That red duck lay an egg, and it is green. That blue duck lay an egg, and it is red. That green duck lay an egg, and it is white.
130    Come on, says those ducks. We got to sing a song. We got to do a dance. So they do. Coyote and that big mistake and those four ducks dance around the eggs. So they dance and sing for a long time, and pretty soon Coyote gets hungry.
131    I know this dance, she says, but you got to close your eyes when you do it or nothing will happen. You got to close your eyes tight. Okay, says those ducks. We can do that. And they do. And that big mistake closes its eyes, too.
132    But Coyote, she don't close her eyes, and all of them start dancing again, and Coyote dances up close to that white duck, and she grabs that white duck by her neck.
133    When Coyote grabs that duck, that duck flaps her wings, and that big mistake hears the noise and opens them eyes. Say, says that big mistake, that's not the way the dance goes.

134   By golly, you're right, says Coyote, and she lets that duck go. I am getting it mixed up with another dance.

135   So they start to dance again. And Coyote is very hungry, and she grabs that blue duck, and she grabs his wings, too. But Coyote's stomach starts to make hungry noises, and that mistake opens them eyes and sees Coyote with the blue duck. Hey, says that mistake, you got yourself mixed up again.

136   That's right, says Coyote, and she drops that duck and straightens out that neck. It sure is good you're around to help me with this dance.

137   They all start that dance again, and, this time, Coyote grab the green duck real quick and tries to stuff it down that greedy throat, and there is nothing hanging out but them yellow duck feet. But those feet are flapping in Coyote's eyes, and she can't see where she is going, and she bumps into the big mistake and the mistake turns around to see what has happened.

138   Ho, says that big mistake, you can't see where you're going with them yellow duck feet flapping in your eyes, and that mistake pulls that green duck out of Coyote's throat. You could hurt yourself dancing like that.

139   You are one good friend, look after me like that, says Coyote.

140   Those ducks start to dance again, and Coyote dances with them, but that red duck says, we better dance with one eye open, so we can help Coyote with this dance. So they dance some more, and, then, those eggs begin to move around, and those eggs crack open. And if you look hard, you can see something inside those eggs.

141   I know, I know, says that Coyote, jump up and down on my chair, shake up my good tea. Indians come out of those eggs. I remember this story, now. Inside those eggs are the Indians Coyote's been looking for.

142   No, I says. You are one crazy Coyote. What comes out of those duck eggs are baby ducks. You better sit down, I says. You may fall and hurt yourself. You may spill my tea. You may fall on top of this story and make it flat.

143   Where are the Indians? says that Coyote. This story is about how Coyote found the Indians. Maybe the Indians are in the eggs with the baby ducks.

144   No, I says, nothing in those eggs but little ducks. Indians will be along in a while. Don't lose your skin.

145   So.

146   When those ducks see what has come out of the eggs, they says, boy, we didn't get that quite right. We better try that again. So they do. They lay them eggs. They dance that dance. They sing that song. Those eggs crack open and out comes some more baby ducks. They do this seven times and each time, they get more ducks.

147   By golly, says those four ducks. We got more ducks than we need. I guess we got to be the Indians. And so they do that. Before Coyote

or that big mistake can mess things up, those four ducks turn into Indians, two women and two men. Good-looking Indians, too. They don't look at all like ducks anymore.

148 But those duck-Indians aren't too happy. They look at each other and they begin to cry. This is pretty disgusting, they says. All this ugly skin. All these bumpy bones. All this awful black hair. Where are our nice soft feathers? Where are our beautiful feet? What happened to our wonderful wings? It's probably all that Coyote's fault because she didn't do the dance right, and those four duck-Indians come over and stomp all over Coyote until she is flat like before. Then they leave. That big mistake leave, too. And that Coyote, she starts to think about a healing song.

149 Psst. Psst.

150 That's it, I says. It is done.

151 But what happens to Coyote, says Coyote. That wonderful one is still flat.

152 Some of these stories are flat, I says. That's what happens when you try to fix this world. This world is pretty good all by itself. Best to leave it alone. Stop messing around with it.

153 I better get going, says Coyote. I will tell Raven your good story. We going to fix this world for sure. We know how to do it now. We know how to do it right.

154 So, Coyote drinks my tea and that one leave. And I can't talk anymore because I got to watch the sky. Got to watch out for falling things that land in piles. When that Coyote's wandering around looking to fix things, nobody in this world is safe.

*(1990)*

# Donna E. Smyth (b. 1943)

**N**ovelist, playwright, short-story writer, and peace activist, Smyth currently teaches English in Nova Scotia. Her works include Quilt (1982) and Subversive Elements (1986). In "Red Hot," Smyth raises questions not only about the abuse of women but also about the boundaries between fiction and reality.

## Red Hot

1  (*In November, 1982, the Crown charged that Jane Stafford of Bangs Falls, Nova Scotia, willfully and deliberately took the life of her common-law husband William [Billy] Stafford. All direct quotations in the following piece are taken from the Liverpool* Advance's *coverage of this case.*)

\*\*\*

2  This is written in the Valley of the Shadow where we read death in the horrorscopes of movie stars, musicians and whales. In the cold northern light, people are building bomb shelters.

\*\*\*

3  This is a ritual. Billy beats Jane like Jane's father beat her mother. Billy beat his first wife and his second wife and he beat Jane like Jane's father beat her mother.

\*\*\*

4  This is written in hunting season when the wild geese on the river talk to each other all night long. Rising in flight into the frozen dawn, shot-gun scatter plucks them from the sky. The old moon, aghast, rolls on her back. The hunter takes another drink of rye.

\*\*\*

5  Smelling like a fetid beast, this city heaves itself into the black and blue night. He forces a stick between her teeth so she cannot speak. Video flicker in a rented room. He strokes her throat with a razor. In the room the watchers groan. He grinds his teeth and says: I'm drilling for oil. Nothing can stop me! The watchers sigh and shift in their chairs. He chains her to the operating table, her feet are in stirrups as

if she is giving birth. He approaches with a scalpel, whispering: Tell me you like it! Tell me you like it!

\*\*\*

6   The forensic firearms expert said: When a shotgun is fired at close range it causes the skull to explode. There was gross destruction of the victim's skull. The truck was full of blood and brain particles. It was like an explosion had taken place.

\*\*\*

7   The late night talk show host smiles with his perfect teeth. He says to his female guest
— In our modern society, surely censorship is a dangerous weapon. Was it Roland Barthes[1] who said censorship is the bourgeois revenge on the erotic principle?
8   Cut to the beer commercial. Four men on a fishing trip. Not a woman in sight. The fish are jumping. They are happy.
9   Flip back to the female guest who never cracks a smile as she says
— This has nothing to do with sex. We're talking about power.

\*\*\*

10   February, 1981. Jane said: "... a friend came to visit our home. We were sitting in the kitchen. Bill wasn't drinking and he went to bed. We were just sitting there talking about old times, not bothering anybody, when he came charging out of the bedroom with a 30-30, put it to her (my friend's) head and told her to get out. He then began beating me with the gun. I was knocked out. ..."

\*\*\*

11   This is a ritual. To be on the football team, he has to prove he is a man. Stick it in a hot dog bun, slather it with mustard. Mustard? Yes, and ketchup too. The works! As if they're going to eat it BUT! Then they bring the ice and he must put it on ice until it melts 'cause he is hot, red hot! Later, in an interview, the coach chuckles
— Well, things maybe got a little out of hand. You know what guys are like.

\*\*\*

12   November, 1982. Pauline, Billy's first wife, said: "He was a very cruel man in the six years I was married to him." He hit me, kicked me when I was pregnant. Once "he almost drowned me in a bucket of water." He beat our children too, "quite badly from the time they were six months old." He took one of the kids and stood her outside the

---

1. Roland Barthes (1915–1980), French literary critic and one of the originators of modern theories of semiotics, which perceive literature, along with gesture and other forms of communication, as an elaborate system of signs.

house and threw knives at her to see how close he could come. Another time he sat the children down on the steps, threatened them with lit cigarettes and then made them eat the butts.

\*\*\*

13 Video rerun. Close-up of her hands clutching the table. Glazed faces in a rented room. Black scarf tied over her mouth so she cannot scream. She is chained face-down on the table, a meat-cutting table. The room smells of smoke and booze and pickled herrings. A meat-cutting table where the saw whines with desire. Her hands clutching. The watchers groan. Whine of the saw rises, louder, louder than ambulance screams.
14   Cut.
15   The talk show host smiles disarmingly
     — Think of *Ulysses*. Think of *Lady Chatterley's Lover*.[2] Think of all the great works of art. Would you really want to censor the human imagination?
16   Cut.

\*\*\*

17 Alan, Jane's teenage son, said that he often found his mother unconscious on the floor after Billy had beaten her. He said that often Billy would fire a gun in the house for no good reason. Once Billy took a shot at Jane while she was putting wood in the stove. Another time he fired when she was in the garden. Even the dog, said Alan. Our St. Bernard was "crazy from the beatings." Billy would "kick the dog in the mouth, bite its nose or even hit it with a piece of wood." We were all scared of Billy. That's what Alan said.

\*\*\*

18 The female guest on the talk show says
     — These tapes show incredible violence against women and children. We asked this particular chain of stores, called Red Hot, to take the tapes off their shelves. They refused. We asked the Attorney-General to do something about it. He set up a committee to study the issue. Our point is: we don't need to study the issue!
19   Cut.
20   To Wayne Gretzky scoring a goal!
21   Cut.
22   Back to the host who now introduces Professor Arnold Armstrong. The Professor has written a scholarly book: *Eros Erectus: Paradigms of Sexuality and Civilization*. Along with his pipe, he brings to the discussion a word of caution

---

2. Both James Joyce's *Ulysses* (1922) and D.H. Lawrence's *Lady Chatterley's Lover* (1928) were originally censored in Britain and in the United States.

— If you interfere with what people do in the privacy of their own homes, you're violating their civil liberties. To quote our Prime Minister: "The state has no business in the bedrooms of the nation."

\*\*\*

23 The judge said: Mrs. Stafford, will you please speak up. We can hardly hear you.

24 Jane said: At first Billy was not violent but after I had Darren, our four-year-old, "things started getting different." "Billy wanted a baby girl" and he said "I was no good" because I had the operation so I couldn't have any more children. He started to beat me and make me do things ...

25 The lawyer said: What kind of things?

26 Jane said: Things in bed.

: Sexually?
: Yes.
: Bondage?
: Yes.
: Bestiality?
: Yes.
: Why didn't you tell someone?
: No one would believe me.
: How did he treat the children?
: He never taught Darren anything good. It was always hit, fight, get what you want. Sometimes Billy would pick him up by the hair, right off his feet, and hold a butcher knife to his throat. Darren was never supposed to cry because Billy told him "men don't cry."

\*\*\*

27 November, 1982. In one night the Vancouver Wimmin's Fire Brigade burned two of the Red Hot shops. On the shelves the ghostly videotape figures writhed and hissed. Red hot. Red hot. The fireman had trouble putting out this purgatorial blaze. The Attorney-General spluttered and said: Taking the law into their own hands is no solution. Our Committee has been studying the issue for six months! The man-in-the-street, interviewed, said: They can't do this to me! In the privacy of my own home I can do what I want. That's what democracy is all about. We're not living in Soviet Russia. At least not yet.

\*\*\*

28 Jane said: "I stayed in the truck; whenever he passed out in the truck I'd have to stay until he woke up. I just sat there; everything he had said about what he was going to do started sinking in. He said he was going to burn out Margaret Joudrey, my friend who I consider like a mother, and he said he was going to *deal* with Alan. All this started sinking in and I finally said to hell with it. I wasn't going to live like

that anymore. ... I put the gun in the window (the gun Alan brought me from the house) and pulled the trigger. ..."

\*\*\*

29   Cut.
30   Professor Armstrong has forgotten his pipe, he is well-launched into his subject
— Society is always trying to chain up the erotic impulse like they locked up de Sade[3] in a madhouse. To the liberal man of conscience, de Sade is a revolutionary figure. A hero!
31   The female guest tries to interrupt
— But I. ...
32   And is cut off by the host who says
— I'm sorry. We're running out of time again.
33   Cut.
34   To the streets where the firemen are putting away their gear. The Red Hot shops are charred and smouldering. Into the first delicate light of dawn a car speeds along the Fraser Valley highway. Inside are three women who smell of gasoline and tension and fire. Inside are three women smiling.

\*\*\*

35   November, 1982. After deliberating for 18 hours, the jury returned the verdict that Jane Stafford was NOT GUILTY. The spectator section of the courtroom burst into applause and people shouted: "Praise the Lord!" Jane's neighbour, Roger, said: "I never thought Jane would have enough gumption to do something like that." The Crown said they would appeal. Jane said: Thank you.

\*\*\*

36   This is written in the Valley of the Shadow where the wind whips the sea to bitter fury and the old moon holds the new moon in her arms.

*(1989)*

---

3. The Marquis de Sade (1740–1814), French novelist who celebrated gaining sexual pleasure from physical cruelty to others in his novel *Justine* (1791). The term "sadism" is derived from his name.

# Alice Walker (b. 1944)

The daughter of Georgia sharecroppers, Walker established her literary reputation as an editor and writer of poetry and fiction. The Color Purple (1982), which examines the effects of racism, won the Pulitzer Prize for Fiction in 1983. Other works include The Third Life of Grange Copeland (1970), Meridian (1976), and The Temple of My Familiar (1989).

## Nineteen Fifty-Five

1955

1   The car is a brandnew red Thunderbird convertible, and it's passed the house more than once. It slows down real slow now, and stops at the curb. An older gentleman dressed like a Baptist deacon gets out on the side near the house, and a young fellow who looks about sixteen gets out on the driver's side. They are white, and I wonder what in the world they doing in this neighborhood.

2   Well, I say to J.T., put your shirt on, anyway, and let me clean these glasses offa the table.

3   We had been watching the ballgame on TV. I wasn't actually watching, I was sort of daydreaming, with my foots up in J.T.'s lap.

4   I seen 'em coming on up the walk, brisk, like they coming to sell something, and then they rung the bell, and J.T. declined to put on a shirt but instead disappeared into the bedroom where the other television is. I turned down the one in the living room; I figured I'd be rid of these two double quick and J.T. could come back out again.

5   Are you Gracie Mae Still? asked the old guy, when I opened the door and put my hand on the lock inside the screen.

6   And I don't need to buy a thing, said I.

7   What makes you think we're sellin'? he asks, in that hearty Southern way that makes my eyeballs ache.

8   Well, one way or another and they're inside the house and the first thing the young fellow does is raise the TV a couple of decibels. He's about five feet nine, sort of womanish looking, with real dark white skin and a red pouting mouth. His hair is black and curly and he looks like a Loosianna creole.

9. About one of your songs, says the deacon. He is maybe sixty, with white hair and beard, white silk shirt, black linen suit, black tie and black shoes. His cold gray eyes look like they're sweating.

10. One of my songs?

11. Traynor here just loves your songs. Don't you, Traynor? He nudges Traynor with his elbow. Traynor blinks, says something I can't catch in a pitch I don't register.

12. The boy learned to sing and dance livin' around you people out in the country. Practically cut his teeth on you.

13. Traynor looks up at me and bites his thumbnail.

14. I laugh.

15. Well, one way or another they leave with my agreement that they can record one of my songs. The deacon writes me a check for five hundred dollars, the boy grunts his awareness of the transaction, and I am laughing all over myself by the time I rejoin J.T.

16. Just as I am snuggling down beside him though I hear the front door bell going off again.

17. Forgit his hat? asks J.T.

18. I hope not, I say.

19. The deacon stands there leaning on the door frame and once again I'm thinking of those sweaty-looking eyeballs of his. I wonder if sweat makes your eyeballs pink because his are sure pink. Pink and gray and it strikes me that nobody I'd care to know is behind them.

20. I forgot one little thing, he says pleasantly. I forgot to tell you Traynor and I would like to buy up all of those records you made of the song. I tell you we sure do love it.

21. Well, love it or not, I'm not so stupid as to let them do that without making 'em pay. So I says, Well, that's gonna cost you. Because, really, that song never did sell all that good, so I was glad they was going to buy it up. But on the other hand, them two listening to my song by themselves, and nobody else getting to hear me sing it, give me a pause.

22. Well, one way or another the deacon showed me where I would come out ahead on any deal he had proposed so far. Didn't I give you five hundred dollars? he asked. What white man — and don't even need to mention colored — would give you more? We buy up all your records of that particular song: first, you git royalties. Let me ask you, how much you sell that song for in the first place? Fifty dollars? A hundred, I say. And no royalties from it yet, right? Right. Well, when we buy up all of them records you gonna git royalties. And that's gonna make all them race record shops sit up and take notice of Gracie Mae Still. And they gonna push all them other records of yourn they got. And you no doubt will become one of the big name colored recording artists. And then we can offer you another five hundred dollars for letting us do all this for you. And by God you'll be sittin' pretty! You can go out and buy you the kind of outfit a star should have. Plenty sequins and yards of red satin.

23  I had done unlocked the screen when I saw I could get some more money out of him. Now I held it wide open while he squeezed through the opening between me and the door. He whipped out another piece of paper and I signed it.

24  He sort of trotted out to the car and slid in beside Traynor, whose head was back against the seat. They swung around in a u-turn in front of the house and then they were gone.

25  J.T. was putting his shirt on when I got back to the bedroom. Yankees beat the Orioles 10-6, he said. I believe I'll drive out to Paschal's pond and go fishing. Wanta go?

26  While I was putting on my pants J.T. was holding the two checks.

27  I'm real proud of a woman that can make cash money without leavin' home, he said. And I said *Umph*. Because we met on the road with me singing in first one little low-life jook after another, making ten dollars a night for myself if I was lucky, and sometimes bringin' home nothing but my life. And J.T. just loved them times. The way I was fast and flashy and always on the go from one town to another. He loved the way my singin' made the dirt farmers cry like babies and the womens shout Honey, hush! But that's mens. They loves any style to which you can get 'em accustomed.

## 1956

28  My little grandbaby called me one night on the phone: Little Mama, Little Mama, there's a white man on the television singing one of your songs! Turn on channel 5.

29  Lord, if it wasn't Traynor. Still looking half asleep from the neck up, but kind of awake in a nasty way from the waist down. He wasn't doing too bad with my song either, but it wasn't just the song the people in the audience was screeching and screaming over, it was that nasty little jerk he was doing from the waist down.

30  Well, Lord have mercy. I said, listening to him. If I'da closed my eyes, it could have been me. He had followed every turning of my voice, side streets, avenues, red lights, train crossings and all. It give me a chill.

31  Everywhere I went I hear Traynor singing my song, and all the little white girls just eating it up. I never had so many ponytails switched across my line of vision in my life. They was so *proud*. He was a *genius*.

32  Well, all that year I was trying to lose weight anyway and that and high blood pressure and sugar kept me pretty well occupied. Traynor had made a smash from a song of mine. I still have seven hundred dollars of the original one thousand dollars in the bank, and I felt if I could just bring my weight down, life would be sweet.

## 1957

33  I lost ten pounds in 1956. That's what I give myself for Christmas. And J.T. and me and the children and their friends and grandkids of all description had just finished dinner — over which I had put on nine and a half of my lost ten — when who should appear at the front door but Traynor. Little Mama, Little Mama! It's that white man who sings ─── ─── ───. The children didn't call it my song anymore. Nobody did. It was funny how that happened. Traynor and the deacon had bought up all my records, true, but on his record he had put "written by Gracie Mae Still." But that was just another name on the label, like "produced by Apex Records."

34  On the TV he was inclined to dress like the deacon told him. But now he looked presentable.

35  Merry Christmas, said he.

36  And same to you, Son.

37  I don't know why I called him Son. Well, one way or another they're all our sons. The only requirement is that they be younger than us. But then again Traynor seemed to be aging by the minute.

38  You looks tired, I said. Come on in and have a glass of Christmas cheer.

39  J.T. ain't never in his life been able to act decent to a white man he wasn't working for, but he poured Traynor a glass of bourbon and water, then he took all the children and grandkids and friends and whatnot out to the den. After a while I heard Traynor's voice singing the song, coming from the stereo console. It was just the kind of Christmas present my kids would consider cute.

40  I looked at Traynor, complicit. But he looked like it was the last thing in the world he wanted to hear. His head was pitched forward over his lap, his hands holding his glass and his elbows on his knees.

41  I done sung that song seem like a million times this year, he said. I sung it on the Grand Ole Opry, I sung it on the Ed Sullivan show. I sung it on Mike Douglas, I sung it at the Cotton Bowl, the Orange Bowl. I sung it at Festivals. I sung it at Fairs. I sung it overseas in Rome, Italy, and once in a submarine *underseas*. I've sung it and sung it, and I'm making forty thousand dollars a day offa it, and you know what, I don't have the faintest notion what that song means.

42  Whatchumean, what do it mean? It mean what it says. All I could think was: these suckers is making forty thousand a *day* offa my song and now they gonna come back and try to swindle me out of the original thousand.

43  It's just a song, I said. Cagey. When you fool around with a lot of no count mens you sing a bunch of 'em. I shrugged.

44  Oh, he said. Well. He started brightening up. I just come by to tell you I think you are a great singer.

45  He didn't blush, saying that. Just said it straight out.

46     And I brought you a little Christmas present too. Now you take this little box and you hold it until I drive off. Then you take it outside under the first streetlight back up the street aways in front of that green house. Then you open the box and see ... Well, just *see*.

47     What had come over this boy, I wondered, holding the box. I looked out the window in time to see another white man come up and get in the car with him and then two more cars full of white mens start out behind him. They was all in long black cars that looked like a funeral procession.

48     Little Mama, Little Mama, what it is? One of my grandkids came running up and started pulling at the box. It was wrapped in gay Christmas paper — the thick, rich kind that it's hard to picture folks making just to throw away.

49     J.T. and the rest of the crowd followed me out the house, up the street to the streetlight and in front of the green house. Nothing was there but somebody's gold-grille white Cadillac. Brandnew and most distracting. We got to looking at it so till I almost forgot the little box in my hand. While the others were busy making 'miration I carefully took off the paper and ribbon and folded them up and put them in my pants pocket. What should I see but a pair of genuine solid gold caddy keys.

50     Dangling the keys in front of everybody's nose, I unlocked the caddy, motioned for J.T. to git in on the other side, and us didn't come back home for two days.

## 1960

51 Well, the boy was sure nuff famous by now. He was still a mite shy of twenty but already they was calling him the Emperor of Rock and Roll.

52     Then what should happen but the draft.

53     Well, says J.T. There goes all this Emperor of Rock and Roll business.

54     But even in the army the womens was on him like white on rice. We watched it on the News.

> *Dear Gracie Mae* [he wrote from Germany],
>
> *How you? Fine I hope as this leaves me doing real well. Before I come in the army I was gaining a lot of weight and gitting jittery from making all them dumb movies. But now I exercise and eat right and get plenty of rest. I'm more awake than I been in ten years.*
> *I wonder if you are writing any more songs?*
> *Sincerely,*
> *Traynor*

55 I wrote him back:

*Dear Son,*

*We is all fine in the Lord's good grace and hope this finds you the same. J.T. and me be out all times of the day and night in that car you give me — which you know you didn't have to do. Oh, and I do appreciate the mink and the new self-cleaning oven. But if you send anymore stuff to eat from Germany I'm going to have to open up a store in the neighborhood just to get rid of it. Really, we have more than enough of everything. The Lord is good to us and we don't know Want.*

*Glad to here you is well and gitting your right rest. There ain't nothing like exercising to help that along. J.T. and me work some part of every day that we don't go fishing in the garden.*

*Well, so long Soldier.*
*Sincerely,*
*Gracie Mae*

56 He wrote:

*Dear Gracie Mae,*

*I hope you and J.T. like that automatic power tiller I had one of the stores back home send you. I went through a mountain of catalogs looking for it — I wanted something that even a woman could use.*

*I've been thinking about writing some songs of my own but every time I finish one it don't seem to be about nothing I've actually lived myself. My agent keeps sending me other people's songs but they just sound mooney. I can hardly git through 'em without gagging.*

*Everybody still loves that song of yours. They ask me all the time what do I think it means, really. I mean, they want to know just what I want to know. Where out of your life did it come from?*
*Sincerely,*
*Traynor*

# 1968

57 I didn't see the boy for seven years. No. Eight. Because just about everybody was dead when I saw him again. Malcolm X, King, the president and his brother[1] and even J.T. J.T. died of a head cold. It just settled in his head like a block of ice, he said, and nothing we did moved it until one day he just leaned out the bed and died.

---

1. Malcolm X (1925–1965), African-American founder of the Black Muslim movement. Martin Luther King, Jr. (1929–1968), U.S. civil rights leader who successfully led a movement of non-violent resistance against racial segregation in the United States. John F. Kennedy (1917–1963), U.S. president who supported racial integration. Robert F. Kennedy (1925–1968), the president's brother who served as U.S. attorney general. All four were killed by assassins.

58   His good friend Horace helped me put him away, and then about a year later Horace and me started going together. We was sitting out on the front porch swing one summer night, dusk-dark, and I saw this great procession of lights winding to a stop.

59   Holy Toledo! said Horace. (He's got a real sexy voice like Ray Charles.[2]) Look *at* it. He meant the long line of flashy cars and the white men in white summer suits jumping out on the drivers' sides and standing at attention. With wings they could pass for angels, with hoods they could be the Klan.

60   Traynor comes waddling up the walk.

61   And suddenly I know what it is he could pass for. An Arab like the ones you see in storybooks. Plump and soft and with never a care about weight. Because with so much money, who cares? Traynor is almost dressed like someone from a storybook too. He has on, I swear, about ten necklaces. Two sets of bracelets on his arms, at least one ring on every finger, and some kind of shining buckles on his shoes, so that when he walks you get quite a few twinkling lights.

62   Gracie Mae, he says, coming up to give me a hug. J.T.

63   I explain that J.T. passed. That this is Horace.

64   Horace, he says, puzzled but polite, sort of rocking back on his heels, Horace.

65   That's it for Horace. He goes in the house and don't come back.

66   Looks like you and me is gained a few, I say.

67   He laughs. The first time I ever heard him laugh. It don't sound much like a laugh and I can't swear that it's better than no laugh at a'tall.

68   He's gitting fat for sure, but he's still slim compared to me. I'll never see three hundred pounds again and I've just about said (excuse me) fuck it. I got to thinking about it one day an' I thought: aside from the fact that they say it's unhealthy, my fat ain't never been no trouble. Men always have loved me. My kids ain't never complained. Plus they's fat. And fat like I is I looks distinguished. You see me coming and know somebody's *there*.

69   Gracie Mae, he says, I've come with a personal invitation to you to my house tomorrow for dinner. He laughed. What did it sound like? I couldn't place it. See them men out there? he asked me. I'm sick and tired of eating with them. But if you come to dinner tomorrow we can talk about the old days. You can tell me about that farm I bought you.

70   I sold it, I said.

71   You did?

72   Yeah, I said. I did. Just cause I said I like to exercise by working in a garden didn't mean I wanted five hundred acres! Anyhow, I'm a city girl now. Raised in the country it's true. Dirt poor — the whole bit — but that's all behind me now.

73   Oh well, he said. I didn't mean to offend you.

---

2. African-American rhythm and blues singer who became famous during the 1950s.

74   We sat a few minutes listening to the crickets.
75   Then he said: You wrote that song while you was still on the farm, didn't you, or was it right after you left?
76   You had somebody spying on me? I asked.
77   You and Bessie Smith[3] got into a fight over it once, he said.
78   You *is* been spying on me!
79   But I don't know what the fight was about, he said. Just like I don't know what happened to your second husband. Your first one died in the Texas electric chair. Did you know that? Your third one beat you up, stole your touring costumes and your car and retired with a chorine[4] to Tuskegee. He laughed. He's still there.
80   I had been mad, but suddenly I calmed down. Traynor was talking very dreamily. It was dark but seems like I could tell his eyes weren't right. It was like *something* was sitting there talking to me but not necessarily with a person behind it.
81   You gave up on marrying and seem happier for it. He laughed again. I married but it never went like it was supposed to. I never could squeeze any of my own life either into it or out of it. It was like singing somebody else's record. I copied the way it was supposed to be *exactly* but I never had a clue what marriage meant.
82   I bought her a diamond ring big as your fist. I bought her clothes. I built her a mansion. But right away she didn't want the boys to stay there. Said they smoked up the bottom floor. Hell, there were *five* floors.
83   No need to grieve, I said. No need to. Plenty more where she comes from.
84   He perked up. That's part of what that song means, ain't it? No need to grieve. Whatever it is, there's plenty more down the line.
85   I never really believed that way back when I wrote the song, I said. It was all bluffing then. The trick is to live long enough to put your young bluffs to use. Now if I was going to sing that song today I'd tear it up. 'Cause I done lived long enough to know it's *true*. Them words could hold me up.
86   I ain't lived that long, he said.
87   Look like you on your way, I said. I don't know why, but the boy seemed to need some encouraging. And I don't know, seem like one way or another you talk to rich white folks and you end up reassuring *them*. But what the hell, by now I feel something for the boy. I wouldn't be in his bed all alone in the middle of the night for nothing. Couldn't be nothing worse than being famous the world over for something you don't even understand. That's what I tried to tell Bessie. She wanted that same song. Overheard me practising it one

---

3. Bessie Smith (c. 1898–1937), Southern-American singer who became famous during the 1920s as the "Empress of the Blues."
4. Chorus dancer (derogatory).

day, said, with her hands on her hips: Gracie Mae, I'ma sing your song tonight. I *likes* it.

88   Your lips be too swole to sing, I said. She was mean and she was strong, but I trounced her.

89   Ain't you famous enough with your own stuff? I said. Leave mine alone. Later on, she thanked me. By then she was Miss Bessie Smith to the World, and I was still Miss Gracie Mae Nobody from Notasulga.

90   The next day all these limousines arrived to pick me up. Five cars and twelve bodyguards. Horace picked that morning to start painting the kitchen.

91   Don't paint the kitchen, fool, I said. The only reason that dumb boy of ours is going to show me his mansion is because he intends to present us with a new house.

92   What you gonna do with it? he asked me, standing there in his shirt-sleeves stirring the paint.

93   Sell it. Give it to the children. Live in it on weekends. It don't matter what I do. He sure don't care.

94   Horace just stood there shaking his head. Mama you sure looks *good*, he says. Wake me up when you git back.

95   *Fool*, I say, and pat my wig in front of the mirror.

96   The boy's house is something else. First you come to this mountain, and then you commence to drive up this road that's lined with magnolias. Do magnolias grow on mountains? I was wondering. And you come to lakes and you come to ponds and you come to deer and you come up on some sheep. And I figure these two is sposed to represent England and Wales. Or something out of Europe. And you just keep on coming to stuff. And it's all pretty. Only the man driving my car don't look at nothing but the road. Fool. And then *finally*, after all this time, you begin to go up the driveway. And there's more magnolias — only they're not in such good shape. It's sort of cool up this high and I don't think they're gonna make it. And then I see this building that looks like if it had a name it would be The Tara Hotel.[5] Columns and steps and outdoor chandeliers and rocking chairs. Rocking chairs? Well, and there's the boy on the steps dressed in a dark green satin jacket like you see folks wearing on TV late at night, and he looks sort of like a fat dracula with all that house rising behind him, and standing beside him there's this little white vision of loveliness that he introduces as his wife.

97   He's nervous when he introduces us and he says to her: This is Gracie Mae Still, I want you to know me. I mean ... and she gives him a look that would fry meat.

---

5. From Tara, the home of Scarlett O'Hara in Margaret Mitchell's novel, *Gone With the Wind*.

98   Won't you come in, Grace May, she says, and that's the last I see of her.

99   He fishes around for something to say or do and decides to escort me to the kitchen. We go through the entry and the parlor and the breakfast room and the dining room and the servants' passage and finally get there. The first thing I notice is that, altogether, there are five stoves. He looks about to introduce me to one.

100  Wait a minute, I say. Kitchens don't do nothing for me. Let's go sit on the front porch.

101  Well, we hike back and we sit in the rocking chairs rocking until dinner.

102 Gracie Mae, he says down the table, taking a piece of fried chicken from the woman standing over him, I got a little surprise for you.

103  It's a house, ain't it? I ask, spearing a chitlin.[6]

104  You're getting *spoiled*, he says. And the way he says *spoiled* sounds funny. He slurs it. It sounds like his tongue is too thick for his mouth. Just that quick he's finished the chicken and is now eating chitlins, *and* a pork chop. *Me* spoiled, I'm thinking.

105  I already got a house. Horace is right this minute painting the kitchen. I bought that house. My kids feel comfortable in that house.

106  But this one I bought you is just like mine. Only a little smaller.

107  I still don't need no house. And anyway who would clean it?

108  He looks surprised.

109  Really, I think, some peoples advance *so* slowly.

110  I hadn't thought of that. But what the hell. I'll get you somebody to live in.

111  I don't want other folks living 'round me. Makes me nervous.

112  You *don't*? It *do*?

113  What I want to wake up and see folks I don't even know for?

114  He just sits there downtable staring at me. Some of that feeling is in the song, ain't it? Not the words, the *feeling*. What I want to wake up and see folks I don't even know for? But I see twenty folks a day I don't even know, including my wife.

115  This food wouldn't be bad to wake up to though, I said. The boy had found the genius of corn bread.

116  He looked at me real hard. He laughed. Short. They want what you got but they don't want you. They want what I got only it ain't mine. That's what makes 'em so hungry for me when I sing. They getting the flavor of something but they ain't getting the thing itself. They like a pack of hound dogs trying to gobble up a scent.

117  You talking 'bout your fans?

118  Right. Right. He says.

---

6. Chitterlings are pigs' intestines, cleaned and fried with spices, a popular Southern dish.

119   Don't worry 'bout your fans, I say. They don't know their asses from a hole in the ground. I doubt there's a honest one in the bunch.

120   That's the point. Dammit, that's the point! He hits the table with his fist. It's so solid it don't even quiver. You need a honest audience! You can't have folks that's just gonna lie right back to you.

121   Yeah, I say, it was small compared to yours, but I had one. It would have been worth my life to try to sing 'em somebody else's stuff that I didn't know nothing about.

122   He must have pressed a buzzer under the table. One of his flunkies zombies up.

123   Git Johnny Carson, he says.

124   On the phone? asks the zombie.

125   On the phone, says Traynor, what you think I mean, git him offa the front porch? Move your ass.

126   So two weeks later we's on the Johnny Carson show.

127   Traynor is all corseted down nice and looks a little bit fat but mostly good. And all the women that grew up on him and my song squeal and squeal. Traynor says: The lady who wrote my first hit record is here with us tonight, and she's agreed to sing it for all of us, just like she sung it forty-five years ago. Ladies and Gentlemen, the great Gracie Mae Still!

128   Well, I had tried to lose a couple of pounds my own self, but failing that I had me a very big dress made. So I sort of rolls over next to Traynor, who is dwarfed by me, so that when he puts his arms around back of me to try to hug me it looks funny to the audience and they laugh.

129   I can see this pisses him off. But I smile out there at 'em. Imagine squealing for twenty years and not knowing why you're squealing? No more sense of endings and beginnings than hogs.

130   It don't matter, Son, I say. Don't fret none over me.

131   I commence to sing. And I sound — wonderful. Being able to sing good ain't all about having a good singing voice a'tall. A good singing voice helps. But when you come up in the Hard Shell Baptist church like I did you understand early that the fellow that sings is the singer. Them that waits for programs and arrangements and letters from home is just good voices occupying body space.

132   So there I am singing my own song, my own way. And I give it all I got and enjoy every minute of it. When I finish Traynor is standing up clapping and clapping and beaming at first me and then the audience like I'm his mama for true. The audience claps politely for about two seconds.

133   Traynor looks disgusted.

134   He comes over and tries to hug me again. The audience laughs.

135   Johnny Carson looks at us like we both weird.

136   Traynor is mad as hell. He's supposed to sing something called a love ballad. But instead he takes the mike, turns to me and says: Now see if my imitation still holds up. He goes into the same song, *our* song, I think, looking out at his flaky audience. And he sings it just the way he always did. My voice, my tone, my inflection, everything. But he forgets a couple of lines. Even before he's finished the matronly squeals begin.

137   He sits down next to me looking whipped.

138   It don't matter, Son, I say, patting his head. You don't even know those people. Try to make the people you know happy.

139   Is that in the song? he asks.

140   Maybe. I say.

## 1977

141   For a few years I hear from him, then nothing. But trying to lose weight takes all the attention I got to spare. I finally faced up to the fact that my fat is the hurt I don't admit, not even to myself, and that I been trying to bury it from the day I was born. But also when you git real old, to tell the truth, it ain't as pleasant. It gits lumpy and slack. So one day I said to Horace, I'ma git this shit offa me.

142   And he fell in with the program like he always try to do and Lord such a procession of salads and cottage cheese and fruit juice!

143   One night I dreamed Traynor had split up with his fifteenth wife. He said: *You meet 'em for no reason. You date 'em for no reason. You marry 'em for no reason. I do it all but I swear it's just like somebody else doing it. I feel like I can't remember Life.*

144   The boy's in trouble, I said to Horace.

145   You've always said that, he said.

146   I have?

147   Yeah. You always said he looked asleep. You can't sleep through life if you wants to live it.

148   You not such a fool after all, I said, pushing myself up with my cane and hobbling over to where he was. Let me sit down on your lap, I said, while this salad I ate takes effect.

149   In the morning we heard that Traynor was dead. Some said fat, some said heart, some said alcohol, some said drugs. One of the children called from Detroit. Them dumb fans of his on a crying rampage, she said. You just ought to turn on the TV.

150   But I didn't want to see 'em. They was crying and crying and didn't even know what they was crying for. One day this is going to be a pitiful country, I thought.

(1981)

# Lee Maracle (b. 1950)

Born in Vancouver of Métis and Salish parents, Maracle did not complete high school, but studied at Simon Fraser University in 1987. Education is a central concern of her work, which remains true to the principles of Native oratory. A gifted poet, novelist, short story writer, and commentator, Maracle draws her readers into her work to "become the trickster, the architect of great social transformations at whatever level [they] choose."

## Yin Chin

*for Sharon Lee, whose real name is Sky, and for Jim Wong-Chu*

1. she is tough,
   she is verbose,
   she has lived a thousand lives

2. she is sweet,
   she is not,
   she is blossoming
   and dying every moment

3. a flower
   unsweetened by rain
   untarnished by simpering
   uncuckolded by men
   not coquettish enough
   for say the gals
   who make a career of shopping
   at the Pacific Centre Mall

4. PACIFIC CENTRE, my gawd
   do North Americans never tire
   of claiming the centre
   of the universe, the Pacific and
   everywhere else ...

5. I am weary
   of North Americans
   so I listen to SKY

6 Standing in the crowded college dining hall, coffee in hand, my face is drawn to a noisy group of Chinese youth; I mentally cancel them out. No place to sit — no place meaning there aren't any Indians in the room. It is a reflexive action on my part to assume that any company that isn't Indian company is generally unacceptable, but there it was: the absence of Indians, not chairs, determined the absence of a space for me. Soft of heart, guilt-ridden liberals might argue defensively that such sweeping judgement is not different from any of the generalizations made about us. So be it; after all, it is not their humanity I am calling into question. It is mine. Along with that thought dances another. I have lived in this city in the same neighbourhood as Chinese people for over twenty-two years now and don't know a single Chinese person.

7 It scares me just a little. It wasn't always that way. The memory of a skinny little waif drops into the frame of moving pictures rolling across my mind. Unabashed, she stands next to the door of Mad Sam's market across from the Powell Street[1] grounds, surveying "Chinamen" with accusatory eyes. Once a month on a Saturday the process repeats itself: the little girl of noble heart studies the old men. Not once in all her childhood years did she ever see an old man steal a little kid. She gave up, not because she became convinced that the accusation was unfounded, but because she got too big to worry about it.

8 "Cun-a-muck-ah-you-da-puppy-shaw, that's Chinee for how are you," and the old Pa'pa-y-ah would laugh. "Don't wander around town or the old Chinamen will get you, steal you, … Chinkee, chinkee Chinaman went down town, turned around the corner and his pants fell down," and other such truck is buried somewhere in the useless information file tucked in the basement of my mind, but the shape of my social life is frighteningly influenced by those absurd sounds. The movie is just starting to lag and the literary theme of the pictures is coming into focus when a small breath of air, a gentle touch of a small woman's hand invites me to sit. How embarrassing. I'd been gaping and gawking at a table-load of Hans long enough for my coffee to cool.

9 It doesn't take long. Invariably, when people of colour get together they discuss white people. They are the butt of our jokes, the fountain of our bitterness and pain and the infinite well-spring of every dilemma life ever presented to us. The humour eases the pain, but always whites figure front and centre of our joint communication. If I had a dollar for every word ever said about them, instead of to them, I'd be the richest welfare bum in the country. No wonder they suffer from inflated egoism.

10 I sit at the table-load of Chinese people and towards the end of the hour I want to tell them about Mad Sam's, Powell Street and the old men. Wisely, I think now, I didn't. Our sense of humour was different then. In the face of a crass white world we had erased so much of ourselves, and

---

1. Thoroughfare in Vancouver's Chinatown.

sketched so many cartoon characters of white people over top of the emptiness inside, that it would have been too much for us to face the fact that we really did feel just like them. I sat at that table more than a dozen times but not once did it occur to any of us that we were friends. Eventually, the march of a relentless clock, my hasty departure from college the following semester and my failure to return for fifteen years took its toll — now even their names escape me.

11   Last Saturday — seems like a hundred years later — was different. This time the table-load of people was Asian and Native. We laughed at ourselves and spoke very seriously about our writing. "We really believe we are writers," someone said, and the room shook with the hysteria of it all. We ran on and on about our growth and development, and not once did the white man ever enter the room. It just seemed too incredible that a dozen Hans and Natives could sit and discuss all things under heaven, including racism, and not talk about white people. It had only taken a half-dozen revolutions in the third world, seventeen riots in America, one hundred demonstrations against racism in Canada and thirty-seven dead Native youth in my life to become. I could have told them about the waif, but it didn't seem relevant. We had crossed a millennium of bridges over rivers swollen with the floodwaters of dark humanity's tenacious struggle to extricate ourselves from oppression, and we knew it. We had been born during the first sword wound that the third world swung at imperialism. We were children of that wound, invincible, conscious and movin' on up. We could laugh because we were no longer a joke. But somewhere along the line we forgot to tell the others, the thousands of our folks who still tell their kids about old Chinamen.

* * *

12   It's Tuesday and I'm circling the block at Gore and Powell trying to find a parking space, windows open, driving like I belong here. A sharp, "Don't come near me, why you bother me?" jars me loose. An old Chinese woman swings a ratty old umbrella at a Native man who is pushing her, cursing her and otherwise giving her a hard time. I lean toward the passenger side and shout at him from the safety of my car: "Leave her alone, asshole."

13   "Shuddup you f.ck.ng rag-head." I jump out of the car without bothering to park it. No one honks; they just stare at me. The man sees my face and my cowichan,[2] bends deeply and says sarcastically that he didn't know I was a squaw. Well, I'm no pacifist, I admit: I belt him, give him a what for, and the coward leaves. I help the old woman across the street, then return to park my car. She stays there, where I left her, still shaking, so I stop to try to quell her fear.

---

2. Usually the word is capitalized. It refers to the heavy, handknit sweaters made and sometimes worn by the Cowichan band.

14    She isn't afraid. She is ashamed of her own people — men who passed her by, walking around her or crossing the street to avoid trying to rescue her from the taunts of one of my people. The world rages around inside me while she copiously describes every Chinese man who saw her and kept walking. I listen to her in silence and think of me and old Sam again.

15    Mad Sam was a pioneer of discount foods. Slightly overripe bananas (great for peanut-butter-and-banana bannock sandwiches), bruised apples and day-old bread were always available at half the price of Safeway's, and we shopped there regularly for years. I am not sure if he sold meat. In any case, we never bought meat; we were fish-eaters then. I doubt very much that Sam knew we called him "Mad" but I know now that "mad" was intended for the low prices and the crowds in his little store, not for him. In the fifties, there were still storeowners who concerned themselves with their customers, established relationships with them, exchanged gossip and shared a few laughs. Sam was good to us.

16    If you press your nose up against the window to the left of the door you can still see me standing there, ghost-like, skinny brown body with huge eyes riveted on the street and the Powell Street grounds. Sometimes my eyes take a slow shift from left to right, then right to left. I'm watchin' ol' Chinamen, makin' sure they don't grab little kids. Once a month for several years I assume my post and keep my private vigil. No one on the street seems to know what I'm doing or why, but it doesn't matter. The object of my vigil is not appreciation but catchin' the old Chinamen in the act.

17    My nose is pressed up against the window pane; the cold circles the end of my flattened nose; it feels good. Outside, the window pane is freckled with crystal water drops; inside, it is smooth and dry, but for a little wisp of fog from my breath. Round o's of water splotch onto the clear glass. Not perfectly round, but just the right amount of roundness that allows you to call them o's. Each o is kind of wobbly and different, like on the page at school when you first print o's for teacher.

18    I can see the rain-distorted street scene at the park through the round o's of water. There are no flowers or grass in this park, no elaborate floral themes or landscape designs, just a dozen or so benches around a wasteland of gravel, sand and comfrey root (weeds), and a softball backstop at one end. (What a bloody long time ago that was, mama.)

19    Blat. A raindrop hits the window, scrunching up the park bench I am looking at. The round o of rain makes the park bench wiggle towards my corner of the store. I giggle.

20    "Mad Sam's ... Mad Sam's ... Mad Sam's?" What begins as a senseless repetition of a household phrase ends as a question. I know that Mad Sam is a Chinaman ... Chinee, the old people call them — but then, the old people can't speak goot Inklish. But what in the world

makes him mad? I breathe at the window. It fogs up. The only kind of mad I know is when everyone runs aroun' hollering and kicking up dust.

21   I rock back and forth while my finger traces out a large circle which my hand had cleared. Two old men on the bench across the street break my thoughts of Sam's madness. One of them rises. He is wearing one of those grey tweed wool hats that people think of as English and associate with sports cars. He has a cane, a light beige cane. He half bends at the waist before he leaves the bench, turns, and with his arms stretched out from his shoulders flails them back and forth a few times, accentuating his words to the other old man seated there.

22   It would have looked funny if Pa'pa-y-ah had done it, or ol' Mike, but I am acutely aware that this is a Chinaman. Ol' Chinamen are not funny. They are serious, and the words of the world echo violently in my ears: "Don't wander off or the ol' Chinamen will get you and eat you." I wonder about the fact that mama has never warned me about them.

23   A woman with a black car coat and a white pill box hat disturbs the scene. Screech, the door of her Buick opens. Squeak, slam, it bangs shut. There she be, blonde as all get out, slightly hippy, heaving her bare leg, partially constrained by her skirt, onto the bumper of her car and cranking at whatever has to be cranked to make the damn thing go. There is something humorously inelegant about a white lady with spiked heels, tight skirt and a pill box hat cranking up a '39 Buick. (Thanks, mama, for having me soon enough to have seen it.) All of this wonderfulness comes squiggling to me through a little puddle of clear rain on the window. The Buick finally takes off and from the tail end of its departure I can see the little old man still shuffling his way across the street. Funny, all the cars stop for him. Odd, the little Chinee boy talks to him, unafraid.

24   Shuffle, shuffle, plunk of his cane, shuffle, shuffle, plunk; on he trudges. The breath from the corner near my window comes out in shorter and louder gasps. It punctuates the window with an on-again, off-again choo-choo rhythm of clarity. Breath and fog, shuffle, shuffle, plunk, breath and fog. BOOM! And the old man's face is right on mine. My scream is indelicate. Mad Sam and mama come running.

25   "Whatsa matter?" ... "Wah iss it?" from Sam and mama respectively.

26   Half hesitating, I point out the window. "The Chinaman was looking at me." I can see that this is not the right answer. Mama's eyes yell *for pete's sake* and her cheeks shine red with shame — not embarrassment, shame. Sam's face is clearly, definably hurt. Not the kind of hurt that shows when adults burn themselves or something, but the kind of hurt you can sometimes see in the eyes of people who have been cheated. The total picture spells something I cannot define.

27   Grandmothers, you said if I was ever caught doing nothing you would take me away for all eternity. The silence is thick, cloying and paralyzing. It stops my brain and stills my emotions. It deafens my

ears to the rain. I cannot look out to see if the old man is still there. No grannies come to spare me.

28   My eyes fall unseeing on a parsnip just exactly in front of my face. They rest there until everyone stops looking at my treacherous little body and resumes talking about whatever they were talking about before I brought the world to a momentary halt with my astounding stupidity. What surprises me now, years later, is that they did eventually carry on as though nothing were wrong.

29   The floor sways beneath me, while I try hard to make it swallow me. A hand holding a pear in front of my face jars my eyes loose from the parsnip.

30   "Here," the small, pained smile on Sam's face stills the floor, but the memory remains a moving moment in my life.

\* \* \*

31   The old woman is holding my hands, saying she feels better now. All that time I wasn't thinking about what she said, or speaking. I just nodded my head back and forth and relived my memory of Mad Sam's.

32   "How unkind of the world to school us in ignorance" is all I say, and I make my way back to the car.

*(1990)*

# Guy Vanderhaeghe (b. 1951)

Born in Saskatchewan, Vanderhaeghe worked as a teacher, researcher, and archivist before turning to writing. He won the Governor General's Award for fiction for his first book, Man Descending (1982), and for The Englishman's Boy (1996). He regards himself "as a writer who celebrates ... the endurance of the ordinary person whose life is a series of small victories fashioned from small resources."

## Drummer

1  You'd think my old man was the Pope's nephew or something if you'd seen how wild he went when he learned I'd been sneaking off Sundays to Faith Baptist Church. Instead of going to eleven o'clock Mass like he figured I was.

2  Which is kind of funny. Because although Mom is solid R.C. — eight o'clock Mass and saying a rosary at the drop of a hat — nobody ever accused Pop of being a religious fanatic by no means. He goes to confession regular like an oil change, every five thousand miles, or Easter, whichever comes first.

3  Take the Knights of Columbus. He wouldn't join those guys for no money. Whenever Mom starts in on him about enlisting he just answers back that he can't afford the outlay on armour and where'd he keep a horse? Which is his idea of a joke. So it isn't exactly as if he was St. Joan of Arc himself to go criticizing me.

4  And Pop wouldn't have been none the wiser if it wasn't for my older brother Gene, the prick. Don't think I don't know who told. But I can't expect nothing different from that horse's ass.

5  So, as I was saying, my old man didn't exactly take it all in stride. "Baptists! *Baptists!* I'm having your head examined. Do you hear me? I'm having it *examined*! Just keep it up and see if I don't, you crazy little pecker. They roll in the aisles, Baptists, for chrissakes!"

6  "I been three times already and nobody rolled in an aisle once."

7  "Three times? *Three times?* Now it all comes out. Three, eh?" He actually hits himself in the forehead with the heel of his palm. Twice. "Jesus Christ Almighty, I'm blessed with a son like this? What's the matter with you? Why can't you ever do something I can understand?"

8   "Like wrecking cars?" This is a swift kick in the old fun sack. Pop's just getting over Gene's totalling off the first new car he's bought in eight years. A 1966 Chevy Impala.

9   "Shut your smart mouth. Don't go dragging your brother into this. Anyway what he done to the car was *accidental*. But not you. Oh no, you marched into that collection of religious screwballs, holy belly-floppers, and linoleum-beaters under your own steam. On purpose. For God's sake, Billy, that's no religion that — it's exercise. Stay away from them Baptists."

10  "Can't," I says to him.

11  "Can't? *Can't?* Why the hell not?"

12  "Matter of principle."

13  They teach us that in school, matters of principle. I swear it's a plot to get us all slaughtered the day they graduate us out the door. It's their revenge, see? Here we are reading books in literature class about some banana who's only got one oar in the water to start with, and then he pops it out worrying about principles. Like that Hamlet, or what's his name in *A Tale of Two Cities*.[1] Ever notice how many of those guys are alive at the end of those books they teach us from?

14  "I'll principle you," says the old man.

15  The only teacher who maybe believes all that crock of stale horse-shit about principles is Miss Clark, who's fresh out of wherever they bake Social Studies teachers. She's got principles on the brain. For one thing, old Clarkie has pretty nearly wallpapered her room with pictures of that Negro, Martin Luther King, and some character who's modelling the latest in Wabasso sheets and looks like maybe he'd kill for a hamburger — Gandhi is his name — and that hairy old fart Tolstoy, who wrote the books you need a front-end loader to lift. From what Clarkie tells us, I gather they're what you call non-violent shit-disturbers.

16  Me too. Being a smart-ass runs in the Simpson family. It's what you call hereditary, like a disease. That's why all of a sudden, before I even *think* for chrissakes, I hear myself lecturing the old man in this fruity voice that's a halfway decent imitation of old Clarkie, and I am using the exact words which I've heard her say myself.

17  "Come, come, surely by this day and age everybody has progressed to the point where we can all agree on the necessity of freedom of worship. If we can't agree on anything else, at least we can agree on that."

18  I got news for her. My old man don't agree to no such thing. He up and bangs me one to the side of the head. A backhander special. You see, nobody in our house is allowed an opinion until they're twenty-one.

19  Of course, I could holler Religious Persecution. Not that it would do any good. But it's something I happen to know quite a bit about,

---

1. Novel by Charles Dickens about the French Revolution.

seeing as Religious Persecution was my assignment in Social Studies that time we studied Man's Inhumanity to Man. The idea was to write a two-thousand-word report proving how everybody has been a shit to everybody else through the ages, and where did it ever get them? This is supposed to improve us somehow, I guess.

20    Anyway, as usual anything good went fast. Powbrowski got A. Hitler, Keller put dibs on Ivan the Terrible, Langly asked for Genghis Khan. By the time old Clarkie got around to me there was just a bunch of crap left like No Votes For Women. So I asked, please, could I do a project on Mr. Keeler? Keeler is the dim-witted bat's fart who's principal of our school.

21    For being rude, Miss Clark took away my "privilege" of picking and said I had to do Religious Persecution. Everybody was avoiding that one like the plague.

22    Actually, I found Religious Persecution quite interesting. It's got principles too, number one being that whatever you're doing to some poor son of a bitch — roasting his chestnuts over an open fire, or stretching his pant-leg from a 29-incher to a 36-incher on the rack — why, you're doing it for his own good. So he'll start thinking right. Which is more or less what my old man was saying when he told me I can't go out of the house on Sundays any more. He says to me, "You aren't setting a foot outside that door [he actually points to it] of a Sunday until you come to your senses and quit with all the Baptist bullshit."

23    Not that that's any heavy-duty torture. What he don't know is that these Baptists have something called Prayer, Praise and Healing on Wednesday nights. My old man hasn't locked me up Wednesday nights yet by no means.

24    I figure if my old man wants somebody to blame for me becoming a Baptist he ought to take a peek in my older brother Gene's direction. He started it.

25    Which sounds awful funny if you know anything about Gene. Because if Gene was smart enough to have ever thought about it, he'd come out pretty strong against religion, since it's generally opposed to most things he's in favour of.

26    Still, nobody thinks the worse of my brother for doing what he likes to do. They make a lot of excuses for you in a dinky mining town that's the arsehole of the world if you bat .456 and score ninety-eight goals in a thirty-five-game season. Shit, last year they passed the hat around to all the big shots on the recreation board and collected the dough for one of Gene's liquor fines and give it to him on the q.t.

27    But I'm trying to explain my brother. If I had to sum him up I'd probably just say he's the kind of guy doesn't have to dance. What I mean is, you take your average, normal female: they slobber to dance. The guys that stand around leaning against walls are as popular to

them as syphilis. You don't dance, you're a pathetic dope — even the ugly ones despise you.

28   But not Gene. He don't dance and they all cream. You explain it. Do they figure he's too superior to be bothered? Because it's not true. I'm his brother and I know. The dink just can't dance. That simple. But if I mention this little fact to anybody, they look at me like I been playing out in the sun too long. Everybody around here figures Mr. Wonderful could split the fucking atom with a hammer and a chisel if he put his mind to it.

29   Well, almost everybody. There's a born doubter in every crowd. Ernie Powers is one of these. He's the kind of stupid fuck who's sure they rig the Stanley Cup and the Oscars and nobody ever went up in space. Everything is a hoax to him. Yet he believes professional wrestling is on the up and up. You wonder — was he dropped on his head, or what? Otherwise you got to have a plan to grow up that ignorant.

30   So it was just like Einstein to bet Gene ten dollars he couldn't take out Nancy Williams. He did that while we were eating a plate of chips and gravy together in the Rite Spot and listening to Gene going on about who's been getting the benefit of his poking lately. Powers, who is a very jealous person because he's going steady with his right hand, says, oh yeah sure, maybe her, but he'd bet ten bucks somebody like Nancy Williams in 11B wouldn't even go out with Gene.

31   "Get serious," says my brother when he hears that. He considers himself irresistible to the opposite sex.

32   "Ten bucks. She's strictly off-limits even to you, Mr. Dreamboat. It's all going to waste. That great little gunga-poochy-snuggy-bum, that great matched set. Us guys in 11B, you know what we call them? The Untouchables. Like on TV."

33   "What a fucking sad bunch. Untouchables for you guys, maybe. If any of you queers saw a real live piece of pelt you'd throw your hat over it and run."

34   "Talk's cheap," says Ernie, real offended. "You don't know nothing about her. My sister says Miss High-and-Mighty didn't go out for cheerleading because the outfits were *too revealing*. My sister says Nancy Williams belongs to some religion doesn't allow her to dance. Me I saw her pray over a hard-boiled egg for about a half-hour before she ate it in the school lunch-room. Right out where everybody could see, she prayed. No way somebody like that is going to go out with you, Simpson. If she does I'll eat my shorts."

35   "Start looking for the ten bucks, shitface, and skip dinner, because I'm taking Nancy Williams to the Christmas Dance," my brother answers him right back. Was Gene all of a sudden hostile, or was he hostile? I overheard our hockey coach say one time that my brother Gene's the kind of guy rises to a challenge. The man's got a point. I lived with Gene my whole life, which is sixteen years now, and I ought to know. Unless he gets mad he's useless as tits on a boar.

36   You better believe Gene was mad. He called her up right away from the pay phone in the Rite Spot. It was a toss-up as to which of those two jerks was the most entertaining. Powers kept saying, "There's no way she'll go out with him. No way." And every time he thought of parting with a ten-spot, a look came over his face like he just pinched a nut or something. The guy's so christly tight he squeaks when he walks. He was sharing *my* chips and gravy, if you know what I mean?

37   And then there was Gene. I must say, I've always enjoyed watching him operate. I mean, even on the telephone he looks so sincere I could just puke. It's not unconscious by no means. My brother explained to me once what his trick is. To look that way you got to think that way is his motto. "What I do, Billy," he told me once, "is make myself believe, really believe, say … well, that an H-bomb went off, or that some kind of disease which only attacks women wiped out every female on the face of the earth but the one I'm talking to. That makes her the last piece of tail on the face of the earth, Billy! It's just natural then to be extra nice." Even though he's my brother, I swear to God he had to been left on our doorstep.

38   Of course, you can't argue with success. As soon as Gene hung up and smiled, Powers knew he was diddled. Once. But my brother don't show much mercy. Twice was coming. It turned out that Nancy Williams had a cousin staying with her for Christmas vacation. She wondered if maybe Gene could get this cousin a date? When Powers heard that, he pretty nearly went off in his pants. Nobody'll go out with him. He's fat and he sweats and he never brushes his teeth, there's stuff grows on them looks like that crap that floats on top of a slough. Even the really desperate girls figure no date is less damaging to their reputations than a date with Powers. You got to hold the line somewhere is how they look at it.

39   So Ernie's big yap cost him fifteen dollars. He blew that month's baby bonus (which his old lady gives him because he promises to finish school) and part of his allowance. The other five bucks is what he had to pay when Gene sold him Nancy Williams' cousin. It damn near killed him.

40   All right. Maybe I ought to've said something when Gene marched fat Ernie over to the Bank of Montreal to make a withdrawal on this account Powers has had since he was seven and started saving for a bike. He never got around to getting the bike because he couldn't bring himself to ever see that balance go down. Which is typical.

41   Already then I *knew* Ernie wasn't taking the cousin to no Christmas Dance. I'd heard once too often from that moron how Whipper Billy Watson would hang a licking on Cassius Clay, or how all the baseball owners get together in the spring to decide which team will win the World Series in the fall. He might learn to keep his hole shut for once.

42   The thing is *I'd* made up my mind to take the cousin. For nothing. It just so happens that, Gene being mad, he'd kind of forgot he's not

allowed to touch the old man's vehicle. Seeing as he tied a chrome granny knot around a telephone pole with the last one.

43   Gene didn't realize it yet but he wasn't going nowhere unless I drove. And I was going to drive because I'd happened to notice Nancy Williams around. She seemed like a very nice person who maybe had what Miss Clark says are principles. I suspected that if that was true, Gene for once was going to strike out, and no way was I going to miss *that*. Fuck, I'd have killed to see that. No exaggeration.

44   On the night of the Christmas Dance it's snowing like a bitch. Not that it's cold for December, mind you, but snowing. Sticky, sloppy stuff that almost qualifies for sleet, coming down like crazy. I had to put the windshield wipers on. In December yet.

45   Nancy Williams lives on the edge of town way hell and gone, in new company housing. The mine manager is the dick who named it Green Meadows. What a joke. Nobody lives there seen a blade of grass yet nor pavement neither. They call it Gumboot Flats because if it's not frozen it's mud. No street-lights neither. It took me a fuck of a long time to find her house in the dark. When I did I shut off the motor and me and Gene just sat.

46   "Well?" I says after a bit. I was waiting for Gene to get out first.

47   "Well what?"

48   "Well, maybe we should go get them?"

49   Gene didn't answer. He leans across me and plays "Shave and a haircut, two bits" on the horn.

50   "You're a geek," I tell him. He don't care.

51   We wait. No girls. Gene gives a couple of long, long blasts on the hooter. I was wishing he wouldn't. This time somebody pulls open the living-room drapes. There stands this character in suspenders, for chrissakes, and a pair of pants stops about two inches shy of his armpits. He looked like somebody's father and what you'd call belligerent.

52   "I think he wants us to come to the door."

53   "He can want all he like. Jesus Murphy, it's snowing out there. I got no rubbers."

54   "Oh, Christ," I says, "I'll go get them, Gene. It's such a big deal."

55   Easier said than done. I practically had to present a medical certificate. By the time Nancy's father got through with me I was starting to sound like that meatball Chip on *My Three Sons*.[2] Yes sir. No sir. He wasn't too impressed with the hornblowing episode, let me tell you. And then Nancy's old lady totes out a Kodak to get some "snaps" for Nancy's scrapbook. I didn't say nothing but I felt maybe they were getting evidence for the trial in case they had to slap a charge on me later. You'd have to see it to believe it. Here I was standing with Nancy and

---

2. Popular television comedy series of the 1960s.

her cousin, grinning like I was in my right mind, flash bulbs going off in my face, nodding away to the old man, who was running a safe-driving clinic for yours truly on the sidelines. Gene, I says to myself, Gene, you're going to pay.

56  At last, after practically swearing a blood oath to get his precious girls home, undamaged, by twelve-thirty, I chase the women out the door. And while they run through the snow, giggling, Stirling Moss[3] delays me on the doorstep, in this blizzard, showing me for about the thousandth time how to pull a car out of a skid on ice. I kid you not.

57  From that point on everything goes rapidly downhill.

58  Don't get me wrong. I got no complaints against the girls. Doreen, the cousin, wasn't going to break no mirrors, and she sure was a lot more lively than I expected. Case in point. When I finally get to the car, fucking near frozen, what do I see? Old Doreen hauling up about a yard of her skirt, which she rolled around her waist like the spare tire on a fat guy. Then she pulled her sweater down to hide it. You bet I was staring.

59  "Uncle Bob wouldn't let me wear my mini," she says. "Got a smoke? I haven't had one for days."

60  It seems she wasn't the only one had a bit of a problem with the dress code that night. In the back seat I could hear Nancy apologizing to Gene for the outfit her mother had made her special for the dance. Of course, I thought Nancy looked quite nice. But with her frame she couldn't help, even though she was got up a bit peculiar. What I mean is, she had on this dress made out of the same kind of shiny material my mother wanted for drapes. But the old man said she couldn't have it because it was too heavy. It'd pull the curtain rods off the wall.

61  I could tell poor old Nancy Williams sure was nervous. She just got finished apologizing for how she looked and then she started in suck-holing to Gene to please excuse her because she wasn't the world's best dancer. As a matter of fact this was her first dance ever. Thank heavens for Doreen, who was such a good sport. She'd been teaching her to dance all week. But it takes lots and lots of practice to get the hang of it. She hoped she didn't break his toes stepping on them. Ha ha ha. Just remember, she was still learning.

62  Gene said he'd be glad to teach her anything he figured she needed to know.

63  Nancy didn't catch on because she doesn't have that kind of mind. "That would be sweet of you, Gene," she says.

64  The band didn't show because of the storm. An act of God they call it. I'll say. So I drove around this dump for about an hour while Gene tried to molest Nancy. She put up a fair-to-middling struggle from

---

3. (b. 1929), British racing car driver, six-time Grand Prix winner.

what I could hear. The stuff her dress was made of was so stiff it crackled when she moved. Sort of like tin foil. Anyway, the two of them had it snapping and crackling like a bonfire there in the back seat while they fought a pitched battle over her body. She wasn't having none of that first time out of the chute.

65 "Gene!"
66 "Well for chrissakes, relax!"
67 "Don't take the Lord's name in vain."
68 "What's that supposed to mean?"
69 "Don't swear."
70 "Who's swearing?"
71 "Don't snap my nylons, Gene. Gene, what in the world are you ... Gene!"
72 "Some people don't know when they're having a good time," says Doreen. I think she was a little pissed I hadn't parked and give her some action. But Lord knows what might've happened to Nancy if I'd done that.
73 Then, all of a sudden, Nancy calls out, sounding what you'd call desperate, "Hey, everybody, who wants a Coke!"
74 "Nobody wants a Coke," mumbles Gene, sort of through his teeth.
75 "Well, maybe we could go some place?" Meaning somewhere well-lit where this octopus will lay off for five seconds.
76 "I'll take you some place," Gene mutters. "You want to go somewhere, we'll go to Zipper's. Hey Billy, let's take them to Zipper's."
77 "I don't know, Gene ..."
78 The way I said that perked Doreen up right away. As far as she was concerned, anything was better than driving around with a dope, looking at a snowstorm. "Hey," she hollers, "that sounds like *fun*!" Fun like a mental farm.
79 That clinched it though. "Sure," says Gene, "we'll check out Zipper's."
80 What could I say?
81 Don't get me wrong. Like everybody else I go to Zipper's and do stuff you can't do any place else in town. That's not it. But I wouldn't take anybody nice there on purpose. And I'm not trying to say that Zipper and his mother are bad people neither. It's just that so many shitty things have happened to those two that they've become kind of unpredictable. If you aren't used to that it can seem pretty weird.
82 I mean, look at Zipper. This guy is a not entirely normal human being who tries to tattoo himself with geometry dividers and Indian ink. He has this home poke on his arm which he claims is an American bald eagle but looks like a demented turkey or something. He did it himself, and the worst is he doesn't know how homely that bird is. The dumb prick shows it to people to admire.
83 Also, I should say a year ago he quits school to teach himself to be a drummer. That's all. He doesn't get a job or nothing, just sits at home and drums, and his mother, who's a widow and doesn't know any

better, lets him. I guess that that's not any big surprise. She's a pretty hopeless drunk who's been taking her orders from Zipper since he was six. That's when his old man got electrocuted out at the mine.

84  Still, I'm not saying that the way Zipper is is entirely his fault. Though he can be a real creep all right. Like once when he was about ten years old Momma Zipper gets a jag on and passes out naked in the bedroom, and he lets any of his friends look at his mother with no clothes on for chrissakes, if they pay him a dime. His own mother, mind you.

85  But in his defence I'd say he's seen a lot of "uncles" come and go in his time, some of which figured they'd make like the man of the house and tune him in. For a while there when he was eleven, twelve maybe, half the time he was coming to school with a black eye.

86  Now you take Gene, he figures Zipper's house is heaven on earth. Of course, nothing's entirely free. At Zipper's you got to bring a bottle or a case of beer and give Mrs. Zipper a few snorts, then everything is hunky-dory. Gene had a bottle of Five Star stashed under the back seat for the big Christmas Dance, so we were okay in that department.

87  But that night the lady of the house didn't seem to be around, or mobile anyway. Zipper himself came to the door, sweating like a pig in a filthy T-shirt. He'd been drumming along to the radio.

88  "What do you guys want?" says Zipper.

89  Gene holds up the bottle. "Party time."

90  "I'm practising," says Zipper.

91  "So you're practising. What's that to us?"

92  "My old lady's sleeping on the sofa," says Zipper, opening the door wide. "You want to fuck around here you do it in the basement." Which means his old lady'd passed out. Nobody sleeps through Zipper on the drums.

93  "Gene," Nancy was looking a bit shy, believe me.

94  My brother didn't let on he'd even heard her. "Do I look particular? You know me, Zip."

95  Zipper looked like maybe he had to think about that one. To tell the truth, he didn't seem quite all there. At last he says, "Sure. Sure, I know you. Keep a cool tool." And then, just like that, he wanders off to his drums, and leaves us standing there.

96  Gene laughs and shakes his head. "What a meatball."

97  It makes me feel empty lots of times when I see Zipper. He's so skinny and yellow and his eyes are always weepy-looking. They say there's something gone wrong with his kidneys from all the gas and glue he sniffed when he was in elementary school.

98  Boy, he loves his drums though. Zipper's really what you'd call dedicated. The sad thing is that the poor guy's got no talent. He just makes a big fucking racket and he don't know any better. You see, Zipper really thinks he's going to make himself somebody with those drums, he really does. Who'd tell him any different?

99   Gene found some dirty coffee cups in the kitchen sink and started rinsing them out. While he did that I watched Nancy Williams. She hadn't taken her coat off, in fact she was hugging it tight to her chest like she figured somebody was going to tear it off of her. I hadn't noticed before she had on a little bit of lipstick. But now her face had gone so pale it made her mouth look bright and red and pinched like somebody had just slapped it, hard.

100   Zipper commenced slamming away just as the four of us got into the basement. Down there it sounded as if we were right inside a great big drum and Zipper was beating the skin directly over our heads.

101   And boy, did it *stink* in that place. Like the sewer had maybe backed up. But then there were piles of dirty laundry humped up on the floor all around an old wringer washing machine, so that could've been the smell too.

102   It was cold and sour down there and we had nothing to sit on but a couple of lawn chairs and a chesterfield that was all split and stained with what I think was you know what. Nancy looked like she wished she had a newspaper to spread out over it before she sat down. As I said before, you shouldn't never take anybody nice to Zipper's.

103   Gene poured rye into the coffee mugs he'd washed out and passed them around. Nancy didn't want hers. "No thank you," she told him.

104   "You're embarrassing me, Nancy," says Doreen. The way my date was sitting in the lawn chair beside me in her make-do mini I knew why Gene was all scrunched down on that wrecked chesterfield.

105   "You know I don't drink, Doreen." Let me explain that when Nancy said that it didn't sound snotty. Just quiet and well-mannered like when a polite person passes up the parsnips. Nobody in their right mind holds it against them.

106   "You don't do much, do you?" That was Gene's two bits' worth.

107   "I'll say," chips in Doreen.

108   Nancy doesn't answer. I could hear old Zipper crashing and banging away like a madman upstairs.

109   "You don't do much, do you?" Gene's much louder this time.

110   "I suppose not." I can barely hear her answer because her head's down. She's checking out the backs of her hands.

111   "Somebody in your position ought to try harder," Doreen pipes up. "You don't make yourself too popular when you go spoiling parties."

112   Gene shoves the coffee mug at Nancy again. "Have a drink."

113   She won't take it. Principles.

114   "Have a drink!"

115   "Whyn't you lay off her?"

116   Gene's pissed off because he can't make Nancy Williams do what he says, so he jumps off the chesterfield and starts yelling at me. "Who's going to make me?" he hollers. "You? You going to make me?"

117   I can't do nothing but get up too. I never won a fight with my brother yet, but that don't mean I got to lay down and die for him.

"You better take that sweater off," I says, pointing, "it's mine and I don't want blood on it." He always wears my clothes.

That's when the cousin Doreen slides in between us. She's the kind of girl loves fights. They put her centre stage. That is, if she can wriggle herself in and get involved in breaking them up. Fights give her a chance to act all emotional and hysterical like she can't stand all the violence. Because she's so sensitive. Blessed are the peacemakers.

"Don't fight! Please, don't fight! Come on, Gene," she cries, latching on to his arm, "don't fight over her. Come away and cool down. I got to go to the bathroom. You show me where the bathroom is, Gene. Okay?"

"Don't give me that. You can find the bathroom yourself." Old Gene has still got his eyes fixed on me. He's acting the role. Both of them are nuts.

"Come on, Gene, I'm scared to go upstairs with that Zipper person there! He's so strange, I don't know what he might get it in his head to do. Come on, take me upstairs." Meanwhile this Doreen, who is as strong as your average sensitive ox, is sort of dragging my brother in the direction of the stairs. Him pretending he don't really want to go and have a fuss made over him, because he's got this strong urge to murder me or cripple me or something.

"You wait" is all he says to me.

"Ah, quit it or I'll die of shock," I tell him.

"Please, Gene. That Zipper person is *weird*."

At last he goes with her. I hear Gene on the stairs. "Zipper ain't much," he says, "I know lots of guys crazier than him."

I look over to Nancy sitting quietly on that grungy chesterfield, feet together, hands turned palms up on her lap. Her dress kind of sticks out from under the hem of her coat all stiff and shiny and funny-looking.

"I shouldn't have let her make me this dress," she says, angry. "We ought to have gone downtown and bought a proper one. But she had this *material*." She stops, pulls at the buttons of her coat and opens it. "Look at this thing. No wonder Gene doesn't like it, I bet."

At first I don't know what to say when she looks at me like that, her face all white except for two hot spots on her cheekbones. Zipper is going nuts upstairs. He's hot tonight. It almost sounds like something recognizable. "Don't pay Gene any attention," I say, "he's a goof."

"It's awful, this dress."

She isn't that dumb. But a person needs a reason for why things go wrong. I'm not telling her she's just a way to win ten dollars and prove a point.

"Maybe it's because I wouldn't drink that whiskey? Is that it?"

"Well, kind of. That's part of it. He's just a jerk. Take it from me, I know. Forget it."

133 "I never even thought he knew I was alive. Never guessed. And here I was, crazy about him. Just crazy. I'd watch him in the hallway, you know? I traded lockers with Susan Braithwaite just to get closer to his. I went to all the hockey games to see him play. I worshipped him."

134 The way she says that, well, it was too personal. Somebody oughtn't say that kind of a thing to a practical stranger. It was worse than if she'd climbed out of her clothes. It made me embarrassed.

135 "And funny thing is, all that time he really did think I was cute. He told me on the phone, But he never once thought to ask me out because I'm a Baptist. He was sure I couldn't go. Because I'm a Baptist he thought I couldn't go. But he thought I was cute all along."

136 "Well, yeah."

137 "And now," she says, "look at this. I begged and begged Dad to let me come. I practically got down on my hands and knees. And all those dancing lessons and everything and the band doesn't show. Imagine."

138 "Gene wouldn't have danced with you anyway. He doesn't dance."

139 Nancy smiled at me. As if I was mental. She didn't half believe me.

140 "Hey," I says, just like that, you never know what's going to get into you, "Nancy, you want to dance?"

141 "Now?"

142 "Now. Sure. Come on. We got the one-man band, Zipper, upstairs. Why not?"

143 "What'll Gene say?"

144 "To hell with Gene. Make him jealous."

145 She was human at least. She liked the idea of Gene jealous.

146 "Okay."

147 And here I got a confession to make. I go on all the time about Gene not being able to dance. Well, me neither. But I figured what the fuck. You just hop around and hope to hell you don't look too much like you're having a convulsion.

148 Neither of us knew how to get started. We just stood gawking at one another. Upstairs Zipper was going out of his tree. It sounded like there was four of him. As musical as a bag of hammers he is.

149 "The natives are restless tonight, Giles," I says. I was not uncomfortable. Let me tell you another one.

150 "Pardon?"

151 "Nothing. It was just dumb."

152 Nancy starts to sway from side to side, shuffling her feet. I figure that's the signal. I hop or whatever. So does she. We're out of the gates, off and running.

153 To be perfectly honest, Nancy Williams can't dance for shit. She gets this intense look on her face like she's counting off in her head, and starts to jerk. Which gets some pretty interesting action out of the notorious matched set but otherwise is pretty shoddy. And me? Well, I'm none too co-ordinated myself, so don't go getting no mental picture of Fred Astaire or whoever.

154    In the end what you had was two people who can't dance, dancing to the beat of a guy who can't drum. Still, Zipper didn't know no better and at the time neither did we. We were just what you'd call mad dancing fools. We danced and danced and Zipper drummed and drummed and we were all together and didn't know it. Son of a bitch, the harder we danced the hotter and happier Nancy Williams' face got. It just smoothed the unhappiness right out of it. Mine too, I guess.

155    That is, until all of a sudden it hit her. She stops dead in her tracks and asks, "Where's Doreen and Gene?"

156    Good question. They'd buggered off in my old man's car. Zipper didn't know where.

157    The rest of the evening was kind of a horror story. It took me a fair while to convince Nancy they hadn't gone for Cokes or something and would be right back. In the end she took it like a trooper. The only thing she'd say was, "That Doreen. *That Doreen,*" and shake her head. Of course she said it about a thousand times. I was wishing she'd shut up, or maybe give us a little variety like, "*That Gene.*" No way.

158    I had a problem. How to get Cinderella home before twelve-thirty, seeing as Gene had the family chariot. I tried Harvey's Taxi but no luck. Harvey's Taxi is one car and Harvey, and both were out driving lunches to a crew doing overtime at the mine.

159    Finally, at exactly twelve-thirty, we struck out on foot in this blizzard. Jesus, was it snowing. There was slush and ice water and every kind of shit and corruption all over the road. Every time some hunyak roared by us we got splattered by a sheet of cold slop. The snow melted in our hair and run down our necks and faces. By the time we went six blocks we were soaked. Nancy was the worst off because she wasn't dressed too good with nylons and the famous dress and such. I seen I had to be gentleman so I stopped and give her my gloves, and my scarf to tie around her head. The two of us looked like those German soldiers I seen on TV making the death march out of Russia, on that series *Canada at War.* That was a very educational series. It made you think of man's inhumanity to man quite often.

160    "I could just die," she kept saying. "Dad is going to kill me. This is my last dance ever. I could just die. I could just die. *That Doreen.* Honestly!"

161    When we stumbled up her street, all black because of the lack of street-lights, I could see that her house was all lit up. Bad news. I stopped on the corner. Just then it quits snowing. That's typical.

162    She stares at the house. "Dad's waiting."

163    "I guess I better go no further."

164    Nancy Williams bends down and feels her dress where it sticks out from under her coat. "It's soaked. I don't know how much it cost a yard. I could just die."

165    "Well," I says, repeating myself like an idiot, "I guess I better go no further." Then I try and kiss her. She sort of straight-arms me. I get the palm of my own glove in the face.

166    "What're you doing?" She sounds mad.

167    "Well, you know — "

168    "I'm not *your* date," she says, real offended. "I'm your brother's date."

169    "Maybe we could go out some time?"

170    "I won't be going anywhere for a long time. Look at me. He's going to kill me."

171    "Well, when you do? I'm in no hurry."

172    "Don't you understand? Don't you understand? Daddy will never let me go out with anybody named Simpson again. Ever. Not after tonight."

173    "Ever?"

174    "I can't imagine what you'd have to do to redeem yourself after this mess. That's how Daddy puts it — you've got to redeem yourself. I don't even know how I'm going to do it. And none of it's my fault."

175    "Yeah," I says, "he'll remember me. I'm the one he took the picture of."

176    She didn't seem too upset at not having me calling. "Everything is ruined," she says. "If you only knew."

177    Nancy Williams turns away from me then and goes up that dark, dark street where there's nobody awake except at her house. Wearing my hat and gloves.

178 Nancy Williams sits third pew from the front, left-hand side. I sit behind her, on the other side so's I can watch her real close. Second Sunday I was there she wore her Christmas Dance dress.

179    Funny thing, everything changes. At first I thought I'd start going and maybe that would redeem myself with her old man. Didn't work. He just looks straight through me.

180    You ought to see her face when she sings those Baptist hymns. It gets all hot and happy-looking, exactly like it did when we were dancing together and Zipper was pounding away there up above us, where we never even saw him. When her face gets like that there's no trouble in it, by no means.

181    It's like she's dancing then, I swear. But to what I don't know. I try to hear it. I try and try. I listen and listen to catch it. Christ, somebody tell me. What's she dancing to? Who's the drummer?

(1982)

# Rohinton Mistry (b. 1952)

Born into the Parsi community in Bombay and educated at the University of Bombay, Mistry immigrated to Canada in 1975. He worked for a bank and completed a B.A. in English and philosophy at the University of Toronto. When he won two Hart House Prizes for his first short stories, he committed to writing full time. His first collection, Tales from Firozsha Baag (1987), was shortlisted for a Governor General's Award; Such a Long Journey (1991) received the Governor General's Award, among others; A Fine Balance (1995) won the Giller Prize.

## Swimming Lessons

1. The old man's wheelchair is audible today as he creaks by in the hallway: on some days it's just a smooth whirr. Maybe the way he slumps in it, or the way his weight rests has something to do with it. Down to the lobby he goes, and sits there most of the time, talking to people on their way out or in. That's where he first spoke to me a few days ago. I was waiting for the elevator, back from Eaton's with my new pair of swimming-trunks.
2. "Hullo," he said. I nodded, smiled.
3. "Beautiful summer day we've got."
4. "Yes," I said, "it's lovely outside."
5. He shifted the wheelchair to face me squarely. "How old do you think I am?"
6. I looked at him blankly, and he said, "Go on, take a guess."
7. I understood the game; he seemed about seventy-five although the hair was still black, so I said, "Sixty-five?" He made a sound between a chuckle and a wheeze: "I'll be seventy-seven next month." Close enough.
8. I've heard him ask that question several times since, and everybody plays by the rules. Their faked guesses range from sixty to seventy. They pick a lower number when he's more depressed than usual. He reminds me of Grandpa as he sits on the sofa in the lobby, staring out vacantly at the parking lot. Only difference is, he sits with the stillness of stroke victims, while Grandpa's Parkinson's disease would bounce his thighs and legs and arms all over the place. When he could no longer hold the *Bombay Samachar* steady enough to read, Grandpa

took to sitting on the veranda and staring emptily at the traffic passing outside Firozsha Baag. Or waving to anyone who went by in the compound: Rustomji, Nariman Hansotia in his 1932 Mercedes-Benz, the fat ayah Jaakaylee with her shopping-bag, the *kuchrawalli* with her basket and long bamboo broom.

9   The Portuguese woman across the hall has told me a little about the old man. She is the communicator for the apartment building. To gather and disseminate information, she takes the liberty of unabashedly throwing open her door when newsworthy events transpire. Not for Portuguese Woman the furtive peerings from thin cracks or spyholes. She reminds me of a character in a movie, *Barefoot In The Park* I think it was, who left empty beer cans by the landing for anyone passing to stumble and give her the signal. But PW does not need beer cans. The gutang-khutang of the elevator opening and closing is enough.

10  The old man's daughter looks after him. He was living alone till his stroke, which coincided with his youngest daughter's divorce in Vancouver. She returned to him and they moved into this low-rise in Don Mills. PW says the daughter talks to no one in the building but takes good care of her father.

11  Mummy used to take good care of Grandpa, too, till things became complicated and he was moved to the Parsi General Hospital. Parkinsonism and osteoporosis laid him low. The doctor explained that Grandpa's hip did not break because he fell, but he fell because the hip, gradually growing brittle, snapped on that fatal day. That's what osteoporosis does, hollows out the bones and turns effect into cause. It has an unusually high incidence in the Parsi community, he said, but did not say why. Just one of those mysterious things. We are the chosen people where osteoporosis is concerned. And divorce. The Parsi community has the highest divorce rate in India. It also claims to be the most westernized community in India. Which is the result of the other? Confusion again, of cause and effect.

12  The hip was put in traction. Single-handed, Mummy struggled valiantly with bedpans and dressings for bedsores which soon appeared like grim spectres on his back. *Mamaiji*, bent double with her weak back, could give no assistance. My help would be enlisted to roll him over on his side while Mummy changed the dressing. But after three months, the doctor pronounced a patch upon Grandpa's lungs, and the male ward of Parsi General swallowed him up. There was no money for a private nursing home. I went to see him once, at Mummy's insistence. She used to say that the blessings of an old person were the most valuable and potent of all, they would last my whole life long. The ward had rows and rows of beds; the din was enormous, the smells nauseating, and it was just as well that Grandpa passed most of his time in a less than conscious state.

13  But I should have gone to see him more often. Whenever Grandpa went out, while he still could in the days before parkinsonism, he

would bring back pink and white sugar-coated almonds for Percy and me. Every time I remember Grandpa, I remember that; and then I think: I should have gone to see him more often. That's what I also thought when our telephone-owning neighbour, esteemed by all for that reason, sent his son to tell us the hospital had phoned that Grandpa died an hour ago.

14   *The postman rang the doorbell the way he always did, long and continuous; Mother went to open it, wanting to give him a piece of her mind but thought better of it, she did not want to risk the vengeance of postmen, it was so easy for them to destroy letters; workers nowadays thought no end of themselves, strutting around like peacocks, ever since all this Shiv Sena agitation about Maharashtra or Maharashtrians, threatening strikes and Bombay* bundh *all the time, with no respect for the public; bus drivers and conductors were the worst, behaving as if they owned the buses and were doing favours to commuters, pulling the bell before you were in the bus, the driver purposely braking and moving with big jerks to make the standees lose their balance, the conductor so rude if you did not have the right change.*

15   *But when she saw the airmail envelope with a Canadian stamp her face lit up, she said wait to the postman, and went in for a fifty paisa piece, a little* baksheesh *for you, she told him, then shut the door and kissed the envelope, went in running, saying my son has written, my son has sent a letter, and Father looked up from the newspaper and said, don't get too excited, first read it, you know what kind of letters he writes, a few lines of empty words, I'm fine, hope you are all right, your loving son — that kind of writing I don't call letter-writing.*

16   *Then Mother opened the envelope and took out one small page and began to read silently, and the joy brought to her face by the letter's arrival began to ebb; Father saw it happening and knew he was right, he said read aloud, let me also hear what our son is writing this time, so Mother read: My dear Mummy and Daddy, Last winter was terrible, we had record-breaking low temperatures all through February and March, and the first official day of spring was colder than the first official day of winter had been, but it's getting warmer now. Looks like it will be a nice warm summer. You asked me about my new apartment. It's small, but not bad at all. This is just a quick note to let you know I'm fine, so you won't worry about me. Hope everything is okay at home.*

17   *After Mother put it back in the envelope, Father said everything about his life is locked in silence and secrecy. I still don't understand why he bothered to visit us last year if he had nothing to say; every letter of his has been a quick note so we won't worry — what does he think we worry about, his health, in that country everyone eats well whether they work or not, he should be worrying about us with all the black market and rationing, has he forgotten already how he used to go to the ration-shop and wait in line every week; and what kind of apartment description is that, not bad at all; and if it is a Canadian weather report I need from*

*him, I can go with Nariman Hansotia from A Block to the Cawasji Framji Memorial Library and read all about it, there they get newspapers from all over the world.*

18   The sun is hot today. Two women are sunbathing on the stretch of patchy lawn at the periphery of the parking lot. I can see them clearly from my kitchen. They're wearing bikinis and I'd love to take a closer look. But I have no binoculars. Nor do I have a car to saunter out to and pretend to look under the hood. They're both luscious and gleaming. From time to time they smear lotion over their skin, on the bellies, on the inside of the thighs, on the shoulders. Then one of them gets the other to undo the string of her top and spread some there. She lies on her stomach with the straps undone. I wait. I pray that the heat and haze make her forget, when it's time to turn over, that the straps are undone.

19   But the sun is not hot enough to work this magic for me. When it's time to come in, she flips over, deftly holding up the cups, and reties the top. They arise, pick up towels, lotions and magazines, and return to the building.

20   This is my chance to see them closer. I race down the stairs to the lobby. The old man says hullo. "Down again?"

21   "My mailbox," I mumble.

22   "It's Saturday," he chortles. For some reason he finds it extremely funny. My eye is on the door leading in from the parking lot.

23   Through the glass panel I see them approaching. I hurry to the elevator and wait. In the dimly lit lobby I can see their eyes are having trouble adjusting after the bright sun. They don't seem as attractive as they did from the kitchen window. The elevator arrives and I hold it open, inviting them in with what I think is a gallant flourish. Under the fluorescent glare in the elevator I see their wrinkled skin, aging hands, sagging bottoms, varicose veins. The lustrous trick of sun and lotion and distance has ended.

24   I step out and they continue to the third floor. I have Monday night to look forward to, my first swimming lesson. The high school behind the apartment building is offering, among its usual assortment of macramé and ceramics and pottery classes, a class for non-swimming adults.

25   The woman at the registration desk is quite friendly. She even gives me the opening to satisfy the compulsion I have about explaining my non-swimming status.

26   "Are you from India?" she asks. I nod. "I hope you don't mind my asking, but I was curious because an Indian couple, husband and wife, also registered a few minutes ago. Is swimming not encouraged in India?"

27   "On the contrary," I say. "Most Indians swim like fish. I'm an exception to the rule. My house was five minutes walking distance from Chaupatty beach in Bombay. It's one of the most beautiful beaches in

Bombay, or was, before the filth took over. Anyway, even though we lived so close to it, I never learned to swim. It's just one of those things."

28 "Well," says the woman, "that happens sometimes. Take me, for instance. I never learned to ride a bicycle. It was the mounting that used to scare me, I was afraid of falling." People have lined up behind me. "It's been very nice talking to you," she says, "hope you enjoy the course."

29 The art of swimming had been trapped between the devil and the deep blue sea. The devil was money, always scarce, and kept the private swimming clubs out of reach; the deep blue sea of Chaupatty beach was grey and murky with garbage, too filthy to swim in. Every so often we would muster our courage and Mummy would take me there to try and teach me. But a few minutes of paddling was all we could endure. Sooner or later something would float up against our legs or thighs or waists, depending on how deep we'd gone in, and we'd be revulsed and stride out to the sand.

30 Water imagery in my life is recurring. Chaupatty beach, now the high-school swimming pool. The universal symbol of life and regeneration did nothing but frustrate me. Perhaps the swimming pool will overturn that failure.

31 When images and symbols abound in this manner, sprawling or rolling across the page without guile or artifice, one is prone to say, how obvious, how skilless; symbols, after all, should be still and gentle with dewdrops, tiny, yet shining with a world of meaning. But what happens when, on the page of life itself, one encounters the ever-moving, all-engirdling sprawl of the filthy sea? Dewdrops and oceans both have their rightful places; Nariman Hansotia certainly knew that when he told his stories to the boys of Firozsha Baag.

32 The sea of Chaupatty was fated to endure the finales of life's everyday functions. It seemed that the dirtier it became, the more crowds it attracted: street urchins and beggars and beachcombers, looking through the junk that washed up. (Or was it the crowds that made it dirtier? — another instance of cause and effect blurring and evading identification.)

33 Too many religious festivals also used the sea as repository for their finales. Its use should have been rationed, like rice and kerosene. On Ganesh Chaturthi, clay idols of the god Ganesh, adorned with garlands and all manner of finery, were carried in processions to the accompaniment of drums and a variety of wind instruments. The music got more frenzied the closer the procession got to Chaupatty and to the moment of immersion.

34 Then there was Coconut Day, which was never as popular as Ganesh Chaturthi. From a bystander's viewpoint, coconuts chucked into the sea do not provide as much of a spectacle. We used the sea, too, to deposit the leftovers from Parsi religious ceremonies, things

such as flowers, or the ashes of the sacred sandalwood fire, which just could not be dumped with the regular garbage but had to be entrusted to the care of Avan Yazad, the guardian of the sea. And things which were of no use but which no one had the heart to destroy were also given to Avan Yazad. Such as old photographs.

35   After Grandpa died, some of his things were flung out to sea. It was high tide; we always checked the newspaper when going to perform these disposals; an ebb would mean a long walk in squelchy sand before finding water. Most of the things were probably washed up on shore. But we tried to throw them as far out as possible, then waited a few minutes; if they did not float back right away we would pretend they were in the permanent safekeeping of Avan Yazad, which was a comforting thought. I can't remember everything we sent out to sea, but his brush and comb were in the parcel, his *kusti*, and some Kemadrin pills, which he used to take to keep the parkinsonism under control.

36   Our paddling session stopped for lack of enthusiasm on my part. Mummy wasn't too keen either, because of the filth. But my main concern was the little guttersnipes, like naked fish with little buoyant penises, taunting me with their skills, swimming underwater and emerging unexpectedly all around me, or pretending to masturbate — I think they were too young to achieve ejaculation. It was embarrassing. When I look back, I'm surprised that Mummy and I kept going as long as we did.

37   I examine the swimming-trunks I bought last week. Surf King, says the label, Made in Canada-Fabriqué Au Canada. I've been learning bits and pieces of French from bilingual labels at the supermarket too. These trunks are extremely sleek and stream-lined hipsters, the distance from waistband to pouch tip the barest minimum. I wonder how everything will stay in place, not that I'm boastful about my endowments. I try them on, and feel that the tip of my member lingers perilously close to the exit. Too close, in fact, to conceal the exigencies of my swimming lesson fantasy: a gorgeous woman in the class for non-swimmers, at whose sight I will be instantly aroused, and she, spying the shape of my desire, will look me straight in the eye with her intentions; she will come home with me, to taste the pleasures of my delectable Asian brown body whose strangeness has intrigued her and unleashed uncontrollable surges of passion inside her throughout the duration of the swimming lesson.

38   I drop the Eaton's bag and wrapper in the garbage can. The swimming-trunks cost fifteen dollars, same as the fee for the ten weekly lessons. The garbage bag is almost full. I tie it up and take it outside. There is a medicinal smell in the hallway; the old man must have just returned to his apartment.

39   PW opens her door and says, "Two ladies from the third floor were lying in the sun this morning. In bikinis."

40   "That's nice," I say, and walk to the incinerator chute. She reminds me of Najamai in Firozsha Baag, except that Najamai employed a bit more subtlety while going about her life's chosen work.

41   PW withdraws and shuts her door.

42   *Mother had to reply because Father said he did not want to write to his son till his son had something sensible to write to him, his questions had been ignored long enough, and if he wanted to keep his life a secret, he would get no letters from his father.*

43   *But after Mother started the letter he went and looked over her shoulder, telling her what to ask him, because if they kept on writing the same questions, maybe he would understand how interested they were in knowing about things over there; Father said go on, ask him what his work is at the insurance company, tell him to take some courses at night school, that's how everyone moves ahead over there, tell him not to be discouraged if his job is just clerical right now, hard work will get him ahead, remind him he is a Zoroastrian:* manashni, gavashni, kunashni, *better write the translation also: good thoughts, good words, good deeds — he must have forgotten what it means, and tell him to say prayers and do* kusti *at least twice a day.*

44   *Writing it all down sadly, Mother did not believe he wore his* sudra *and* kusti *any more, she would be very surprised if he remembered any of the prayers; when she had asked him if he needed new* sudras *he said not to take any trouble because the Zoroastrian Society of Ontario imported them from Bombay for their members, and this sounded like a story he was making up, but she was leaving it in the hands of God, ten thousand miles away there was nothing she could do but write a letter and hope for the best.*

45   *Then she sealed it, and Father wrote the address on it as usual because his writing was much neater than hers, handwriting was important in the address and she did not want the postman in Canada to make any mistake; she took it to the post office herself, it was impossible to trust anyone to mail it ever since the postage rates went up because people just tore off the stamps for their own use and threw away the letter, the only safe way was to hand it over the counter and make the clerk cancel the stamps before your own eyes.*

46   Berthe, the building superintendent, is yelling at her son in the parking lot. He tinkers away with his van. This happens every fine-weathered Sunday. It must be the van that Berthe dislikes because I've seen mother and son together in other quite amicable situations.

47   Berthe is a big Yugoslavian with high cheekbones. Her nationality was disclosed to me by PW. Berthe speaks a very rough-hewn English, I've overheard her in the lobby scolding tenants for late rents and leaving dirty lint screens in the dryers. It's exciting to listen to her, her words fall like rocks and boulders, and one can never tell where or how the next few will drop. But her Slavic yells at her son are a dif-

ferent matter, the words fly swift and true, well-aimed missiles that never miss. Finally, the son slams down the hood in disgust, wipes his hands on a rag, accompanies mother Berthe inside.

48  Berthe's husband has a job in a factory. But he loses several days of work every month when he succumbs to booze, a word Berthe uses often in her Slavic tirades on those days, the only one I can understand, as it clunks down heavily out of the tight-flying formation of Yugoslavian sentences. He lolls around in the lobby, submitting passively to his wife's tongue-lashings. The bags under his bloodshot eyes, his stringy moustache, stubbled chin, dirty hair are so vulnerable to the poison-laden barbs (poison works the same way in any language) emanating from deep within the powerful watermelon bosom. No one's presence can embarrass or dignify her into silence.

49  No one except the old man who arrives now. "Good morning," he says, and Berthe turns, stops yelling, and smiles. Her husband rises, positions the wheelchair at the favourite angle. The lobby will be peaceful as long as the old man is there.

*

50  It was hopeless. My first swimming lesson. The water terrified me. When did that happen, I wonder, I used to love splashing at Chaupatty, carried about by the waves. And this was only a swimming pool. Where did all that terror come from? I'm trying to remember.

51  Armed with my Surf King I enter the high school and go to the pool area. A sheet with instructions for the new class is pinned to the bulletin board. All students must shower and then assemble at eight by the shallow end. As I enter the showers three young boys, probably from a previous class, emerge. One of them holds his nose. The second begins to hum, under his breath: Paki Paki, smell like curry. The third says to the first two: pretty soon all the water's going to taste of curry. They leave.

52  It's a mixed class, but the gorgeous woman of my fantasy is missing. I have to settle for another, in a pink one-piece suit, with brown hair and a bit of a stomach. She must be about thirty-five. Plain-looking.

53  The instructor is called Ron. He gives us a pep talk, sensing some nervousness in the group. We're finally all in the water, in the shallow end. He demonstrates floating on the back, then asks for a volunteer. The pink one-piece suit wades forward. He supports her, tells her to lean back and let her head drop in the water.

54  She does very well. And as we all regard her floating body, I see what was not visible outside the pool: her bush, curly bits of it, straying out of the pink Spandex V. Tongues of water lapping against her delta, as if caressing it teasingly, make the brown hair come alive in the most tantalizing manner. The crests and troughs of little waves, set off by the movement of our bodies in a circle around her, dutifully irrigate her; the curls alternately wave free inside the crest, then adhere to her

wet thighs, beached by the inevitable trough. I could watch this forever, and I wish the floating demonstration would never end.

55 Next we are shown how to grasp the rail and paddle, face down in the water. Between practising floating and paddling, the hour is almost gone. I have been trying to observe the pink one-piece suit, getting glimpses of her straying pubic hair from various angles. Finally, Ron wants a volunteer for the last demonstration, and I go forward. To my horror he leads the class to the deep end. Fifteen feet of water. It is so blue, and I can see the bottom. He picks up a metal hoop attached to a long wooden stick. He wants me to grasp the hoop, jump in the water, and paddle, while he guides me by the stick. Perfectly safe, he tells me. A demonstration of how paddling propels the body.

56 It's too late to back out; besides, I'm so terrified I couldn't find the words to do so even if I wanted to. Everything he says I do as if in a trance. I don't remember the moment of jumping. The next thing I know is, I'm swallowing water and floundering, hanging on to the hoop for dear life. Ron draws me to the rails and helps me out. The class applauds.

57 We disperse and one thought is on my mind: what if I'd lost my grip? Fifteen feet of water under me. I shudder and take deep breaths. This is it. I'm not coming next week. This instructor is an irresponsible person. Or he does not value the lives of non-white immigrants. I remember the three teenagers. Maybe the swimming pool is the hang-out of some racist group, bent on eliminating all non-white swimmers, to keep their waters pure and their white sisters unogled.

58 The elevator takes me upstairs. Then gutang-khutang. PW opens her door as I turn the corridor of medicinal smells. "Berthe was screaming loudly at her husband tonight," she tells me.

59 "Good for her," I say, and she frowns indignantly at me.

60 The old man is in the lobby. He's wearing thick wool gloves. He wants to know how the swimming was, must have seen me leaving with my towel yesterday. Not bad, I say.

61 "I used to swim a lot. Very good for the circulation." He wheezes. "My feet are cold all the time. Cold as ice. Hands too."

62 Summer is winding down, so I say stupidly, "Yes, it's not so warm any more."

63 The thought of the next swimming lesson sickens me. But as I comb through the memories of that terrifying Monday, I come upon the straying curls of brown pubic hair. Inexorably drawn by them, I decide to go.

64 It's a mistake, of course. This time I'm scared even to venture in the shallow end. When everyone has entered the water and I'm the only one outside, I feel a little foolish and slide in.

65 Instructor Ron says we should start by reviewing the floating technique. I'm in no hurry. I watch the pink one-piece pull the swim-suit down around her cheeks and flip back to achieve perfect flotation.

And then reap disappointment. The pink Spandex triangle is perfectly streamlined today, nothing strays, not a trace of fuzz, not one filament, not even a sign of post-depilation irritation. Like the airbrushed parts of glamour magazine models. The barrenness of her impeccably packaged apex is a betrayal. Now she is shorn like the other women in the class. Why did she have to do it?

66 The weight of this disappointment makes the water less manageable, more lung-penetrating. With trepidation, I float and paddle my way through the remainder of the hour, jerking my head out every two seconds and breathing deeply, to continually shore up a supply of precious, precious air without, at the same time, seeming too anxious and losing my dignity.

67 I don't attend the remaining classes. After I've missed three, Ron the instructor telephones. I tell him I've had the flu and am still feeling poorly, but I'll try to be there the following week.

68 He does not call again. My Surf King is relegated to an unused drawer. Total losses: one fantasy plus thirty dollars. And no watery rebirth. The swimming pool, like Chaupatty beach, has produced a stillbirth. But there is a difference. Water means regeneration only if it is pure and cleansing. Chaupatty beach was filthy, the pool was not. Failure to swim through filth must mean something other than failure of rebirth — failure of symbolic death? Does that equal success of symbolic life? death of a symbolic failure? death of a symbol? What is the equation?

69 *The postman did not bring a letter but a parcel, he was smiling because he knew that every time something came from Canada his baksheesh was guaranteed, and this time because it was a parcel Mother gave him a whole rupee, she was quite excited, there were so many stickers on it besides the stamps, one for Small Parcel, another Printed Papers, a red sticker saying Insured; she showed it to Father, and opened it, then put both hands on her cheeks, not able to speak because the surprise and happiness was so great, tears came to her eyes and she could not stop smiling, till Father became impatient to know and finally got up and came to the table.*

70 *When he saw it he was surprised and happy too, he began to grin, then hugged Mother saying our son is a writer, and we didn't even know it, he never told us a thing, here we are thinking he is still clerking away at the insurance company, and he has written a book of stories, all these years in school and college he kept his talent hidden, making us think he was just like one of the boys in the Baag, shouting and playing the fool in the compound, and now what a surprise; then Father opened the book and began reading it, heading back to the easy chair, and Mother so excited, still holding his arm, walked with him, saying it was not fair him reading it first, she wanted to read it too, and they agreed that he would read the first story, then give it to her so she could also read it, and they would take turns in that manner.*

71   *Mother removed the staples from the padded envelope in which he had mailed the book, and threw them away, then straightened the folded edges of the envelope and put it away safely with the other envelopes and letters she had collected since he left.*

72   The leaves are beginning to fall. The only ones I can identify are maple. The days are dwindling like the leaves. I've started a habit of taking long walks every evening. The old man is in the lobby when I leave, he waves as I go by. By the time I'm back, the lobby is usually empty.

73   Today I was woken up by a grating sound outside that made my flesh crawl. I went to the window and saw Berthe raking the leaves in the parking lot. Not in the expanse of patchy lawn on the periphery, but in the parking lot proper. She was raking the black tarred surface. I went back to bed and dragged a pillow over my head, not releasing it till noon.

74   When I return from my walk in the evening, PW, summoned by the elevator's gutang-khutang, says, "Berthe filled six black garbage bags with leaves today."

75   "Six bags!" I say. "Wow!"

76   Since the weather turned cold, Berthe's son does not tinker with his van on Sundays under my window. I'm able to sleep late.

77   Around eleven, there's a commotion outside. I reach out and switch on the clock radio. It's a sunny day, the window curtains are bright. I get up, curious, and see a black Olds Ninety-Eight in the parking lot, by the entrance to the building. The old man is in his wheelchair, bundled up, with a scarf wound several times round his neck as though to immobilize it, like a surgical collar. His daughter and another man, the car-owner, are helping him from the wheelchair into the front seat, encouraging him with words like: that's it, easy does it, attaboy. From the open door of the lobby, Berthe is shouting encouragement too, but hers is confined to one word: yah, repeated at different levels of pitch and volume, with variations on vowel-length. The stranger could be the old man's son, he has the same jet black hair and piercing eyes.

78   Maybe the old man is not well, it's an emergency. But I quickly scrap that thought — this isn't Bombay, an ambulance would have arrived. They're probably taking him out for a ride. If he is his son, where has he been all this time, I wonder.

79   The old man finally settles in the front seat, the wheelchair goes in the trunk, and they're off. The one I think is the son looks up and catches me at the window before I can move away, so I wave, and he waves back.

80   In the afternoon I take down a load of clothes to the laundry room. Both machines have completed their cycles, the clothes inside are waiting to be transferred to dryers. Should I remove them and place them on top of a dryer, or wait? I decide to wait. After a few minutes,

two women arrive, they are in bathrobes, and smoking. It takes me a while to realize that these are the two disappointments who were sunbathing in bikinis last summer.

81   "You didn't have to wait, you could have removed the clothes and carried on, dear," says one. She has a Scottish accent. It's one of the few I've learned to identify. Like maple leaves.

82   "Well," I say, "some people might not like strangers touching their clothes."

83   "You're not a stranger, dear," she says, "you live in this building, we've seen you before."

84   "Besides, your hands are clean," the other one pipes in. "You can touch my things any time you like."

85   Horny old cow. I wonder what they've got on under their bathrobes. Not much, I find, as they bend over to place their clothes in the dryers.

86   "See you soon," they say, and exit, leaving me behind in an erotic wake of smoke and perfume and deep images of cleavages. I start the washers and depart, and when I come back later, the dryers are empty.

87   PW tells me, "The old man's son took him out for a drive today. He has a big beautiful black car."

88   I see my chance, and shoot back: "Olds Ninety-Eight."

89   "What?"

90   "The car," I explain, "it's an Oldsmobile Ninety-Eight."

91   She does not like this at all, my giving her information. She is visibly nettled, and retreats with a sour face.

92   *Mother and Father read the first five stories, and she was very sad after reading some of them, she said he must be so unhappy there, all his stories are about Bombay, he remembers every little thing about his childhood, he is thinking about it all the time even though he is ten thousand miles away, my poor son, I think he misses his home and us and everything he left behind, because if he likes it over there why would he not write stories about that, there must be so many new ideas that his new life could give him.*

93   *But Father did not agree with this, he said it did not mean that he was unhappy, all writers worked in the same way, they used their memories and experiences and made stories out of them, changing some things, adding some, imagining some, all writers were very good at remembering details of their lives.*

94   *Mother said, how can you be sure that he is remembering because he is a writer, or whether he started to write because he is unhappy and thinks of his past, and wants to save it all by making stories of it; and Father said that is not a sensible question, anyway, it is now my turn to read the next story.*

95   The first snow has fallen, and the air is crisp. It's not very deep, about two inches, just right to go for a walk in. I've been told that immigrants from hot countries always enjoy the snow the first year, maybe

for a couple of years more, then inevitably the dread sets in, and the approach of winter gets them fretting and moping. On the other hand, if it hadn't been for my conversation with the woman at the swimming registration desk, they might now be saying that India is a nation of non-swimmers.

96  Berthe is outside, shovelling the snow off the walkway in the parking lot. She has a heavy, wide pusher which she wields expertly.

97  The old radiators in the apartment alarm me incessantly. They continue to broadcast a series of variations on death throes, and go from hot to cold and cold to hot at will, there's no controlling their temperature. I speak to Berthe about it in the lobby. The old man is there too, his chin seems to have sunk deeper into his chest, and his face is yellowish grey.

98  "Nothing, not to worry about anything," says Berthe, dropping rough-hewn chunks of language around me. "Radiator no work, you tell me. You feel cold, you come to me, I keep you warm," and she opens her arms wide, laughing. I step back, and she advances, her breasts preceding her like the gallant prows of two ice-breakers. She looks at the old man to see if he is appreciating the act: "You no feel scared, I keep you safe and warm."

99  But the old man is staring outside, at the flakes of falling snow. What thoughts is he thinking as he watches them? Of childhood days, perhaps, and snowmen with hats and pipes, and snowball fights, and white Christmases, and Christmas trees? What will I think of, old in this country, when I sit and watch the snow come down? For me, it is already too late for snowmen and snowball fights, and all I will have is thoughts about childhood thoughts and dreams, built around snowscapes and winter-wonderlands on the Christmas cards so popular in Bombay; my snowmen and snowball fights and Christmas trees are in the pages of Enid Blyton's[1] books, dispersed amidst the adventures of the Famous Five, and the Five Find-Outers, and the Secret Seven. My snowflakes are even less forgettable than the old man's, for they never melt.

100  It finally happened. The heat went. Not the usual intermittent coming and going, but out completely. Stone cold. The radiators are like ice. And so is everything else. There's no hot water. Naturally. It's the hot water that goes through the rads and heats them. Or is it the other way around? Is there no hot water because the rads have stopped circulating it? I don't care, I'm too cold to sort out the cause and effect relationship. Maybe there is no connection at all.

101  I dress quickly, put on my winter jacket, and go down to the lobby. The elevator is not working because the power is out, so I take the stairs. Several people are gathered, and Berthe has announced that she

---

1. British author (1887–1968) of over 600 books for children.

has telephoned the office, they are sending a man. I go back upstairs. It's only one floor, the elevator is just a bad habit. Back in Firozsha Baag, they were broken most of the time. The stairway enters the corridor outside the old man's apartment, and I think of his cold feet and hands. Poor man, it must be horrible for him without heat.

102 As I walk down the long hallway, I feel there's something different but I can't pin it down. I look at the carpet, the ceiling, the wallpaper: it all seems the same. Maybe it's the freezing cold that imparts a feeling of difference.

103 PW opens her door: "The old man had another stroke yesterday. They took him to the hospital."

104 The medicinal smell. That's it. It's not in the hallway any more.

105 *In the stories that he'd read so far Father said that all the Parsi families were poor or middle-class, but that was okay; nor did he mind that the seeds for the stories were picked from the sufferings of their own lives; but there should also have been something positive about Parsis, there was so much to be proud of: the great Tatas and their contribution to the steel industry, or Sir Dinshaw Petit in the textile industry who made Bombay the Manchester of the East, or Dadabhai Naoroji in the freedom movement, where he was the first to use the word* swaraj, *and the first to be elected to the British Parliament where he carried on his campaign; he should have found some way to bring some of these wonderful facts into his stories, what would people reading these stories think, those who did not know about Parsis — that the whole community was full of cranky, bigoted people; and in reality it was the richest, most advanced and philanthropic community in India, and he did not need to tell his own son that Parsis had a reputation for being generous and family-oriented. And he could have written something also about the historic background, how Parsis came to India from Persia because of Islamic persecution in the seventh century, and were the descendants of Cyrus the Great and the magnificent Persian Empire. He could have made a story of all this, couldn't he?*

106 *Mother said what she liked best was his remembering everything so well, how beautifully he wrote about it all, even the sad things, and though he changed some of it, and used his imagination, there was truth in it.*

107 *My hope is, Father said, that there will be some story based on his Canadian experience, that way we will know something about our son's life there, if not through his letters then in his stories; so far they are all about Parsis in Bombay, and the one with a little about Toronto, where a man perches on top of the toilet, is shameful and disgusting, although it is funny at times and did make me laugh, I have to admit, but where does he get such an imagination from, what is the point of such a fantasy; and Mother said that she would also enjoy some stories about Toronto and the people there; it puzzles me, she said, why he writes nothing about it, especially since you say that writers use their own experience to make stories out of.*

108     Then Father said this is true, but he is probably not using his Toronto experience because it is too early; what do you mean, too early, asked Mother and Father explained it takes a writer about ten years time after an experience before he is able to use it in his writing, it takes that long to be absorbed internally and understood, thought out and thought about, over and over again, he haunts it and it haunts him if it is valuable enough, till the writer is comfortable with it to be able to use it as he wants; but this is only one theory I read somewhere, it may or may not be true.

109     That means, said Mother that his childhood in Bombay and our home here is the most valuable thing in his life just now, because he is able to remember it all to write about it, and you were so bitterly saying he is forgetting where he came from; and that may be true, said Father, but that is not what the theory means, according to the theory he is writing of these things because they are far enough in the past for him to deal with objectively, he is able to achieve what critics call artistic distance, without emotions interfering; and what do you mean emotions, said Mother, you are saying he does not feel anything for his characters, how can he write so beautifully about so many sad things without any feelings in his heart?

110     But before Father could explain more, about beauty and emotion and inspiration and imagination, Mother took the book and said it was her turn now and too much theory she did not want to listen to, it was confusing and did not make as much sense as reading the stories, she would read them her way and Father could read them his.

111 My books on the windowsill have been damaged. Ice has been forming on the inside ledge, which I did not notice, and melting when the sun shines in. I spread them in a corner of the living room to dry out.

112     The winter drags on. Berthe wields her snow pusher as expertly as ever, but there are signs of weariness in her performance. Neither husband nor son is ever outside with a shovel. Or anywhere else, for that matter. It occurs to me that the son's van is missing, too.

113     The medicinal smell is in the hall again, I sniff happily and look forward to seeing the old man in the lobby. I go downstairs and peer into the mailbox, see the blue and magenta of an Indian aerogramme with Don Mills, Ontario, Canada in Father's flawless hand through the slot.

114     I pocket the letter and enter the main lobby. The old man is there, but not in his usual place. He is not looking out through the glass door. His wheelchair is facing a bare wall where the wallpaper is torn in places. As though he is not interested in the outside world any more, having finished with all that, and now it's time to see inside. What does he see inside, I wonder? I go up to him and say hullo. He says hullo without raising his sunken chin. After a few seconds his grey countenance faces me. "How old do you think I am?" His eyes are dull and glazed; he is looking even further inside than I first presumed.

115 "Well, let's see, you're probably close to sixty-four,"
116 "I'll be seventy-eight next August." But he does not chuckle or wheeze. Instead, he continues softly, "I wish my feet did not feel so cold all the time. And my hands." He lets his chin fall again.
117 In the elevator I start opening the aerogramme, a tricky business because a crooked tear means lost words. Absorbed in this while emerging, I don't notice PW occupying the centre of the hallway, arms folded across her chest: "They had a big fight. Both of them have left."
118 I don't immediately understand her agitation. "What ... who?"
119 "Berthe. Husband and son both left her. Now she is all alone."
120 Her tone and stance suggest we should not be standing here talking but do something to bring Berthe's family back. "That's very sad," I say, and go in. I picture father and son in the van, driving away, driving across the snow-covered country, in the dead of winter, away from wife and mother; away to where? how far will they go? Not son's van nor father's booze can take them far enough. And the further they go, the more they'll remember, they can take it from me.

121 *All the stories were read by Father and Mother, and they were sorry when the book was finished, they felt they had come to know their son better now, yet there was much more to know, they wished there were many more stories; and this is what they mean, said Father, when they say that the whole story can never be told, the whole truth can never be known; what do you mean, they say, asked Mother, who they, and Father said writers, poets, philosophers. I don't care what they say, said Mother, my son will write as much or as little as he wants to, and if I can read it I will be happy.*
122 *The last story they liked the best of all because it had the most about Canada, and now they felt they knew at least a little bit, even if it was a very little bit, about his day-to-day life in his apartment; and Father said if he continues to write about such things he will become popular because I am sure they are interested there in reading about life through the eyes of an immigrant, it provides a different viewpoint; the only danger is if he changes and becomes so much like them that he will write like one of them and lose the important difference.*

123 The bathroom needs cleaning. I open a new can of Ajax and scour the tub. Sloshing with mug from bucket was standard bathing procedure in the bathrooms of Firozsha Baag, so my preference now is always for a shower. I've never used the tub as yet; besides, it would be too much like Chaupatty or the swimming pool, wallowing in my own dirt. Still, it must be cleaned.
124 When I've finished, I prepare for a shower. But the clean gleaming tub and the nearness of the vernal equinox give me the urge to do something different today. I find the drain plug in the bathroom cabinet, and run the bath.

125 I've spoken so often to the old man, but I don't know his name. I should have asked him the last time I saw him, when his wheelchair was facing the bare wall because he had seen all there was to see outside and it was time to see what was inside. Well, tomorrow. Or better yet, I can look it up in the directory in the lobby. Why didn't I think of that before? It will only have an initial and a last name, but then I can surprise him with: hullo Mr. Wilson, or whatever it is.

126 The bath is full. Water imagery is recurring in my life: Chaupatty beach, swimming pool, bathtub. I step in and immerse myself up to the neck. It feels good. The hot water loses its opacity when the chlorine, or whatever it is, has cleared. My hair is still dry. I close my eyes, hold my breath, and dunk my head. Fighting the panic, I stay under and count to thirty. I come out, clear my lungs and breathe deeply.

127 I do it again. This time I open my eyes under water, and stare blindly without seeing, it takes all my will to keep the lids from closing. Then I am slowly able to discern the underwater objects. The drain plug looks different, slightly distorted; there is a hair trapped between the hole and the plug, it waves and dances with the movement of the water. I come up, refresh my lungs, examine quickly the overwater world of the washroom, and go in again. I do it several times, over and over. The world outside the water I have seen a lot of, it is now time to see what is inside.

128 The spring session for adult non-swimmers will begin in a few days at the high school. I must not forget the registration date.

129 The dwindled days of winter are now all but forgotten; they have grown and attained a respectable span. I resume my evening walks, it's spring, and a vigorous thaw is on. The snowbanks are melting, the sound of water on its gushing, gurgling journey to the drains is beautiful. I plan to buy a book of trees, so I can identify more than the maple as they begin to bloom.

130 When I return to the building, I wipe my feet energetically on the mat because some people are entering behind me, and I want to set a good example. Then I go to the board with its little plastic letters and numbers. The old man's apartment is the one on the corner by the stairway, that makes in number 201. I run down the list, come to 201, but there are no little white plastic letters beside it. Just the empty black rectangle with holes where the letters would be squeezed in. That's strange. Well, I can introduce myself to him, then ask his name.

131 However, the lobby is empty. I take the elevator, exit at the second floor, wait for the gutang-khutang. It does not come: the door closes noiselessly, smoothly. Berthe has been at work, or has made sure someone else has. PW's cue has been lubricated out of existence.

132 But she must have the ears of a cockroach. She is waiting for me. I whistle my way down the corridor. She fixes me with an accusing

look. She waits till I stop whistling, then says: "You know the old man died last night."

133   I cease groping for my key. She turns to go and I take a step towards her, my hand still in my trouser pocket. "Did you know his last name?" I ask, but she leaves without answering.

(1987)

# Lynda Barry (b. 1956)

Lynda Barry is a Wisconsin-born author, illustrator, playwright, and contributor to various periodicals. "Automatic Timer," a story that plays with the idea of photographic representation, captures the voice of youthful adolescence. Barry herself has said that childhood is "the only place to go if you're looking for answers."

## Automatic Timer

1   My father. For a long time I thought about him and then I didn't think about him and then yesterday I started thinking about him again. I was in the basement, and for no reason I went around under the steps and suddenly saw his camera case on this high shelf, and it was like that thing of where you're drowning and your whole life flashes in front of your eyes. Except it wasn't my whole life. It was just one day from a million years ago when he lived with us still and this room was glowing glowing red from the darkroom light. I was standing on a chair, watching his hand pull a piece of paper back and forth under the water, him saying, "Watch honey, now watch." And then I saw the reverse disappearing ghost of my face showing itself slow onto that paper, and him saying what he always said when he did something like that. "Okay, honey. Who's the best dad?"

2   Some nights he would tilt out the lamp shade in the front room and set his stacks of pictures on a TV tray under it. I'd watch him smoking and coloring me and sister and my mom with Q-Tips and oils and special midget paint tubes and then, for his last finishing touch, he would draw on our eyelashes with a tiny red pencil with Life Magazine printed on the side. He would ask me to hold it up for him to look at and I'd watch him lean back and "Ahhhhhhh. Another Perfect Masterpiece by Raymond Robert Arkins!" And then my mother would see it and yell at him for making us look like a bunch of Mexican whores.

3   Mom found a picture of another lady colored the same way. It was in the street in front of our house. I guess it fell out of his car. It was Pat, the checker at his store. Pat with the small teeth who did a wink to my mom and rang our meat up really cheap. Pat colored in and smiling under a tire mark, with her hands up behind her head and no

top on. My mom put it on our front door with so many rows of Scotch tape that it looked like Pat was sinking in a deep aquarium.

4   I can remember the sound of my dad's feet coming up the steps and then stopping. Then him coming in and saying it didn't mean anything.

5   A long time later, when my dad left, my mother took everything that ever belonged to him and put it out on the front porch for Goodwill. Afterwards, I remember coming into the kitchen and seeing her holding her curved fingernail scissors, flipping through all our photo books and cutting his head out of every picture there was of him. I remember the pile of my dad's heads in the ashtray, her cigarette burning on top, and her singing along with the radio. I remember hearing the bathroom door close, me sneaking into the kitchen and taking three pictures to save. One of him and her holding me, one of him squatting on a beach in an Air Force uniform, and one of him laughing with his eyes shut, holding a dog I didn't know and a glass of beer. The last picture he had colored. He colored the dog in blue.

6   I reached my hand up and pulled down the camera. It was the kind with the flip-open top viewer and I remembered once how I watched him and Pat drunk through it, them singing upside down at the company picnic. My mom was at work and Dad took me and my sister. He kept singing "Welcome to my world" and she kept laughing. I won the footrace and I ran to show him my silver dollar, then me seeing them kissing, and then her trying to act nice to me, and later in the car him telling me how lucky he was to have a kid like me. A kid who understood his saying Don't Make Waves.

7   I saw a yellow number eight through the square glass window. There was still film. My hand started to kind of freak out. It was like a backwards version of that Alfred Hitchcock Hour where the camera comes from something like the thirteenth dimension and can take pictures of the future. The moral of it was something like, Don't Mess with Your Regular Life. I put the camera back on the shelf, and then I took it back down. I put it under my shirt and walked up the stairs past my mom in the kitchen.

8   My friend Vicky Talluso's brother Victor has a darkroom in their rec room bathroom and said for two joints he would develop the film for me. I had one roach. He said okay. Me and Vicky stood in the pitch dark and I could hear Victor dropping things and saying "Fuck." Then he handed me a container and he said keep shaking it and he lit the roach and Vicky lit a Kool and Mrs. Talluso pounded on the door yelling "What in the hell is going on in there?" She made us come out and each blow on her nose and busted Victor and Vicky for smoking and made me go home.

9   This morning at school Vicky came running across the parking lot saying she had a present for me. She opened her folder and handed me some pictures. "Only three came out," she said. The first one was of Pat in front of a car. Then two kids at a birthday with Pat smiling and talking on the phone. Then my dad and Pat with their arms around each other, kissing.

10   I remembered the sound of the automatic timer. How my dad would set it and run fast across the room to get into the picture.

11   "Who's it of?" Vicky says.

*(1990)*

# GLOSSARY

**Accent**  Accent, or stress, is emphasis on one syllable in relation to another or others when a word is spoken. It is a prominent feature of speech in English and has, since the fourteenth century, been the basis of rhythmic pattern in the language. *See* SCANSION.

**Accentual verse** and **accentual-syllabic verse**  The most common formal verse measure or METRE is either accentual (where each line of verse has a uniform number of stressed syllables but not of unstressed ones) or accentual-syllabic (where each line has a uniform number of stressed and unstressed syllables). For an example of accentual-syllabic verse, see the quotation from Alexander Pope under SCANSION. Syllabic verse (where the unit of measurement is the number of syllables exclusively) is much less common. Rarer still (but common in classical Greek and Latin) is quantitative verse, which is based on vowel length. *See also* METRE.

**Action**  In any literary work, not only what the CHARACTERS do or say, but also what happens to them. In some works, the action also includes what the characters feel and how they respond psychologically. *See also* PLOT.

**Allegory**  (a) A NARRATIVE where the sequence of events develops a symbolic pattern of ideas making a moral or philosophical statement. (b) A form of symbolism where CHARACTERS and incidents are presented not for what they signify in themselves but for philosophical, historical, or other references that lie outside the text.

**Alliteration**  The close recurrence of consonants for poetic effect, especially at the beginning of words and in stressed syllables.

**Allusion**  A reference in a literary work to something (a person, place, work of art, statement, or object of any kind) that is external to the text.

**Antagonist** See CHARACTER.

**Anti-hero** In twentieth-century literary works, a major CHARACTER who is presented as having qualities antithetical either to those of the traditional HERO or to those of the romantic hero of popular FICTION. Anti-heroes are typically ineffectual and passive, but they may also be obnoxious and obtuse. See HERO/HEROINE.

**Antithesis** A device of expression that balances opposing concepts to make a contrast. In VERSE, antithesis may occur between lines or between parts of single lines.

**Archetype** In literary criticism, a term borrowed from psychology employed to discuss the significance of an IMAGE, CHARACTER, situation, etc. Archetypes are recurring configurations that appear in myth, religion, folklore, fantasy, and dreams, as well as in art and literature. In addition to operating essentially at the subconscious level, archetypes recur universally in human experience: psychologist Carl Jung saw them as manifestations of what he called the "collective unconscious." Archetypal criticism is one of several methods of reading a text. For example, one may trace the "Divine Child" archetype in the character of Sylvy in Sarah Orne Jewett's "A White Heron." See MOTIF.

**Assonance** The close repetition of the same or similar vowel sounds in stressed syllables.

**Ballad** A song that tells a story. Usually anonymous in origin, popular or folk ballads were transmitted from generation to generation for centuries by oral tradition. Instead of a fixed text, they employed composition formulas such as REFRAINS, stock phrases, iambic METRE, a preferred STANZA FORM, and swift ACTION. Literary ballads are those written in the STYLE of the traditional ballad and were first introduced in the Romantic period.

**Blank verse** Unrhymed IAMBIC PENTAMETER (see also METRE).

**Cacophony** The use of harsh sounds for poetic effect. The opposite of EUPHONY. See also DISSONANCE and ONOMATOPOEIA.

**Cadence** In VERSE, a rhythmic unit based not on a standard line length or on METRE, but on the spontaneous character of informal speech. See FREE VERSE.

**Caesura** A pause in a line of VERSE. Because its placement may vary from line to line, it is a useful device for altering rhythmic emphasis or flow without breaking away from a metrical pattern. *See* example under SCANSION.

**Canon**  Originally a body of sacred texts accepted by the Christian churches, the term was later applied to secular works accepted by experts as genuine works of particular authors. In contemporary literary terms, the canon consists of works regarded as classics and normally treated in university courses on literature.

**Caricature**  Ludicrously exaggerated CHARACTERIZATION.

***Carpe diem***  (Latin, "seize the day.") A THEME or viewpoint expressed frequently in love LYRICS, but occurring as well in other literature, that since youth is fleeting and death certain, there should be no restraint in enjoying life's pleasures.

**Character**  A fictional person in a literary work who may be either purely imaginary or based upon someone real. Many works employ a central character or protagonist, whose ACTIONS are the main focus of attention and represent a struggle against opposing forces that are often summed up in the person of an antagonist. Characters have been variously classified as flat (two-dimensional) or rounded (three-dimensional), types or individuals, and dynamic or static. Dynamic characters undergo change as a result of their experiences. They are frequently attractive because they are unpredictable. Static characters do not necessarily lack depth and complexity. They can be equally full of dramatic interest when a work is organized to allow for progressive revelation of their inner qualities that are not clear at the outset.

**Characterization**  The means an author employs in presenting and developing CHARACTERS. Writers may either describe the qualities of characters directly or present them through ACTION and DIALOGUE. The former TECHNIQUE provides a quick impression; the latter method is a slow, cumulative one, but allows for depth and complexity. Characterization also varies according to the writer's NARRATIVE PERSPECTIVE.

**Closure**  A term borrowed from parliamentary procedure that refers to the call for conclusion to a debate. In literature, it refers to the principle that works should not end arbitrarily, that they ought to conclude with the ACTION, feeling, or exposition being in some sense complete.

**Comedy**  While comedy employs WIT and HUMOUR to make amusing comment on human folly and social values, it frequently strives to instruct as well as delight. Whether it is written as poetry, FICTION, or drama, comedy is usually associated with happy endings, CHARACTERS that are more survivors of trials than victims of fate, and NARRATIVES that sustain a light-hearted TONE. Farce is less subtle than comedy; its characters are frequently more improbable or exaggerated and their situations more ludicrous. Slapstick is even more far-fetched as a representation of life: the characters are more boisterous, the ACTION more physical and violent, and the verbal HUMOUR more at the level of gags, jokes, and insults. *See also* SATIRE.

**Comic relief**   A comic or humorous passage included in works that are basically non-comic in order to relieve tension or dispel excessive gloom. In TRAGEDY, it is also used to heighten the tragic effect.

**Conceit**   A striking or, frequently, outlandish comparison.

**Conflict**   In literary NARRATIVE, the struggle between opposing forces embodied either in the interaction between CHARACTERS or in the mind of the central figure.

**Connotation**   An association or suggestion attached to a word in addition to its literal meaning. In times of war, for example, propagandists have exploited pleasant associations in words like "pacification" in an attempt to justify unusually severe methods of social control such as bombing civilian targets.

**Consonance**   The close recurrence of consonants with differing vowel sounds in the middle and at the end of words. *See* ALLITERATION.

**Convention**   In literature, the customary practice of writers, such as paragraph indentation or chapters in novels. Conventions are rules agreed on between author and reader but seldom made explicit.

**Couplet**   A pair of rhyming VERSE lines. The two most popular forms in English are the four-stress, or octosyllabic, couplet and the five-stress, or heroic, couplet.

**Dénouement**   The resolution of PLOT CONFLICT in a literary work.

**Dialect**   A non-standard variety of language specific to a region or social group.

**Dialogue**   The conversational language spoken by the CHARACTERS in a literary work. Dialogue may appear to resemble actual speech but at best is always a stylized version of what a character might actually say in a situation. Good dialogue attempts to record the idiom of characters as psychologically and socially observed.

**Diction**  The author's choice of words. Diction may be either formal or informal, obscure or familiar, ornate or plain, depending on the context or the writer's purpose. *See* OBSCURITY.

**Discourse**  A term current in the humanities and social sciences, especially since the 1960s, which insists on language as social practice sustainable within particular social and cultural contexts. Discourse analysis in literary and other studies is concerned with the uses of discourse in running written or spoken conversation. A discourse community or culture is one that shares assumptions, beliefs, and modes of exchange.

**Dissonance**  Deliberate placement of words for inharmonious effect. It contrasts with CACOPHONY, which also aims at discordance but employs words that are themselves harsh.

**Dramatic monologue**  A poem in which the lines are spoken by, and ironically reveal the personality of, a CHARACTER who addresses either a listener who is present or an imagined audience.

**Elegy**  A LYRIC poem expressing a lament for the death of a person or for the passing of an era.

**Enjambment**  A run-on line of VERSE. It occurs when the grammatical sense of a poem forces the reader to finish one line and start the next without a pause. *See also* STANZA.

**Epigram**  A concise but weighty statement, often phrased with WIT and elegance. PARADOX is a favourite epigrammatic device.

**Euphony**  The use of pleasant, harmonious, or musical sounds for poetic effect. The opposite of CACOPHONY.

**Fable**  A brief allegorical TALE told to illustrate a moral. Beast fables are folk tales that use animals to illustrate human shortcomings.

**Fiction**  While the word generally refers to any imagined story, in literary works it means prose fiction in the form of a novel, SHORT STORY, TALE, etc. Even when prose fiction is based on facts or a true story, the process of NARRATION requires much elaboration and this has to be based on invented detail.

If the novel has been typically oriented toward REALISM, freedom of invention has always characterized the popular romance. Romances originated in medieval court tales of love and adventure. From the eighteenth century onward, as the novel with a bias toward CHARACTER development emerged, a distinction arose between the novel and romance. Although the two overlap in works of mixed GENRE, the freedom of romance to go beyond the novel's limits of probability appeals not only to writers of escapist stories but also to those who see it as a more useful vehicle than realism for serious exploration of particular THEMES and subjects. Nathaniel Hawthorne's "The Birthmark" is an example of a short story in the romance vein. While "novel" (usually a work of more than 50 000 words) is the most familiar term for extended works of prose fiction, "novelette" (15 000 to 50 000 words) is a less well-known term for a short novel. The novella (10 000 to 15 000 words) is more of a long story than a short novel. *See* SHORT STORY.

**Figures of speech** and **figurative language**  Figures of speech are devices of expression, basically metaphorical in nature, that enable writers to make suggestions and statements beyond the literal meanings of words, phrases, comparisons, and sentences. Figurative language is effective in literature when it defines or describes something by making striking comparisons either to dissimilar objects or to objects having a partial resemblance. *See* CONCEIT, HYPERBOLE, IRONY, METAPHOR, METONYMY, OXYMORON, PARADOX, PERSONIFICATION, SIMILE, SYMBOL, and SYNECDOCHE.

**First-person narrator**  A term for a story teller who is a CHARACTER in the work being narrated and who writes in the first person ("I"). Also called character narrator. *See* NARRATIVE PERSPECTIVE and NARRATOR.

**Free verse**  Verse that is free of regular METRE and other CONVENTIONS of formal poetry. It relies on the CADENCED phrase, on TONE, on its flexibility and adaptability in relation to its subject, and on its ability to approximate where necessary traditional or formal verse rhythms. *See* CADENCE.

**Genre**  Literary works may be classified into major genres or types such as the novel, the SHORT STORY, the play, the poem, and the essay, and into subgenres such as the problem play or the elegiac poem. Since descriptions of genre and subgenre characteristics are based on our conventional understanding and past experiences of literature, and since there are both hybrid types and many unclassifiable works, definitions of genre cannot be used prescriptively — especially in the assessment of new writing.

**Hero/Heroine**  The central figure around whom the PLOT of a literary work revolves. Originally, before the rise of REALISM, heroes and heroines had noble qualities. In modern literature, the term is often a synonym for PROTAGONIST. Many modern writers employ very ordinary, unheroic central figures. Such protagonists can be timid, awkward, obnoxious, or whatever is required for the author's purpose. *See* ANTI-HERO.

**Humour**   A way of seeing that observes the ludicrous, the comic, and the amusing. While humour shares this tendency with WIT, it is gentler, more tolerant, and warmer in its approach to life. Thus, in SATIRE, where criticism is central to the writer's purpose, humour is as much a leavener of the NARRATIVE as it is a vehicle for commentary. In satire, humour is most effective when combined with art.

**Hyperbole**   Exaggeration or overstatement frequently employed for humorous purposes.

**Iambic pentameter**   The most common ACCENTUAL-SYLLABIC VERSE line in English. Its great expressive range makes it the basis for a variety of traditional forms such as BLANK VERSE, the heroic COUPLET, the heroic QUATRAIN, and several STANZA patterns. *See also* METRE and VERSIFICATION.

**Image** and **Imagery**   In literature, an image is a verbal representation of a sense impression. While images are most obviously recognized as visual, they may also be auditory, olfactory, tactile, and even taste-oriented. Depending on the work or context, images may be either literal or figurative, and they may be either frequently or sparsely employed. Imagery is the term used for images in their aggregate form. Because imagery is patterned throughout a work and related images often concentrated in image clusters, analysis of imagistic detail, and of all language with a FIGURATIVE function, is an essential part of defining the quality, the emotional content, and the meaning of a literary work.

**Irony**   (a) Verbal irony occurs when a statement contradicts its literal meaning. An example of extended verbal irony occurs when events are interpreted through a naïve or unreliable NARRATOR who fails to recognize or admit the significance of what is described. (b) Situational irony occurs when events develop in a pattern opposite to what is expected. *See* Margaret Atwood's "Happy Endings." (c) Dramatic irony occurs when CHARACTERS in a literary work are proceeding without being aware of factors affecting their fate that are known to the audience. Traynor in Alice Walker's "Nineteen Fifty-Five" is such a character.

**Lyric**   A short poem expressing strong personal feeling. As an arrested moment of intense emotion, lyric expression may occur as a tendency in (or in a passage of ) a longer work like a play or a novel.

**Metafiction**   A story or novel, the major THEME of which is the nature of FICTION. Margaret Atwood's story "Happy Endings" is an example.

**Metaphor**   An implied comparison of dissimilar objects. As such, it contrasts with SIMILE, which is an explicit comparison. Metaphors apply words to objects where there is no normal, literal, or expected association ("Life's but a walking shadow").

**Metonymy**   The use of an attribute or association of an object to stand for the object itself (as we might use "Ottawa" to refer to the federal government).

**Metre**   The pattern of stressed and unstressed syllables that STRUCTURES the RHYTHM of formal VERSE in English. (For informal or non-metrical verse, *see* FREE VERSE.) Formal verse is based on a metrical unit of two or three syllables called a foot. The most familiar in English is the iambic, a two-syllable foot where an unstressed is followed by a stressed syllable (William Shakespeare: To bé, or nót to bé). Other feet are the trochaic, where the stressed precedes the unstressed syllable (Sir John Betjeman: Thínk of whát our Nátion stánds for), and two three-syllable feet, the anapestic (˘˘´) and the dactylic (´˘˘). In response to the need for occasional variation from the norm, substitution of one of the other feet can be employed. In addition to any of the four "base" feet, two other variants are employable in substitution: the spondee (two successive stressed syllables) and the pyrrhic (two successive unstressed syllables). *See also* ACCENTUAL VERSE and ACCENTUAL-SYLLABIC VERSE, IAMBIC PENTAMETER, SCANSION, and VERSIFICATION.

*Mimesis*   (Greek, "imitation.") The theory that literary works are a representation of human ACTION. Mimetic theory and criticism focus on the relevance of a work to human experience rather than on its structural features.

**Motif**   One of the unifying elements in a work or a frequently recurring element in a number of works by the same author. It may be a phrase, IMAGE, SYMBOL, citation, or some other narrative detail that recurs and helps to elaborate a THEME.

**Narrator (narration, narrative)**   The narrator is the storyteller in a prose or VERSE narrative. In works of FICTION or poetry in which the narrator is not involved in the ACTION, the narrative VOICE may or may not be authorial (that is, identified with that of the author — *see* SPEAKER). In addition to authorial narrators, CHARACTERS are frequently employed as speakers and storytellers. Narration is the process of telling an audience what happens. While the narrative is the actual account of what happens, it is always a report from a certain perspective (*see* NARRATIVE PERSPECTIVE). Narrative contrasts with DIALOGUE, which, as a record of the speech of the characters, aims to present the action as it happens.

**Narrative perspective**  The point of view or angle from which the ACTION of a literary work is depicted. Character or first-person narration has the perspective of a direct or indirect participant in the action. THIRD-PERSON NARRATION may be omniscient (that is, one that goes beyond the world of the FICTION), or it may be limited. In the case of limited third-person narratives, the perspective is restricted to the perceptual level of the CHARACTERS (*see* the Introduction to Short Fiction). In the case of character narration, narrative perspective varies a great deal according to the reliability of the narrator(s) employed. Some of the variables affecting character narration include the degree to which the narrator is being presented ironically, the degree of the narrator's personal involvement in or with or bias in relation to events and persons described, and the narrator's honesty, intelligence, and powers of observation. Because reliability affects our knowledge of what actually happens in a work, authors often include elements to make us question narrative reliability and thus deliberately present us with problems of interpretation.

**Obscurity**  A quality of language or literature where the writer's meaning is difficult to discern. This may be the result of archaism (the use of words no longer in contemporary speech), neologism (the use of newly coined words), FIGURATIVE LANGUAGE, specialized terminology or technical jargon, slang, or some other unfamiliar form of DICTION or DISCOURSE. It may also be the result of difficult syntax, abstruse thought, or poor writing.

**Ode**  Originally a lengthy poem or praise designed to celebrate a public event, person, achievement, or ideal. Since the Romantic period, when the form became more personal and subjective, the term has been used to describe a dignified formal LYRIC or meditation, usually expressed in a lofty TONE, on a single THEME or specific subject. Aside from its stately manner, it does not require a specific STANZA, METRE, or length.

**Omniscient narrator**  Omniscient means "all-knowing." This is the type of NARRATOR employed by Nathaniel Hawthorne in "The Birthmark." This narrator stands outside the ACTION and comments in the third person from a perspective above the awareness level of the CHARACTERS. *See* NARRATIVE PERSPECTIVE and THIRD-PERSON NARRATOR.

**Onomatopoeia**  The use of words that sound like the objects or ACTIONS referred to.

**Oxymoron** A statement with two apparently contradictory components (W.B. Yeats's "terrible beauty"), which is effective as a result of its incongruity.

**Parable** A TALE illustrating a moral or religious lesson. Often it includes an enigmatic element to arrest the listener's attention. *See* ALLEGORY.

**Paradox** An apparently contradictory statement, as in William Wordsworth's line "The Child is father of the Man."

**Parody** A deliberate and clever imitation of an artistic work or STYLE, often for the purpose of ridicule or mockery.

**Pastoral** Originally, a form of poetry set in a classical rustic Arcadia with shepherds, flowers, flutes, and bucolic emotions. In modern literature, any work that presents rural SETTINGS, THEMES, and CHARACTERS.

**Persona** *See* SPEAKER.

**Personification** The attribution of human qualities to non-human objects.

**Plot** The arrangement of the ACTION and the selection of incidents that best achieve the author's purpose in telling a story.

**Point of View** *See* NARRATIVE PERSPECTIVE.

**Postcolonial** Writing concerned with the culture, history, and politics of former colonies of European empires. Instead of being the objects of European "expert" scrutiny, postcolonial writers become subjects or active agents who offer accounts of their experience that counter traditional imperial NARRATIVES depicting colonized peoples as quaint, inferior, or uncivilized.

**Prose poem** A poem which has abandoned the device of line definition so that as a mode of composition it must be described as prose. However, it retains most of the rhythmic and all of the figurative devices of both formal and FREE VERSE and is fully a poetic form of literary expression.

**Prosody** The study of the theory, history, and principles of METRE and VERSIFICATION.

**Protagonist** *See* CHARACTER.

**Quatrain**  A four-line form with a variety of RHYME SCHEMES, the quatrain is the most familiar STANZA in English. An IAMBIC PENTAMETER version rhyming *abab* is sometimes termed an elegiac and sometimes a heroic quatrain.

**Realism**  In terms of subject matter, realism has come to mean literature that deals with the ordinary commonplace world in preference to the world of exceptional circumstances. CHARACTERS are neither rich nor heroic, SETTINGS are prosaic rather than exotic, and yet there is a serious grappling with moral, social, and psychological dilemmas and a normal range of other THEMES and moods. The surface of life is usually carefully and faithfully observed, a plain STYLE of description is employed, and an unintrusive NARRATIVE PERSPECTIVE is preferred, especially in the handling of character motivation and the presentation of interior consciousness.

**Refrain**  A repeated VERSE line, usually at the end of a STANZA, with a function (whether LYRIC, comic, ironic, etc.) that may change throughout a poem.

**Rhyme**  The repetition of final vowels, or of a combination of final vowels and consonants, in words at the end of, or within, lines of VERSE. *See also* CONSONANCE.

**Rhyme scheme**  The pattern of rhyme within a fixed VERSE form or STANZA. An elegiac QUATRAIN, for instance, follows an *abab* scheme.

**Rhythm**  The flow of language in either free or measured form. Rhythm in VERSE is arranged in either formal or informal patterns. For informal VERSIFICATION, *see* FREE VERSE.

**Satire**  A treatment of subject matter that can appear in any literary GENRE, satire usually employs devices of ridicule and appeals to amusement, scorn, or contempt to comment on or correct some human vice, social evil, or general tendency to folly.

**Scansion**  The analysis of the metrical structure of VERSE. To scan a line of verse is to mark out the ACCENTS or stresses in relation to metrical feet, pauses, and the number of syllables. The following lines from Alexander Pope are scanned as follows:

Trúe wĭt / ĭs ná / tŭre tó / ăd ván / tăge dréssed. /
Whăt óft / wăs thóught, // bŭt n'ér / sŏ wéll / ĕx préssed. /

/ marks the end of each foot, // marks the CAESURA, ´ marks the ACCENT or stress, and ˘ marks the unaccented syllables.

**Sensibility** That part of a writer's or a CHARACTER'S personality that has a capacity for emotional responsiveness and sensitivity. The value of sensibility was heightened in the late eighteenth century when sentimentalism came into fashion in literature and HEROES and HEROINES (and writers) came to be admired for their fine sensitivity to delicate nuances of feeling.

**Setting** In a NARRATIVE or dramatic work, setting involves the place, historical period, and social circumstances of the ACTION. The setting has significant implications for atmosphere, CHARACTER, PLOT, and THEME.

**Shakespearean sonnet** Also known as the English sonnet. *See* SONNET.

**Short story** A relatively brief type of prose FICTION. In the early nineteenth century, a number of writers, including Nathaniel Hawthorne (*see* "The Birthmark"), developed the GENRE out of the sketch and literary essay. While the sketch was a relaxed NARRATIVE, usually written for a newspaper or periodical, with limited development of PLOT, CHARACTER, and THEME, the short story became more compact, complex, and ambitious. The short story is often characterized by its highly crafted STRUCTURE and its use of subtle detail within a compressed spatial format. The short story ranges from 500 to 20 000 words, but normal length is from 2000 to 15 000 words.

**Simile** A comparison usually expressed with "like," "as," or "as if." An explicit form of METAPHOR.

**Sonnet** A poem written in IAMBIC PENTAMETER, consisting of fourteen lines. There are two main patterns: the Italian sonnet, consisting of an octave (rhyming eight lines *abba abba*) and a sestet (six lines rhyming *cde cde*), and the English or SHAKESPEAREAN SONNET, with three QUATRAINS and a final COUPLET (*abab cdcd efef gg*). A variant of the English sonnet is the SPENSERIAN SONNET, notable for its tighter RHYME SCHEME (*abab bcbc cdcd ee*).

**Speaker** Just as we refer to a NARRATOR of a story, we call the person who gives VOICE to a poem the speaker. It is crucial for understanding ironic, satiric, humorous, descriptive, and other intentions in an essay or poem to recognize the kind of speaker employed. Where the speaker is a CHARACTER involved in the ACTION, it is obvious that the sentiments directly expressed are not the poet's — *see* DRAMATIC MONOLOGUE. But, where the speaker is not involved in the action, the persona or voice expressed may or may not be akin to the writer's own. In many short poems, the speaker may reveal only one small aspect of the poet's personality, or the voice is merely one adapted to the evocation of a particular mood or response.

**Spenserian sonnet**   A variant of the English sonnet. *See* SONNET.

**Sprung rhythm**   A distinctive and forceful poetic line developed by Gerard Manley Hopkins. As with trochaic and dactylic feet (*see* METRE), sprung rhythm places the ACCENT on the initial syllable of each foot, but the number of unaccented syllables is irregular.

**Stanza**   Lines of VERSE may be composed in verse paragraphs, or they may be organized into formal units called stanzas. Each stanza provides the poet with a division mark, but frequently the division is blurred for a purpose discernible in the poem. While enjambment may occur as frequently between stanzas as between lines, it does not in any way diminish the impact of the stanza as a forceful unit in a poem.

**Stanza forms**   Some traditional STANZAS are both fixed and elaborate in format (ottava rima, for instance, an eight-line IAMBIC PENTAMETER stanza, rhyming *ababbcc*). Such stanzas are based on a predetermined METRE, RHYME SCHEME, and number of lines and feet per line. Certain basic stanzas like the tercet have fixed variant forms — *see also* COUPLET and QUATRAIN for their variants. While a tercet is a three-line stanza employing a single rhyme, terza rima is a series of tercets with *aba bcb cdc*, interlinking rhymes. BALLADS often alternate tetrameter and trimeter lines in *abcb* quatrains. Rhyme royal is a seven-line iambic pentameter stanza rhyming *ababbcc*. Modern poets frequently design stanzas for specific poems, and although their stanzas may not vary radically from traditional fixed forms, they do not expect readers to link their chosen pattern to a familiar stanza form.

**Stress**   *See* ACCENT.

**Structure**   The organizing principles of a literary work revealed in such obvious elements of a literary framework as chapter, scene, or STANZA divisions as well as more subtle compositional devices such as the arrangement of IMAGES and ideas. Structure affects THEME and meaning and defines the elements that give unity and coherence to a work.

**Style**   A writer's characteristic way of writing, which may or may not be highly distinctive.

**Symbol**   In a literary work, any CHARACTER, ACTION, situation, SETTING, or object can be a symbol if, in addition to having a clear literal function, it represents something beyond itself. Flora, the horse in Alice Munro's "Boys and Girls," is used symbolically to make a statement about the end of an early phase of the NARRATOR's life.

**Synecdoche** The use of the part to stand for the whole ("rhyme" for poem) or the whole to stand for the part ("Canada" for Canadians).

**Tale** An informal or spontaneous literary NARRATIVE. Originally oral in nature, it is now a loosely constructed story that is told with some of the relish of its folk origins. It contrasts with the typically more tightly structured narrative we call the SHORT STORY.

**Technique** A device or method of expression in literature and art.

**Texture** The formal qualities of literary language, as opposed to the content of a work of literature. DICTION, RHYTHM, IMAGERY, FIGURATIVE LANGUAGE, stylistic and prosodic devices, and so on, are aspects of texture, but structural devices such as PLOT and CHARACTER are not.

**Theme** An idea, moral, social observation, or other generalization that can be recognized as underlying or unifying a literary work. Class difference, for example, is a theme in D.H. Lawrence's story "You Touched Me."

**Third-person narrator** A NARRATOR who stands outside the ACTION when telling the story. Third-person narrators may be OMNISCIENT, but more commonly they limit their commentary to the perspective level of the CHARACTERS. *See* NARRATIVE PERSPECTIVE.

**Tone** The cast of VOICE that reveals the SPEAKER'S or writer's attitude to the audience.

**Tragedy** A literary work (most familiar as a classical form of drama) that involves a PROTAGONIST in a series of events leading to a fatal catastrophe. The DÉNOUEMENT, which results in the violent death of the central figure, must seem the inevitable outcome of the struggle of a valiant but tragically flawed HERO/HEROINE against the odds of a fateful situation. Contrast with COMEDY.

**Verse** (a) A single line of poetry. "Verse" is sometimes used to refer to a STANZA. (b) A composition either in METRE or CADENCES that uses the line as a rhythmical unit.

**Versification** The art of making VERSE. Versification is either formal or informal. For informal versification, *see* FREE VERSE. Formal versification employs METRE and a regular line length. Each formal line is named according to its length, with the four-, five-, and six-foot lines being the most familiar (tetrameter, pentameter, hexameter). *See* IAMBIC PENTAMETER. Less well-known are monometer, dimeter, trimeter, and heptameter (the one-, two-, three-, and seven-foot lines). Sometimes line length is measured by syllable (*see* COUPLET for a reference to the octosyllabic line).

**Villanelle**  A poem with five tercets and a final QUATRAIN. The opening and closing lines of the initial tercet provide REFRAINS that are placed in a strict pattern.

**Voice**  Every literary work, whether a brief LYRIC or a long prose NARRATION, has a SPEAKER or PERSONA. The sense of personal presence behind the speaker's words constitutes voice. The term "voice" reminds us that the significance of what is said is qualified by who is speaking, and the speaker's TONE and feeling. *See* SPEAKER.

**Wit**  Originally, wit was associated specifically with quickness of intellect; an instinct for IRONY, variety, and incongruity; and agility of ideas and language. It now tends to mean, at worst, a proclivity to make quips and, at best, the ability to communicate clever, amusing, or surprising observations that have at least a modicum of intellectual substance. Because wit can be incisive, intolerant, and intellectual, it is a useful element in SATIRE.

# CREDITS

*Because some selections are now in the public domain in Canada, not all sources are listed below.*

Atwood, Margaret. "Happy Endings," from *Murder in the Dark* by Margaret Atwood. Used by permission, the Canadian Publishers, McClelland & Stewart, Toronto.

Bambara, Toni Cade. "The Lesson," from *Gorilla, My Love* by Toni Cade Bambara. Copyright © 1972 by Toni Cade Bambara. Reprinted by permission of Random House, Inc.

Barry, Lynda. "Automatic Timer" first appeared in *Mother Jones*. Copyright © 1990 by Lynda Barry. Reprinted with permission of the author.

Faulkner, William. "A Rose for Emily," from *Collected Stories of William Faulkner* by William Faulkner. Copyright © 1930 and renewed 1958 by William Faulkner. Reprinted by permission of Random House, Inc.

Findley, Timothy. "Dreams," from *Stones*. Copyright © Pebble Productions Inc., 1988. Reprinted by permission of Penguin Books Canada Ltd.

Gordimer, Nadine. "Town and Country Lovers," from *A Soldier's Embrace: Stories* (London: Jonathan Cape, 1980), pp. 73–84. Copyright © 1980 by Nadine Gordimer. Originally published in *Harper's and Queen*, Britain.

Hemingway, Ernest. "In Another Country," reprinted with permission of Scribner, an imprint of Simon & Schuster, Inc., from *Men Without Women* by Ernest Hemingway. Copyright 1927 by Charles Scribner's Sons. Copyright renewed 1955 by Ernest Hemingway.

Hughes, Langston. "On the Road," from *Laughing to Keep from Crying*. First published in *Esquire*. Copyright 1935 Esquire, Inc. Reprinted by permission of Harold Ober Associates Inc.

Joyce, James. "The Boarding House," from *Dubliners* by James Joyce. Copyright 1916 by B.W. Heubsch. Definitive text copyright © 1967 by the Estate of James Joyce. Used by permission of Viking Penguin, a division of Penguin Putnam Inc.

King, Thomas. "The One About Coyote Going West," from *One Good Story, That One*, copyright © 1993 by Dead Dog Café Productions Inc. Published in Canada by HarperCollins Publishers Ltd. Reprinted by permission of the author.

Laurence, Margaret. "The Loons," from *A Bird in the House: Stories by Margaret Laurence*. Copyright © 1970 by Margaret Laurence. Used by permission of the Canadian Publishers, McClelland & Stewart, Toronto.

Lawrence, D.H. "You Touched Me," from *Complete Short Stories of D.H. Lawrence* by D.H. Lawrence. Copyright 1922 by Thomas Seltzer, Inc. Renewal copyright 1950 by Frieda Lawrence. Used by permission of Viking Penguin, a division of Penguin Putnam Inc.

MacLeod, Alistair. "The Boat," from *The Lost Salt Gift of Blood*. Used by permission of the Canadian Publishers, McClelland & Stewart, Toronto.

Maracle, Lee. "Yin Chin," from *Sojourner's Truth and Sundogs* (Vancouver: Press Gang Publishers, 1999). Copyright © 1990 Lee Maracle.

Mistry, Rohinton. "Swimming Lessons," from *Tales from the Firozsha Baag* by Rohinton Mistry. Used by permission of the Canadian Publishers, McClelland & Stewart, Toronto.

Munro, Alice. "Boys and Girls," from *Dance of the Happy Shades*. Copyright © 1968 Alice Munro. Used by permission of McGraw-Hill Ryerson Ltd., Canada.

Olsen, Tillie. "I Stand Here Ironing," copyright © 1956, 1957, 1960, 1961 by Tillie Olsen, from *Tell Me a Riddle* by Tillie Olsen. Introduction by John Leonard. Used by permission of Delacorte Press/Seymour Lawrence, a division of Random House, Inc.

Smyth, Donna E. "Red Hot." Copyright by Donna E. Smyth. Reprinted by permission of the author.

Thurber, James. "The Bear Who Let It Alone" and "The Little Girl and the Wolf," from *Fables for Our Time*, Harper and Row. Copyright © 1940

James Thurber. Copyright © renewed 1968 by Helen Thurber and Rosemary Thurber. Reprinted by permission of Rosemary A. Thurber and the Barbara Hogenson Agency.

Vanderhaeghe, Guy. "Drummer," from *Man Descending*. Copyright © 1982 Guy Vanderhaeghe. Reprinted by permission of Macmillan Canada, an imprint of CDG Books Canada Inc.

Walker, Alice. "Nineteen Fifty-Five," from *You Can't Keep a Good Woman Down*. Copyright © 1981 by Alice Walker. Reprinted by permission of Harcourt Company.

Wilson, Ethel. "We Have to Sit Opposite," from *Mrs. Golightly and Other Stories* by Ethel Wilson. Copyright © Ethel Wilson, 1961. Reprinted by permission of Macmillan Canada, an imprint of CDG Books Canada Inc.

# READER REPLY CARD

We are interested in your reaction to *Introduction to Literature: Short Fiction,* by Isobel M. Findlay, Wendy R. Katz, Kenneth A. MacKinnon, Richard J.H. Perkyns, and Gillian Thomas. You can help us to improve this book in future editions by completing this questionnaire.

1. What was your reason for using this book?

    ☐ university course ☐ college course

    ☐ professional development ☐ continuing education course

    ☐ personal interest ☐ other _____

    _____

2. If you are a student, please identify your school and the course in which you used this book.

3. Which chapters or parts of this book did you use? Which did you omit?

4. What did you like best about this book? What did you like least?

5. Please identify any topics you think should be added to future editions.

6. Please add any comments or suggestions.

7. May we contact you for further information?

    Name: _____

    Address: _____

    Phone: _____

    E-mail: _____

(fold here and tape shut)

0116870399-M8Z4X6-BR01

Larry Gillevet
Director of Product Development
HARCOURT CANADA
55 HORNER AVENUE
TORONTO, ONTARIO
M8Z 9Z9

# Introduction to Literature Short Fiction

**Isobel M. Findlay**
UNIVERSITY OF SASKATCHEWAN

**Wendy R. Katz**
**Kenneth A. MacKinnon**
**Richard J.H. Perkyns**
**Gillian Thomas**
ST. MARY'S UNIVERSITY

Harcourt Canada

Toronto  Montreal  Fort Worth  New York  Orlando
Philadelphia  San Diego  London  Sydney  Tokyo

Copyright © 2001 Harcourt Canada Ltd.

All rights reserved. No part of this publication may be reproduced or transmitted in any form or by any means, electronic or mechanical, including photocopy, recording, or any information storage and retrieval system, without permission in writing from the publisher. Reproducing passages from this book without such written permission is an infringement of copyright law.

Requests for permission to photocopy any part of this work should be sent in writing to College Licensing Officer, CANCOPY, 1 Yonge Street, 19th Floor, Toronto, ON, M5E 1E5. Fax: (416) 868-1621. All other inquiries should be directed to the publisher.

Every reasonable effort has been made to acquire permission for copyright material used in this text and to acknowledge such indebtedness accurately. Any errors or omissions called to the publisher's attention will be corrected in future printings.

**Canadian Cataloguing in Publication Data**

Main entry under title:

Introduction to literature. Short fiction

ISBN 0-7747-3695-X

1. Short stories, English.   2. Short stories, American.   3. Short stories, Canadian (English).*   I. Findlay, Isobel.

PN6120.2.I595   2000        823'.0108        C99-932608-2

Acquisitions Editor: Megan Mueller
Senior Developmental Editor: Martina van de Velde
Production Editors: Stephanie Fysh/Emily Ferguson
Production Coordinator: Cheryl Tiongson
Copy Editor: Faith Gildenhuys
Cover Design: The Brookview Group Inc.
Interior Design: The Brookview Group Inc.
Typesetting and Assembly: Bookman Typesetting Co.
Printing and Binding: Tri-Graphic Printing

Cover art: *Unseen Forces* by Ruth Hayes. Watercolour. 11" × 15". Copyright © Ruth Hayes. All rights reserved.

Harcourt Canada
55 Horner Avenue, Toronto, ON, Canada M8Z 4X6
Customer Service
Toll-Free Tel.: 1-800-387-7278
Toll-Free Fax: 1-800-665-7307

This book was printed in Canada.

1  2  3  4  5     04  03  02  01  00